GCSE
MEDIA
STUDIES

Neil Nixon
Lecturer in Media Studies
North West Kent College of Technology

Advisor and Contributor
Mike Edwards, Chief Examiner

Letts
EDUCATIONAL

Letts Educational
Aldine House
Aldine Place
London W12 8AW
Tel: 020 8740 2266
Fax: 020 8743 8451
E-mail: mail@ lettsed.co.uk

First published 1996
Reprinted 1997, 1999 (twice), 2000

British Library Cataloguing in Publication Data
A CIP record for this book is available from the British Library.

ISBN 1 85805 435 4

Printed in Great Britain by The Bath Press, Bath

Letts Educational Ltd, a division of Granada Learning Ltd. Part of the Granada Media Group.

Contents

Contents

Acknowledgements

p.9, fig. 1.2 Copyright © BBC, reproduced with permission; p.11, fig. 1.3 Reproduced with permission of Y Care International; p.12, fig. 1.4 Reproduced with permission of The Royal Exchange Theatre Company; p.13, fig. 1.5 Copyright © Mirror Syndication International, reproduced with permission; p.14, fig. 1.6 Reproduced with permission of Mars U.K. Limited; p.16, fig. 1.7 Still taken from *Sinister Urge*, reproduced with permission of Headliner (Courtesy Kobal); p.18, fig. 1.8 Excerpt from *Mandy & Judy*, reproduced with permission of D.C. Thomson Limited; p.22, fig. 2.1 Reproduced with permission of Hit & Run Music Limited; p.24, fig. 2.2 Reproduced with permission of Rex Features Limited; p.32 Lyrics from the song 'Multinational Corporation' reproduced with kind permission of Earache Records, written by Napalm Death, Copyright © Earache Songs; p.35, fig. 3.2 Reproduced with permission of Kwik Save Stores Limited; p.39 Lyrics from the song 'A Horse With No Name'(Dewey Blunnell) © 1971 Warner Bros Music Ltd, London W1Y 3FA. Reproduced by permission of International Music Publications Ltd; p.45, fig. 4.2 Copyright © 1995 Ragdoll Productions, reproduced with kind permission of Ragdoll Productions and The Redan Company Limited; p.48, fig. 5.1 Copyright © Relay Photos Limited, reproduced with permission; p.48, fig. 5.2 Copyright © Retna Pictures Limited, reproduced with permission; p.50, fig. 5.3 Excerpt from *Catch* magazine, reproduced with permission of D.C. Thomson Limited; p.54, fig. 6.1 Copyright © House of VIZ/John Brown Publishing Limited, reproduced with permission; p.55, fig. 6.2 Copyright © Empics Limited Photo Agency, reproduced with permission; p.56, fig. 6.3 Photograph by Hayley Madden, reproduced with permission of Syndication International Network; p.57, fig. 6.4 Photograph reproduced by permission of Syndication International Network; p.58, fig. 6.5 Copyright © Retna Pictures Limited, reproduced with permission; p.62, fig. 7.1 Excerpt from *Just Seventeen* magazine, reproduced with permission; p.65, fig. 7.2 Copyright © BBC Worldwide Limited 1995, reproduced from *Pingu*, Issue 32. Photographs by The J Allan Cash Photolibrary, reproduced with permission; p.67, fig. 7.3 & fig. 7.4 Excerpts from *Dennis the Menace*, reproduced with permission of D.C. Thomson; p.72, fig. 8.1 Copyright © Retna Pictures Limited, reproduced with permission; p.74, fig. 8.3 Reproduced with permission of *Fortean Times*; p.86, fig. 10.1 Excerpt from *Live & Kicking* magazine, Copyright © BBC Worldwide Publishing 1995; p.96, fig. 11.2 Reproduced with permission of Raw Vision; p.97, fig. 11.3 Reproduced with permission of U.S. Gold Limited; p.101, fig. 12.1 Excerpt from *Radio Times*, Copyright © BBC Worldwide Publishing, 1995; p.105, fig. 12.5 Copyright © Mirror Syndication International, reproduced with permission; p.110, fig. 13.1 Excerpt from *Shoot* magazine, reproduced with permission; p.110, fig. 13.2 Excerpt from *So Jack Ashurst* fanzine, reproduced with permission; p.117, fig. 14.1 Excerpt from New Musical Express, reproduced with permission of New Musical Express, Chart Information Network, MRIB and Steve Double. Billboard Charts © BPI Communications Inc., used with permission of Billboard magazine; p.124, fig. 15.1 Excerpt from *She* magazine, reproduced with permission of The National Magazine Company Limited; p.130 'NIGGERS', by Labi Siffre, reproduced with permission of Xavier Books; p.139, fig. 17.1 Copyright © The Guardian, reproduced with permission; p.140, fig. 17.2 Excerpt from *Radio Times*, Copyright © BBC Worldwide Publishing, 1995.

Introduction

This book is designed to help you get the best results from your GCSE Media Studies course. You will be assessed by coursework and a written paper or a 'controlled test' and this book contains advice on how to cope with both of these. It also includes examples and activities designed to give you a good understanding of the basic ideas behind media studies. Self-test questions allow you to chart your progress.

The book also contains detailed information on the GCSE courses and a discussion of syllabus contents.

Most students simply find it helpful to have all the important information that they need included in one book. While this book can help you, any real success will be based on your own hard work. The book is designed to make this hard work count towards marks by suggesting things that you can do to improve your understanding.

You should also make sure that you understand the purpose of any assignments and coursework set by your teacher. As long as you understand what is expected of you, you will be able to use this book to help you get marks in your coursework assignments and final written paper or test.

Assessment objectives

Your final GCSE result comes in the form of a grade from A★–G. You will be graded on your knowledge of the subject and for meeting a number of stated assessment objectives.

The course will help you to develop a number of skills including:

● the ability to investigate the media
● some technical skills
● how to understand issues that affect the media
● working with others.

In practice you will probably not be given a list of every single course aim but they are covered in this book and your coursework will be designed to cover the aims set out in the syllabus you are following.

Your assessment is based on **assessment objectives**. These are detailed in each syllabus and explain what each student should do. They form a kind of instruction pack for teachers because they ensure that teachers have to set out a course in a certain way to allow students to do everything required by the examining board.

The assessment objectives are split into three categories. These are:

❶ knowledge and understanding

❷ description and analysis

❸ production and evaluation.

The wording on assessment objectives varies slightly between the various syllabuses available but the intention of each objective is broadly the same. This book has been written to cover all of the demands in this area. What matters at this early stage of the book is that you realise that you will be expected to perform in three ways:

❶ Showing that you know and understand the key media concepts and can apply your knowledge in a range of media contexts.

❷ Noting details of the media and making sense of these in the form of your own arguments.

❸ Producing your own practical and production work and putting together arguments that explain it and state how successfully it has been completed.

Three examination boards offer syllabuses in Media Studies at GCSE level in the UK: WJEC, MEG and SEG.

About GCSE Media Studies

There are a number of encouraging things to remember as you start to study the media.

First, everyone knows something about the media. We all use it and like some products more than others. This means that we have some understanding to start with. A lot of the theory you will meet in this book will make sense quite easily. This is because you will already be familiar with it.

The job of the book and your teachers is to help you to understand the words, the ideas and the limits of the different pieces of theory, for example, the theory of genre (see Chapter 5).

Most students starting media studies do not know anything about genres. These are groups of media products which have a similarity of style and content. However, if you were to ask your classmates to describe 'horror' products or talk about the differences between Jungle, Trip Hop and Ambient Techno records, somebody could probably give you a good answer. This person would be talking about genres, although he or she might not know it.

Another piece of good news is that your own ideas will count for a lot, especially in the practical work. There should also be chances to use your own ideas to add examples to written assignments.

Media Studies is as hard as any other GCSE but students tend to like the subject because they often feel more involved than they do with some other GCSE courses. Since you know something about the media and you can use your own ideas, you may well feel motivated to learn the theory that will help you to make these things count for marks.

One final piece of good news is that when you study the media, you are studying an industry. If you manage to understand this point and what it means at an early stage of your media studies course, you should find that this knowledge helps with your GCSE. The job of an industry is to make money and continue to grow if possible. As the products you are studying are made for profit, most of the theory relates to money. Once you realise that you are looking at an industry which is making products to sell to audiences you are likely to understand the whole subject more easily.

Something about you

There is no such thing as a typical GCSE Media Studies student. As the subject is so popular, it attracts a wide range of people who all study for different reasons. Media Studies is now so well established that examining boards know this and have changed their syllabuses to allow flexibility in the examples used and the way that schools and colleges deliver the course.

The framework of theory is the same for all students but, as you will see from this book, there is considerable freedom for you to get involved and use your own ideas.

This means that you can set your own targets, depending on what you want from the course. For example, you may simply want a pass grade to give you the right number of GCSE grades to qualify for a job or another course. In this case, you can master enough theory to make sure that your work reaches the right standard.

On the other hand, you might have definite ideas about getting a job in the media. In this case, you can use all the chances offered by the course to develop your own ideas and learn about the media industry.

How to use this book

The subject-based sections in this book all relate to the subject contents within the syllabuses that you are expected to cover within your course. Each subject-based chapter is designed to give you an understanding of its subject and each follows the same pattern:

1 **What you need to know:** an outline of media theory behind the subject.

2 **Three examples:** which are used to discuss and explore the theory of the chapter.

3 **Help with assignments:** is provided by applying the theory discussed in the examples to practical coursework.

4 **Summary:** short reminders of the important points covered in the chapter.

5 **Self-test questions:** which are designed to check whether you have understood the theory covered by the chapter.

You can use the different chapters and the different elements within the chapters on their own. However, the chapters on representations and issues in representation should be considered together because they deal with the same subject.

As the book has been designed in this way, it is possible to use it for a number of different purposes:

1 For learning – read chapters right through to obtain information about important parts of media theory.

2 For revision – use the summaries to remind you of the important points.

3 For help with assignments – use the index, summaries and examples to help with planning for particular assignments.

Syllabus analysis

The subject areas contained within the syllabuses of the two examining boards vary.

WJEC outlines three areas of 'subject content':

1 media forms and representations

2 media organisations

3 media audiences.

SEG lists four areas of 'subject content':

1 media language: forms and conventions

2 representation

3 institutions

4 audience.

In practice, the two boards want students to cover almost exactly the same ground and the different areas listed above simply show that they divide this important information in a different way. This will become clear as you work your way through the subject-based chapters, but you may find it useful to study the breakdown on page 4 of what these terms mean and how the subjects are divided.

The one major difference between the two examining boards is the way that they test their courses at the end. Both boards split the marks for GCSE Media Studies as follows:

Coursework/assignments – 50 per cent
Written paper or controlled test – 50 per cent

SUBJECT CONTENT: BREAKDOWN

Content area
WJEC – Media forms and representations
SEG – Media language: forms and conventions
        Representations

What this means
This area covers the way that the media develop their own ways of presenting information and using certain images, sounds, etc. It concentrates on how some media products have developed, the way that audience pressures have affected this development and the kind of things that we expect from the media. The WJEC's section on forms and representations covers most of what is included in SEG's two sections.

Content area
WJEC – Media organisations
SEG – Institutions

What this means
The two boards mean the same thing despite using different words. These areas cover the way that the media organise themselves and the way that other organisations around the media operate. The idea of these sections is that students should understand that the organisation of the media and people associated with the media has taken place for a number of reasons. These reasons include working to make the best products, making money and competing efficiently with others in the same industry.

Content area
WJEC – Media audiences
SEG – Audiences

What this means
Both boards are agreed in what they want from audience studies. This area asks students to consider the way that audiences shape the media. There are studies of how audiences make sense of the media, how the media reaches out to audiences and how audiences can influence the media.

The WJEC uses a written paper which provides students with stimulus material and bases the paper on this material. It splits the paper into two sections, each containing five questions. The questions follow a set pattern which is explained in the chapter on the WJEC written paper later in this book.

SEG uses a controlled test. This is a fairly unusual type of assessment and is similar to an assignment done under exam conditions. Students are given a detailed project that requires a number of different activities and this assignment is completed over four hours. The times can be arranged by each centre. The SEG controlled test is explained in a later chapter.

The type of coursework students are expected to complete and the contents of both syllabuses are very similar. This book groups the two together in each subject-based chapter.

Coursework

❶ SEG You must submit three pieces of work of about 1000 words, plus a production supported by an evaluation which is 1000 words in length.

❷ WJEC You must submit three pieces of work. All these can have a practical element but one or two pieces must be the production of a media text for an audience.
Evaluation may be written or oral. Each assignment has a 400–600-word equivalence.

Different teachers find their own way around the areas of the syllabuses and one of the great strengths of GCSE Media Studies is that there are many ways of dealing with the coursework.

Most teachers find time to do work that forms a practice for assignments before they set the actual pieces of assessed coursework. Once you are given tasks in class you should be able to see which area of the syllabus they are covering and this may well give you some idea of how the assignments are planned. For example, one WJEC centre deals with work on industries by comparing comedy on television with comedy in comics. If you were a student in this centre, you would prepare for your assignment by doing a number of class-based tasks that involved comparing two different kinds of media and looking at the way they treated one subject.

Teachers are made aware of submission dates by which the boards must have final marks and work for all students. Your teacher will tell you when these deadlines are in time for your work to be submitted.

Grades

At the end of the GCSE Media Studies course, the most important thing for most students is getting the right grade. Examiners and teachers are made aware of very strict guidelines that determine the grades that students will get. Both of the boards agree on the kind of things that students should do. The descriptions of grades below reflect the demands of both examining boards.

Grade A

For this you must show a sound understanding of the media. You must also use all of the right media terminology and show a real ability to build arguments. This ability is essential when you need to make sense of media products and to put forward reasons for the way they are put together and the reasons for them being put together.

Grade C

For this you must show that you clearly understand questions that were set for assignments and written papers/tests. There should be use of the right media terms and clear attempts to make sense of things and see the reasons for things happening. The important pieces of media theory should be outlined. Candidates must show the right ideas and right understanding in their work. C candidates may fall short of an A Grade simply because there were more mistakes or missed opportunities in their folder. Alternatively, the work may not reach the standards of presentation or the quality of ideas in an A folder.

Grade F

Students still use some of the right terms but don't show much understanding beyond their own use of the media. They may miss important points in arguments and fail to see reasons for the way things happen in the media. At the same time most of the work in the folder will deal with the questions set.

'SPAG' marks

There are five marks specially awarded for standards of 'Spelling, Punctuation and Grammar' (SPAG) in GCSE Media Studies. These marks apply to other subjects as well and a good standard of spelling, punctuation and grammar is sometimes enough to take a Media Studies folder that is on the borderline of two grades up to the higher one.

Examination Boards: addresses

SEG   **Southern Examining Group**
            Stag Hill House, Guildford GU2 5XJ
            Tel: 01483 506506

WJEC   **Welsh Joint Education Committee**
            245 Western Avenue, Cardiff CF5 2YX
            Tel: 01222 265000

Chapter 1
Media languages

1.1 What you need to know

Rules in media languages

Media languages refers to the way that the media use different **rules** to put across messages. The media have developed these rules along with a system of **codes** and **patterns**. Spoken and written languages, like English and German, use rules. An example of a rule in written and spoken English is the way that words have a plural form. So, for instance, the plural of book is books. We can make sense of messages in English because we understand these rules. The same is true of the media.

Each area of the media has different rules for making statements about meaning. For example, scenes in a film in which the camera is placed in the position of the eyes of one of the characters allow the viewer to see exactly what that character is seeing. These shots are often used to say that a character is in danger. Think of any shot you have seen like this – it will probably be from a horror film.

Media language patterns

You need to understand the idea of media languages because it is an important part of media studies. Both of the examining boards require students to look at the way that media texts are put together and to spot the patterns in the way they are constructed. By doing this, you will begin to see the patterns in the way that media products are organised, and that it is our understanding of these patterns that allows us to find meaning in media products.

A media language is a system or code that is used within the media to put across a particular meaning. People who study the media have identified ways in which this happens and which parts of the languages are involved. Imagine, for example, watching a new act on 'Top of the Pops'. The information you get from this first look at the act will help you to form an **impression**. If you see four men with guitars, long hair and tight-fitting clothes, you might expect a heavy metal band. This would be confirmed by an opening crashing chord or riff. If on the other hand, the act featured several people dressed in similar clothes and dancing in a way that looked planned, you might decide that you are watching a dance group.

These impressions are also likely to be supported by the names of the acts. So, for example, Metallica, Iron Maiden and Megadeath are all 'metal' acts. Their names suggest strength. D-Mob is a dance act; its name suggests a group of people, similar to the groups of people who go to dance events.

This information fits into a media language pattern. We can see that the pieces of the language that make up our understanding of music come from a number of different sources. Some come from written languages. The names of bands are based on written languages, usually English. These are often linked to the image of the band. For example, The Beatles is probably the most famous pop/rock band of all time. Its name is a simple pun on the name of an insect using the word 'Beat'. When The Beatles started, the band was part of 'the beat boom', which was based on music with a strong beat.

The 'Top of the Pops' example also shows that media languages might draw their parts from a number of different sources. For instance, in music, the language that links types of music with an audience is made up of **sounds, images and words**.

The examining boards expect you to be able to describe the way in which the media organise information in particular patterns to put across certain messages. You will find this easier to understand once you have studied a few examples.

1.2 A definition of media languages

Functions of language

To understand media languages, we need to look at the role of language in general. People who study language have listed a number of different jobs or **functions of language**:

1 To communicate and make statements.

2 To help us to link ourselves together.

3 To help us to express emotion.

4 To help us to appreciate qualities like beauty.

5 To comment on other messages.

The word 'help' is used in describing the role of language because it is possible to do the above jobs without language. But, most of us would find it difficult to survive without using some form of language.

If we look at each of the functions, we can see that the task of language itself is fairly simple. Media languages do all of the jobs listed for language. A few examples will help you to understand how these languages are put together. We will also see how these languages are linked to other points elsewhere in this book.

Communicating and making statements

In a spoken language a **statement** can be made simply by talking about something. For example, 'I'm bored' is a statement. The media have found other ways of talking about emotions. One reason we value the media so much is that their ways of putting emotions into simple pictures or sounds is often very effective. Look at the example in Fig. 1.1.

Most people think it is important to look after their health and the health of others. Putting these feelings into words can be hard. The leaflet shown in Fig. 1.1 (opposite) is designed to encourage people to become organ donors.

Study the picture of the woman and child. The picture suggests happiness, health and love between the two. The statement made by the picture is very direct. It suggests that donated organs help more people to be as healthy and happy as the woman and child in the picture. You can understand this message simply by looking at the picture and because this understanding is instant, it means more people are likely to take an interest in registering as organ donors.

This book contains many examples of statements made by the media. It is important at this stage that you realise that the media can make statements in a number of ways.

Sounds, pictures and music

Now, try to think of some statements which use language and some that do not. Think of the way that **advertisements** present the products they are selling, for example. These images often make statements about the link between what is being advertised

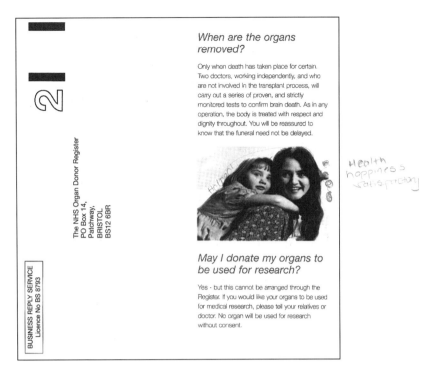

Fig. 1.1

and the type of people who use it. Try your own skills at this. Look again at the leaflet in Fig. 1.1. How would you advertise for people to become organ donors in:

● a radio commercial

● a magazine advert

● a cinema commercial?

The above exercise will have encouraged you to think about the use of sounds, pictures and possibly music to make a statement about the work of a charity. In completing it, you will have used your knowledge of ways in which the media can make statements. This knowledge can help you to gain marks in your GCSE course.

Fig. 1.2

Helping us to link ourselves together

In a spoken and written language like English, much conversation centres around things that have little importance. For example, at a bus stop people often talk about the weather. This conversation might seem dull, but it has an important purpose – it helps people to link themselves together in society. The advantage of talking about trivial things is that they do not divide people. If you suddenly started talking about religion, politics or even football with a total stranger, you might run the risk of an argument.

The appeal of a popular image

The media use a number of **strategies to link audiences**. One way to understand this is to consider a popular image and its appeal to a wide audience. Look at the photo of Noel Edmonds presenting the BBC TV quiz show 'Telly Addicts' (Fig. 1.2). Research has shown that this show is liked by family audiences.

Noel Edmonds is a well-known television personality who has fronted a number of shows aimed at family viewers. He is in his 40s. Although he probably attracts male viewers of his own age to his shows, many of the people who watch him are a different age, gender or colour to Noel Edmonds.

The shows and in particular the presenter offer something that links all these people together. Noel Edmonds presents an **image** of an ordinary, average man. He wears bright casual clothes; his hair cut and beard are well known, but they don't fit current fashion trends. He is youthful but not 'young', and he has a sense of humour but this does not include offensive humour.

This image is perfect for shows aimed at a family audience because it conforms with the views of the majority of people in the UK who belong to average families. It is likely that many of his audience don't spend much time thinking about Noel Edmonds' image.

We can see how well this job of helping people link themselves together works when we consider ways in which it could be threatened. If Noel Edmonds gave up presenting shows like 'Telly Addicts' and 'The House Party', finding a replacement would be crucial. Anyone with a controversial image would be unsuitable.

The images of famous people tend to include qualities that attract some fans and turn other people away. We have seen Noel Edmonds' positive qualities. To get a better insight into this area of media language try the following exercises:

❶ Think of some people who wouldn't want to watch a show presented by Noel Edmonds. List five things about Noel Edmonds that would put them off from watching him.

❷ Imagine that the BBC was looking for a presenter to star alongside David Attenborough in a new wildlife TV series aimed at a family audience of all ages and levels of income. Try to think of one famous person who could take on the job and appeal to this audience. List five points about this person that would help him or her to make a success of their role.

These are simple examples, but they should help you to appreciate the way that a piece of media language, like the image of a famous person, can work to link people who see life in the same way.

Helping us to express emotion

Many media products rely on emotion for their appeal. These products produce emotion from their audience. Because there are so many media products competing for our attention and money, the media usually use emotional ideas and images to try to win **instant appeal** among their audience. There are several ways in which this instant appeal is put across.

There are, however, important differences between the way that we express emotion in real life and the way that media languages do this. In the case of a spoken language, we often discuss things and use words to explain how we feel so as to get others to understand.

A focus for emotion

The media often act as a **focus** for emotion. They say things that we feel and this builds a link between the media and their audiences. The tabloid newspapers, for instance, aim to attract readership by presenting the news in an exciting and sensational way. One example is *The Sun*'s story on the final race of the 1994 world Formula One car championship, in which many British racing fans hoped to see driver Damon Hill clinch the world title with victory. He had a controversial collision with Michael Schumacher during the race and both drivers had to retire. This gave Schumacher the championship. Some people thought that Schumacher had caused the collision deliberately. The following day *The Sun* printed this headline:

SCHU DIRTY RAT

We could say that this is written in English, but it is also typical of a journalistic kind of language that we would not normally use in everyday life. It makes a pun on the first syllable of Schumacher's surname and mimics a famous catchphrase, 'You dirty rat', which has been linked to the gangster roles played by film star James Cagney in the 1930s. The headline suggests that Schumacher cheated and reflects the emotions that many race fans

Fig. 1.3

in Britain felt on the day. The headlines in German newspapers were very different.

Using visual images

When the media try to express emotion, they often copy the way that we do this in real life. The 'Schu dirty rat' headline does this by using the kind of simple phrase that people chant at sports events. Another example can be seen in the advert in Fig. 1.3.

The advert is for a charity appeal and it uses the photo of 'Juanita' to make the reader feel sorry for a number of people who are suffering. Pictures of suffering children often produce a good response for charities because people looking at the photos can see the children as helpless and innocent. This advert is asking for money to give women in developing countries the chance of a good education and a better life. By using a child in an advert aimed at adults with money to donate, the advertisers hope to promote the caring feelings that many adults have for children.

This kind of image is well known to people who take an interest in such adverts. We can say it is part of a media language dealing with emotion because the people who would recognise this advert would understand the meaning behind the picture. They would understand that the young girl was from another country, that her own life wasn't easy or comfortable and that she would be happier if she were helped.

Clichés

Pictures like the one in Fig. 1.3 form part of a media language because they are used again and again. When an image is used in this way, it becomes a **cliché**. This means that we recognise it instantly. There are many examples of emotional clichés in the media such as close-ups of crying faces in films or appealing pictures of animals, both of which are used to get an emotional response from viewers. In all these examples, there is one simple image, from which we understand a great deal.

Can you think of an example when something in the media worked to focus or start an emotion in you? Try to think of a media product that means a lot to you. Even if this product includes words – like film dialogue or song lyrics – try to forget the words and think about the other parts. For example, the sounds of the music in a favourite record are likely to produce emotions for you, as well as the lyrics. If you can remember a sad scene in a film, you should realise that the shots chosen did as much as the dialogue to bring out a sad feeling for you.

These are simple examples of the way in which pieces of a media language work. The examples you thought of may have been quite simple too, but this is important in understanding the way that media language works. Even a short time spent thinking through scenes from films or musical sections of records will help you to realise that the things that made you feel emotional are similar to other film scenes, other parts of different records, etc. The fact that media products tend to use similar ways of producing and focusing emotions shows us that these scenes and sounds are part of a language and do not occur on their own.

Helping us to appreciate qualities like beauty

People who study language believe that one job or function of language is to help us appreciate qualities that we can experience. This is called an **aesthetic** function of language.

In terms of media language, it can be hard to separate this job from other functions of language. For example, a close-up of a beautiful actress or good-looking actor may well be designed to help us to appreciate their qualities of being handsome. Certain types of shot, such as close-ups, are used regularly for this purpose and they form a type of media language. These images are often complicated by the fact that appreciating the good looks of a film star often goes along with feeling an emotion, like affection.

Making sense of images

The media sometimes produce images that rely on shapes, textures, combinations of colour and so on for their appeal. These images often leave an audience confused about their meaning. This means that people have to work harder than usual to make sense of the image.

In cases like this, the images are often valued for some quality of beauty. Look at the leaflet advertising a tour of a serious play by a theatre company (Fig. 1.4). The play is not well known, so showing a character or a scene from the performance on the front of the leaflet would be unlikely to attract large audiences.

Instead, the picture chosen shows a woman swimming on her back but it has been taken in such a way that you have to study the photo carefully to make out the details. The image uses the shape of the woman in the water and the ripples on the water itself as main features. The picture does not seem to have any one meaning.

The play – *The Colleen Bawn* – centres on a woman leading a secret life and facing difficult decisions. Looking at the picture, it is possible to see it as a woman trying to escape pressures or simply doing something that she enjoys. But, the point here is that these suggestions are making a guess at what the picture is about and we would not all agree on its meaning.

Fig. 1.4

In terms of media language, all that can be said is that ideas and emotions are behind most of the media products we see. Because it is often hard to be exact about ideas and emotions, the media have developed ways of suggesting both of these without linking them to one meaning. Fig. 1.4 is an example of this. There is an advantage in using examples which can have more than one meaning. The leaflet might attract larger audiences because a number of different people can read their own meaning into the picture.

To find some examples of this type of media language, visit a large record shop and look at the covers for classical releases. Many of these feature pictures of landscapes, the sea or simply particular things from nature like trees. This doesn't meant that the music is actually about landscapes, the sea, etc.

The idea of using such cover pictures is that audiences should think that the qualities in the cover picture are contained in the music. For example, a freshly snow-covered landscape might be used to feature a classical work that has a sharp and light feel to it. The music might give you a similar feeling to the one you might experience when seeing newly fallen snow. Classical record covers provide one of the best examples of a media language built around feelings or ideas.

You can practise creating such work yourself. Think of something special to you that has more than one meaning, such as a favourite piece of music. Now try to focus on the personal feelings it brings out in you, or simply focus on some feeling that you have. After this, try to invent an image that would describe this feeling to a friend. Avoid using obvious things like pictures of people's faces.

 ## Commenting on other messages

In studies of a written or spoken language this job or function of language is often overlooked. However, in the media this function of language is common. Media languages are built around powerful images, sounds and so on. This means that

Fig. 1.5

audiences understand these **elements** of the media languages as having great power. Many examples of media language rely on things taken from an existing language to use as some kind of comment.

Look at the photo of champion boxer Chris Eubank (Fig. 1.5). A picture like this, taken for publicity purposes, often allows us to see a person or group of people attempting to put across a very definite visual image. Chris Eubank's image is different to that of other boxers. He has styled his look on that of the historic English country gentleman and worn clothes, such as jodhpurs, which have their roots in the past. Eubank's ethnic origin, profession and the time in which he achieved fame all seem to distance him from being the typical country gentleman. His choice of an image based on these clothes means that he is making a comment.

Eubank's image seems to be saying that he is different from other boxers in that he is a cultured person. It is also possible to see his image as making a positive statement about the place of black people in Britain in the 1990s because his clothes are associated with an earlier time when Britain owned and controlled many countries in the world. Eubank was the first black man to be voted Britain's best-dressed man. We can see from this that pieces of media language can be used and updated.

Think about examples you know of media images and ideas that have borrowed from other parts of the media. Can you think of any pop act that has taken an image from another group or from somewhere outside the music business? Are there any characters you know in TV programmes that have images based on other famous characters?

Once you have thought of your own examples, look at the detailed ones given below, in particular the Spangles advert.

1.3 Three examples of media language

EXAMPLE **Spangles advert**

This example clearly illustrates the five jobs of a media language.

Like most adverts, this one has been designed to sell a product – Spangles sweets. Spangles are well remembered by people who were young in the 1960s, and their relaunch in the 1990s was designed to appeal to young people and some of those who had bought the sweets over 30 years ago.

The advert shown in Fig. 1.6 appeared in publications that would allow it to be seen by this broad range of people. For example, it was printed in *The Sun*, the most popular of all British newspapers and magazines.

If we look at the advert in detail, we will see how media language is organised to create a message to an audience.

Fig. 1.6

Making a statement

The clear message is that Spangles are on sale again. In terms of media language, the advert uses some visual tricks linked to news and current affairs to add other messages about Spangles. The fact that the packet of Spangles is close to the camera suggests that the sweets are important, more so than the two people. The serious look on the face of the man also supports this. He is wearing a suit and we tend to associate serious looks and suits with important information.

This visual language is well known to anyone who watches TV news. The importance of the message is also reinforced by the advert being printed in black and white. We tend to think of black and white photographs as showing serious things. This comes from their use in newspapers. All this suggests that the return of Spangles is news in itself.

Linking people together

The style of the advert offers an attractive message to both of the groups of people who might be expected to buy Spangles. This is not easy because the target market for the sweets covers people in their teens to those in their 40s. The advert manages to succeed by presenting the older people with fashions and a style of lettering that they will remember from the 1960s. Because some of these fashions made a come-back in the mid-1990s, the advert also appeals to people who took an interest in the revival of 1960s' style music and clothes.

In terms of media language, the advert presents enough of a 1960s' image to make clear the idea of the link between Spangles and the 1960s. On the other hand, it doesn't link Spangles to any one fashion trend. The general idea of the 1960s, with its youth culture, fashions and fun, is what counts.

By making this point in a general way, the advert appeals to anyone who is interested in enjoying the idea of the 'swinging '60s'. If we look in more detail, we can see that the images chosen are a clever use of media language.

The lettering in particular appeals to a number of different markets. This style of lettering has been widely used. In the 1960s some pop bands used it in their names, but the same style was also used by some rock bands who never appeared in the charts. The fans of both kinds of music often had little respect for each other's tastes. Something similar has happened in the 1990s with dance/rave music fans and the fans of guitar-based groups both having their own places to meet. The 1990s' dance and guitar music scenes have both been influenced by the 1960s, and the type of lettering used in the Spangles advert is known to both dance and guitar music fans of the 1990s.

The lettering is linked in many people's minds to the 'spirit' of the 1960s. Different people have different ideas about this 'spirit', but all would recognise the lettering in the advert. So the lettering helps to link together the different people who might buy Spangles.

Are there other ways that the advert could have used to get across the same message? A photo of a 1960s' pop star, such as P. J. Proby, might have appealed more to the older end of the market. However, those in their teens are unlikely to recognise P. J. Proby, and so his image would not help to sell Spangles to them. On the other hand, a picture of someone wearing 1960s' style clothes at a rave would not appeal to people in their late 30s and 40s. When we consider the problems with these images, the use of the lettering to link the Spangles' buyers together seems to be very effective.

Expressing emotion

The lettering also helps us to understand how the media language used to express emotions works in this advert. It is hard to explain the real meaning of the style of lettering because, as we have seen, the lettering is well known to different groups of people. One particular feature is that it seems to leap out at you from the advert and that you have to work to understand what it says. Lettering like this is linked to music that tends to leap out in a loud way at you and which often demands some work on the part of the listener to make sense of it.

For example, some dance records include samples that fade in and out, and you have to pay attention to pick them out. Compare this with a pop record made by a famous artiste like Cliff Richard for a wide audience. There is usually very little doubt about the words in a Cliff Richard song, and the lettering used for his name is much easier to read.

The lettering and the dance positions of the young people in the advert are all part of a media language that is linked with expressing emotion. The young people look like they are dancing, and the dance poses are easily recognisable. The lettering and the dance positions probably make you think of music, clubs or similar fun things. In terms of a media language, what matters here is that two simple images — a style of lettering and a picture of two young people dancing — can bring all of these different ideas into the mind of someone looking at the advert.

People don't normally look at an advert in such detail. What matters in terms of a media language is that people make a fast and simple connection between what they see in an advert and the ideas behind the images. For example, pictures of young people dancing are a piece of media language that carries a lot of information.

Dancing is usually associated with going out, enjoying oneself and being in a dark place. People often feel a freedom when dancing that they don't find in many other things that they do. This is one reason why dancing in discos and clubs has been a popular pastime for years. If you tried striking the pose of the girl in the Spangles advert on a bus or in a classroom, you would probably be laughed at.

But the fact that many of us recognise dance poses and have some ideas about them being linked to enjoyment and expressing ourselves means that the picture in the advert can put across this idea. To many people, thoughts of dancing have an emotional link. These emotional thoughts might well be personal. If you enjoy dancing, the right kind of picture of people dancing might remind you of your pleasure and bring back this emotion.

When we consider the importance and emotions linked to dancing by so many people, it is easy to see how simple things like the lettering and picture in this advert can have an emotional message.

Appreciating the qualities of the product

We saw earlier how media languages can help us to appreciate qualities like beauty. In the case of adverts the qualities to be appreciated are those of the product.

In many ways, most leading brands of burgers, colas and biscuits resemble each other. This doesn't really matter to the people who buy them. Companies like Coca Cola and Pepsi spend a lot of money on advertising their drinks and developing an image. They know that the image and the experience of their product is what matters to people who buy it. The millions of people who drink Coca Cola every day recognise the taste and if given lemonade instead would notice the difference. The argument that both drinks contain similar ingredients — such as sugar and water — wouldn't stop them complaining.

The same is true of sweets, and the advert for Spangles encourages us to appreciate the qualities of the sweets. Spangles competes with rival brands, like Opal Fruits. The advert is designed to help us appreciate the things that make the experience of Spangles special. The concentration on young people, having a good time and burning up energy, all give a meaning to Spangles — that these sweets give instant pleasure and the taste floods through people's mouths. The advert concentrates on another instant pleasure, dancing, which also gives a good feeling.

Once again, we can see that in terms of media language, the advert is using an image that has a meaning. The meaning allows us to understand more about Spangles. It may be hard to explain, but then it is also difficult to describe the experience of eating sweets.

Commenting on other messages

The Spangles advert attempts to use the 1960s' style as a comment. The advert clearly says that Spangles are different from other sweets because they are rooted in a special time in history.

The lettering also makes a comment — it has links with the 1960s and youth culture and defines the image in the advert which sets it apart from other sweet adverts.

This form of advertising is quite popular and you may find examples in media adverts or even in your own area. Some cafes and restaurants deliberately style themselves on a time in history. They do this by taking items that represent history, such as old clothes and tools, and placing them where customers will see them. We understand this visual language as an attempt to create a kind of meaning. This is exactly the same kind of approach taken by the media language in the Spangles advert.

EXAMPLE ## Film still from a horror film

This example shows a part of media language that has changed little over a period of years.

Plan Nine From Outer Space is a film which has enjoyed cult popularity, since it was first released in 1959, by being well known as 'the worst movie ever made'. In 1995 the film *Ed Wood* was released in the UK. It told the story of the man who directed *Plan Nine From Outer Space*, and to tie in with the release of *Ed Wood*, the video of his earlier film was reissued.

Whatever the reason for the popularity of the film, it will only continue to be watched by audiences for as long as they can understand its meaning. That they can do so is because the media language linked to the film has changed little since the 1950s.

Look closely at Fig. 1.7, it is a film still from another horror film directed by Ed Wood. It tells you a lot. If you were going to note down the things it says, you might produce a list which included the following:

- This is a horror film.

- The man with a knife is a bad character.

- The woman is in danger.

There is truth in all of these points. Even if you've never seen the film, the picture should make sense to you because it includes many familiar things from today's horror films. Monster characters are also a regular feature of horror movies. We often see monster characters attack young people in such films. We also see people who stand for good fighting against monsters of all kinds.

The development of media language in films

The idea of good versus bad and some kind of fight between the two has been used in films since before 1914. In terms of media language, this means that films have developed ways of making the same points by using tried and tested scenes. For this example, it is important to consider the way that this one picture shows us how film has developed a language to present certain ideas.

The setting of the picture at night is also typical of many horror scenes. Mist and graveyards are also common themes of horror films. The combination of mist, the graveyard and night suggests a threat. The darkness and mist stop us from seeing the things that threaten us, and graveyards are linked with death, which is in itself a threat. When all these images are put together in a film, we tend to understand the end result as being one of horror.

In terms of media language, film companies gain much from keeping to a well-known formula. Other chapters in this book look at other types of well-known formulas such as genres and narratives.

Fig. 1.7

From the standpoint of media language, this example clearly shows the way that complicated ideas can be summed up in one still picture from a film. We can say that we are looking at an example of media language because we understand the things we see in this picture and we know that the same features occur in many other films. This example also tells us that media language has changed little since the 1950s. It shows that the things we would recognise today as parts of a media language have been used in the same way for decades. We recognise spoken languages when they get used over a long period of time and the same is true of the languages of the media. The age of this film shows that the points about media language made in this example are true. They are not just the result of recent fashion.

EXAMPLE *Mandy and Judy* **comic**

This example shows the way that a media language develops within a particular media area.

Comic stories have some similarities with TV and film in that they develop through the use of pictures and words. There are, however, some clear differences in length and the fact that comics are based on still pictures while TV and film use moving images.

Media language and the comics market

What matters in studying this example of media language is that we think carefully about why the comic-strip story has developed in the way that it has. Some of this development has been affected by the market for comics.

We need to consider the market for this comic before we study the example in any detail. *Mandy and Judy* is aimed at girls aged 8–12 years. Its readers may move on to read teenage girls' magazines like *Just Seventeen.*

The audience or market for a product matters in terms of media language because media language develops to meet the demands of an audience. We saw above how it is the job of a media language to link people together. By looking at this example we see how media language within the comic works to do this.

Children are more likely to play in an imaginative way then people older than them. The imagination that they use in their play also helps in their understanding of the media. This enables the readers to use their imagination in a number of ways. The lack of colour, sound and movement means that they have to add these for themselves. If you asked the readers of the story about the colour of the main character's clothes, you may get different answers depending on the favourite colour of a particular reader. This can work to make comics more appealing to their readers because every reader can make the character more like themselves.

There are some other points to remember about the market for comics:

● The readers are not particularly well off. Children below teenage years do not usually have much spending money. Comics are often bought for them by parents or others, perhaps as a treat.

● The audience tends to move on from one leisure activity to another very quickly. Their attention span can be very short.

Children's comics meet both these points: they are cheap to buy and are full of stories that can be read quickly.

In terms of media language, this leads to certain ways of putting across a message. Action in the stories comes at a fast rate and most of the frames of a comic story move the story forward. The pictures have enough detail to show where the story is set, but they are not complicated. Their simple style, coupled with the fact that many children's comics are printed in black and white, keeps down costs of production, and therefore the cover price.

Mandy and Judy presents a story in a classic comic style – the example in Fig. 1.8 (overleaf) was published in 1991. The action moves quickly, the scenes are clearly drawn but not cluttered and the story does not take long to read.

If you think about the kind of comics you read when you were younger, you will probably remember them as following the same rules of media language mentioned in this example. The way that children's comics do their job has not changed much in decades because the demand from children for the same kind of product has stayed strong.

Fig. 1.8

1.4 How these examples can help in your assignments

Before you begin this unit, you should remember that the most useful thing you can do to help you get good marks is to read and understand the assignment itself.

The advice here is designed to give you some general help in understanding points that can be used to construct arguments. Used properly these will gain you marks.

The examples of media language in this chapter show that we understand different ways in which the media communicate messages. We have also seen some reasons for the way that media languages have developed.

There are two general ways in which this can help with your work:

1 In studying any media product for an assignment, you should consider how it puts across information and why it has developed this way of presenting information.

2 When producing your own media texts for coursework, you can discuss the way you have coded them and used particular pieces of media language.

When studying an example taken from the media, the following questions about media language will help you to understand any media text:

- Are there any special ways in which the example presents information? If the answer is 'yes', then a good way to get extra marks is to point these out, discuss them and use other examples briefly to show that you understand this point.

- Are there any pictures, sounds, designs and so on in the example that are used elsewhere in other media products? If the answer is 'yes', then you may gain marks by pointing out these examples and adding a few other examples of your own. You can then argue that the existence of many similar examples shows that a media language exists.

- Does the example use an idea from somewhere else? If the answer is 'yes', then you can discuss the borrowed idea or material, state where it came from and mention that one job of a language is to allow people to make comments on other things found in the language. You could briefly suggest what kind of comment was made, using the example of borrowed material that you have found.

- If the example has a particular message that is aimed at one section of an audience, you may be able to point out the thing – such as a picture or sound – that helps to put across the message. If it has a meaning to a particular audience, you could discuss this and use other similar examples to show that it is part of a media language.

When discussing your own work, you could ask yourself the questions above, as well as following the advice below:

- If you have put in a message in a particular way – such as using a character in a video to represent a type of person – you could explain this and briefly mention a few other media examples to show that it is part of a language and not just something you have invented.

- If you have included a way of putting across information that is widely used, you should point this out and quote some examples.

- If you have borrowed or sampled something from another area of the media, then you should mention this and discuss the kind of comment you were hoping to make by doing so. Give other examples to show that you understand the way that media language can allow borrowing or sampling in order to make a comment.

- If you have included something that has a meaning for a small or cult audience, mention this and discuss how media language works to bring together groups of people with a similar view.

Summary

1   A media language works in the same way that other languages work. It is made up of the things we see within the media, like pictures and sounds.

2   Media languages allow us to do the things that other written and spoken languages allow us to do. These include making statements, bringing groups of people together, helping us to express emotion, appreciating qualities like beauty and making comments on other things we find in the language.

3   Media languages develop because of the demands of an audience. For example, children's comics present simply drawn stories for an audience which moves quickly from activity to activity.

4   There are some well-established examples of media language such as film shots of monsters that represent evil.

5   Media languages can change as the demands of audiences change.

6   Some media languages are built on things that have a meaning to a small or cult audience.

7   Media languages can be made up of all the things that the media use to put across their messages to an audience. These include pictures, sounds, lettering, colours, shapes and so on.

Self-test questions

1   In two or three sentences explain the meaning of a 'media language'.
2   Give one example of the way that a media language helps us to communicate.
3   List ten things that might form part of a media language.
4   In three or four sentences, explain why a media language might change over time.
5   In three or four sentences, explain why some parts of a media language might stay the same over time.

Chapter 2
Media forms and conventions

2.1 What you need to know

Media forms are the different parts that make up the mass media, such as newspapers, films, TV programmes, etc.

Conventions are the usual ways in which things are done. In the case of the media, these conventions mean typical features of certain products. So, for example, it is a convention that a newspaper like *The Sun* has a huge headline and at least one picture on the front page.

The difference between forms and conventions

The main difference between forms and conventions is that media producers have more choice about whether to follow convention than they do about whether to follow form.

For example, a pop single may be released in the form of a CD, tape or vinyl. A record company would probably have to release the single on all three if it wanted to make a profit. The forms of release are limited by the kind of equipment people have for listening to music.

There is more choice over convention, however. It is conventional for singles to last between 2½ and 4 minutes because this makes them easy to programme for radio. It is also conventional for singles to have verses, choruses and catchy musical backing. However, some acts release very long singles or records that don't have a chorus. In 1992 the British band The Orb released a single that lasted almost 40 minutes and had no real chorus. This single still made the Top 20 although it ignored media convention.

There are two important things to remember about forms and conventions before you study the detailed examples in unit 2.2.

❶ You are already likely to be familiar with media forms and conventions, so this chapter will not teach you much that is new. Its main aim is to develop your understanding of them.

❷ To get better marks in your GCSE, you will need to write clear arguments explaining the links between forms and conventions and meaning in the media.

2.2 Three examples of media forms and conventions

EXAMPLE **Aswad single**

This example looks at a 'typical' product in one area of the media.

Study the cover of the pop single 'You're No Good' by Aswad (Fig. 2.1). This is a standard single by a reggae band which has had a series of hits and topped the singles charts once. Aswad's image cannot be identified with any one fashion trend. Bands like Aswad tend to have hits on the strength of their records and to build up a following through live performances.

This single was released in 1995 and sold well, but did not become a major hit. In many ways, it is a typical pop single, and the cover is designed to identify it in this way. Because the band lacks an identifiable fashion style, the cover features a 'typical' pop image. Aswad's members are dressed in casual leisure clothes with some fashionable accessories. Although the band has been working since the 1970s, the image is one of youthfulness.

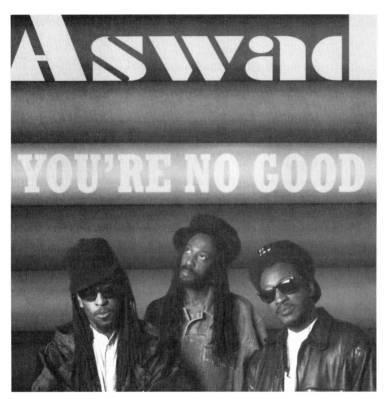

Fig. 2.1

The clear lettering on the cover allows the title of the single and the name of the band to be read without difficulty. Aswad's name has been specially designed so that it is distinctive and therefore easy to remember.

If this picture were shown in colour, the lines across the sleeve behind the band would be red and green, and the lettering would be red. Red, green and gold are the colours associated with Rastafarianism and they have a special meaning within that religion. Reggae music and dreadlocks are also closely linked to the Rastafarian religion. So the cover also aims to attract fans of reggae music.

You can see how a fairly simple cover design, such as this, can work to identify the music as a pop/reggae single.

Within this, we can identify several forms and conventions and look at the way they work.

The pop 'single' as a media form

The sales of the pop single were higher in 1995 than they had been for 10 years. Some people had begun to predict that singles would disappear completely from the record market. Cheap and catchy singles have been a big part of the pop industry for decades. As a form, they have been important in attracting young music fans into the market. Most people buy singles in their early teens before they can afford more expensive albums. Record companies make bigger profits from albums, but singles have always been important because singles buyers are considered to be the album buyers of the future.

A band like Aswad will keep on releasing singles because its live career and album sales will benefit. 'Top of the Pops' appearances and chart singles bring new fans into Aswad concerts and sell albums. Even singles like 'You're No Good', which didn't get the band on to 'Top of the Pops', help a little because they pick up radio air-play and remind people about Aswad.

A throw-away media product

The simplicity of the picture shows that this is, to some extent, a throw-away media product. Pop singles have always been small, portable items, and newer formats like tape and CD mean that singles can be carried in pockets. This helps to identify another aspect of this form. Singles are often carried around from one young person's home to another, listened to and discussed. This is one way that bands gain fans as one person tells friends about the music as they all listen to a single.

When we think about the way that the single is used, we can see why the form developed in this way. The short playing time of singles makes them easy to programme for radio. They also fit easily into young people's conversations and can be listened to in short bursts, for example, on a personal stereo on the way to school or college.

What makes a hit song?

It is difficult to discuss the music in much detail without you being able to hear the record, but there are some basic points that should be made about this particular single. First, reggae is bouncy and danceable music. This type of pop music has always included a heavy dance element because reggae is often used for dancing. Songs that prove to be danceable and catchy are the most common types of hit record.

In terms of conventions, hit songs have musical similarities, and songs which are catchy and memorable have proved to very profitable. This is the reason for old songs in well-known styles being recorded time and time again by pop musicians. Some songs like 'Unchained Melody' have been hits off and on for 40 years. When two actors from the TV programme 'Soldier Soldier' took 'Unchained Melody' to No. 1 in the UK in 1995, the first man to top the charts with the song – Jimmy Young – was working on BBC Radio 2 as a disc jockey and was old enough to qualify for a bus pass!

How Aswad followed convention

It's important to remember this when considering Aswad's single. 'You're No Good' was originally released more than 30 years ago when it appeared in the British charts. Since then, the song has been recorded by many artistes, but it has never again reached the charts. Aswad's own recording of a well-known song that has stood the test of time is a usual tactic of a band trying to have a hit record. We can say that Aswad was following convention.

When the media follow a convention, we can describe this as **conventional**. Aswad's decision to produce a cover version of an old song was a conventional one. The song 'You're No Good' is conventional in being catchy, having a chorus and dealing with the theme of love. The band's appearance in youthful/fashionable clothes is also conventional.

Sometimes, it is hard to identify pop music with any one meaning. A band like Aswad is more of a typical 'pop' band, than a household name like Elton John or Take That. Aswad's survival in the music industry for 20 years has not been built on the kind of international success and major hits that the world's leading performers have enjoyed.

Aswad has been successful mainly on the strength of its music. 'Strength' in this case means that the band has been able to produce music that manages to sound fresh and catchy but also follows the kinds of rules discussed in this example. The band's image has also been important. It has managed to keep enough of a pop image to appeal to the pop market and enough of a reggae image to appeal to the reggae market.

Aswad has achieved its image success by following media conventions. In this example, the band's image is based on the kinds of thing that are hard to pin down in pop images. Pop is linked to ideas like youth, fun and fashion. The picture on the cover manages to show all these things without identifying Aswad with any one fashion style that will eventually look old-fashioned.

In reggae it is conventional to use the rasta colours and dreadlocks as marks of identity. Aswad follows this convention, but avoids too bold a reggae image to allow it to attract a general pop audience.

The band's success lies in its appeal to pop and reggae audiences. Acts who have had hits over many years usually manage to keep a kind of fashionable look without belonging to any one particular trend. If you have ever seen 1960s pictures of Cliff Richard, Tom Jones or Diana Ross in the 1960s, this should be clear.

We have already mentioned some other conventions. The high profile given to the name and the title of the record are conventional in pop music. Success is built on people recognising performers' names and remembering the titles of their records. Because the pop single tends to be a throw-away product, the simple cover design as in our example is also a convention. The cover design allows regular fans to recognise the familiar faces of Aswad. It also gives an instant message about the band and the single in the hope of attracting other record buyers.

EXAMPLE | ## Tabloid newspaper front cover: *The Sun*

This example considers the way that 'typical' forms and conventions are used to produce meaning.

Study the front page of *The Sun* newspaper from 17 June 1995 (Fig. 2.2). This was not a particularly special news day but the papers did find a number of major stories to write about. *The Sun* decided to give priority to the Queen's birthday honours list which included an MBE for England rugby star Rob Andrew. At the time the England team were still in the World Cup. The paper also discussed the future of John Major as prime minister and used a corner of the front page to advertise *The Sun*'s own instant scratch-card game.

Fig. 2.2

There are some points about form and convention to note here because these will help you to understand how forms and conventions can be used to produce meaning.

What is a tabloid newspaper?

In terms of form, *The Sun* is a **tabloid** newspaper. This means that it is smaller in size compared to newspapers such as *The Times*. Tabloid papers are typically slightly smaller than A3 size paper. The word 'tabloid' is usually understood as referring to a newspaper of a certain size, shape and content.

Sometimes it is hard to decide exactly where the limits on a certain kind of newspaper are. For example, some people would say that *The Sun* is a typical tabloid because it is small in size and deals with 'popular' stories. Some other papers of the same size give more attention to politics and business news.

Conventions of tabloid newspapers

In terms of convention, *The Sun* does things in a similar way to the *Daily Mirror*. Both papers have a similar appearance and are often placed together in newsagents' shops. Our front page example shows a number of conventions of tabloid papers.

1 The main story features a celebrity and focuses on a personal angle. In this case, it is a positive one because Rob Andrew's achievement is being celebrated. Tabloid papers are well known for taking negative angles on celebrities and publishing intimate details of their private lives.

2 The headline makes a joke or pun. 'Booty', for example, is a pun because Rob Andrew's kicking prowess on the field had been a major reason for England's rugby success in the years leading up to his receiving the MBE.

3 The layout of pages follows conventional patterns. The front page generally features two stories as in the example, and the main article is given a large headline. Often, large pictures carry most of the story. In this example, the main written part of the story actually appeared on page 2.

4 Tabloid newspapers are known for strongly supporting Britain in general and for supporting the country's national teams when they play in international competitions. The clothes worn by the three rugby players' wives in the picture are all red, and they are holding the English flag of St George (a red cross on a white background).

5 Another tabloid convention is the way that political stories are often based on individuals. The John Major story deals with Mr Major as a person much more than it deals with national politics.

Other national newspapers on the same day featured different stories on their covers. For example, the *Guardian*'s main story was the war in Bosnia.

We can now consider all of this in terms of how forms and conventions produce meaning.

How forms produce meaning

The form and content shown in the example of the front cover of *The Sun* is the result of decisions made by the editors and owners of the newspaper.

The meaning of a media product can be linked to the way that the design is intended to work. The form of *The Sun* involves the paper being smaller than some others and having a shape that makes it easy to hold. The paper can be easily folded and carried and is often read in crowded places such as buses and trains. The paper is designed to be used in this way, and the decision to print it 'tabloid' size was a factor in making *The Sun* the biggest selling daily paper in Britain.

Words like 'popular' are often used to describe the appeal of *The Sun*, and when we consider that the paper is designed to be portable and easily passed around, we can see that the shape and size add to this popularity.

A convention: the human interest story

Conventions also help to add to *The Sun*'s popularity. The paper concentrates on human interest stories and this means that most people are interested in the things that *The Sun* writes about. The fact that a lot of the news in *The Sun* is about people means that you can read and understand these stories without needing much background knowledge.

You do not need to know much about rugby to understand the story about Rob Andrew, for example. The John Major story does have some political points to make, and when any prime minister is in trouble, the political issues are complicated. By dealing mainly with the personality of John Major, *The Sun* simplifies the story a little. This gives the readers a chance to understand this news item without having to get to grips with all the political facts.

In terms of meaning, we need to look at how these conventions usually work. One meaning we could take from this example is that Rob Andrew is a good rugby player. This is true, but it isn't what the examining boards want you to understand. In terms of conventions, we should think about who they would appeal to and why they would have this appeal. Once we have worked this out, we will understand how they produce meaning.

So, for example, the fact that tabloid papers often use a human interest angle means that they can appeal to almost everyone. To test this out, think about your own interests. You will almost certainly spend some time wondering about how some other people live. This is human interest on your part. Almost everyone is curious in this way. If somebody in your area replaced a wall of their house with a sheet of glass it would be hard to avoid the temptation to look in and see what they were doing.

The Sun fulfils the curiosity need in people. In terms of producing meaning, we can see that the human interest approach appeals to almost everyone. The reason it appeals is that we are all curious. One thing that *The Sun*'s treatment of events tells us, is that it is all right to feel this way. Curiosity can often be quite a simple thing, and when a celebrity like Rob Andrew becomes well known, people start to wonder about his life away from sport. The picture of Sara Andrew celebrating her husband's award tells readers something more about the celebrity and his life.

Another example of this is about the way that tabloid newspapers tend to support sports teams. Most of us have fairly simple feelings of support for our teams when they play abroad in international competitions. The tabloids tend to reflect these feelings and this supports the way we see the world.

Criticisms of the tabloid press

The tabloids are often criticised for printing damaging stories about famous people and for oversimplifying complicated issues. On the other hand, these papers are more popular than the ones that go into more depth about news stories. They are certainly more popular than papers like the *Daily Telegraph* or *The Times* which feature the kind of stories that sometimes demand a certain level of knowledge from readers if they are to be understood.

Another consistent area of criticism, especially of *The Sun* and *The Sport*, concerns the way they tend to treat women in their stories. Some people argue that these papers make women appear less intelligent than men and that the topless pictures they use simply exploit women. The defence for this from papers like *The Sun* suggests that such pictures are simply 'fun'.

It might be possible to argue that the front page illustrated here suggests that Rob Andrew's wife is only seen as important because of her marriage to a famous sportsman. Some people, especially equal opportunities groups, have argued in this way for years. Others, especially editors and readers of tabloids, have said that these papers are simply meeting a need. It is beyond dispute that *The Sun* remains the most popular daily paper in Britain and so the 'need' that it meets seems to be shared by many people.

Meeting the needs of readers

While it is easy to criticise the tabloids, we must understand that their conventions in treating the news have made them popular. The tabloids do reflect the views of most of their readers, who could choose not to buy the papers. The conventions we have seen in the front page of *The Sun* create the message for its readers. While it may be hard to identify this message exactly, we can say that the continued success of a paper like *The Sun* shows that it is meeting the needs of its readers. These readers find meaning in the way *The Sun* treats the news and clearly feel that the paper is right to reflect certain opinions.

Other areas of meaning

There are also other areas of meaning created by certain conventions seen on this front page. We have mentioned already that the concentration on John Major in the political story shows that a paper like *The Sun* treats politics in terms of personalities. Someone who took the view of *The Sun* in this respect would probably see politics very much as being about politicians themselves.

Tabloids often make a particular point about mentioning the age of people who are featured in stories. The Rob Andrew feature mentions the age of his wife and those of two other team-mates' wives. Tabloids use age a great deal and this creates the idea that age is important.

There are entire books written on meanings found in the media, but this short example is intended to show how forms and conventions can produce meaning. The detail we have gathered from studying one page of a popular paper is enough to show how meanings can be developed by both of these.

We have seen how form can carry its own meaning and that the repetition of conventions can lead to people developing certain views of the world.

EXAMPLE | ## *Zine Zone Fanzine* cover

This example shows that forms and conventions can change.

Form and convention can change. This is due to changing markets and changing technology in the media.

Look at the front cover of *Zine Zone* (Fig. 2.3), a **fanzine** which is produced in London and sold in record shops and through small ads in publications like *New Musical Express*. 'Fanzine' is a recent word – it does not appear in dictionaries. A fanzine is a publication, usually produced by a few people and printed cheaply. Some fanzines are simply pasted together and then photocopied; others are produced using desk top publishing software packages. *Zine Zone* is called a fanzine, but it is really a collection of odd items that the editors have collected from a number of sources. Some of the items are printed in foreign languages. Other items include music coverage and phone numbers including one for 10 Downing Street.

Fig 2.3

Small-circulation magazines as a form

Zine Zone is fairly new because it is only recently that small-circulation magazines like this have been able to make a profit. *Zine Zone* is still photocopied, but there are now many small-circulation magazines which are produced on a desk-top publishing system. In the last 20 years the cost of producing magazines has fallen sharply compared to other costs. This has meant that almost anyone who wants to can now produce their own publication and sell it. Producing magazines cheaply means that it is possible to make a profit on very small sales.

Fanzines: form and meaning

Zine Zone is A5 size – the size of a sheet of A4 paper folded over. This is an unusual size for a magazine, but in the fanzine end of the market, this size is normal because A4 sheets are easily photocopied and when folded can be posted easily. Most sales of such magazines are by post.

The fact that fanzines are produced in a size that can be mailed has given them their own meaning. People who get fanzines through the post often feel that their opinions are special or unusual in some way. Fanzines deal with the kind of material that does not get published in more popular papers and magazines. The form of a fanzine adds to this feeling of being special.

Fanzines: conventions and meaning

The conventions of fanzines also add to the meaning of the readership being special. Because costs have to be kept low, much of the material in fanzines is photocopied. Some images are taken from other magazines (sometimes without permission), and the writing relies on attitude and ideas for its appeal. For these reasons, fanzines often have a feel of being put together quickly.

Their appeal lies partly in the fact that they say things that other publications would not dare to print and that, in some cases, they bend and break the law. To some readers, this gives fanzines a slightly daring image.

The fanzine market is expanding quickly and it is impossible for the law to watch over everything that is printed in this format. The idea of fanzines being exciting and underground makes them more attractive to some readers. In other cases, fanzines simply deal with a particular subject, like the career of a pop star, that is overlooked by other publications. Fanzines are improving in terms of quality as the technology available to produce them also improves.

A developing media form

There is a lot more to fanzines than this short write-up has been able to cover but in terms of this chapter what matters is that this example clearly shows a form of the media that is still developing. We can see that as fanzines have developed they have taken on a form and a few conventions. These have been determined by the demands of the audience. The form has been determined by the audience getting fanzines through the post. The conventions have been determined by the need to keep fanzines different from mainstream publications and by the need to make the audience feel special. The form and conventions are likely to continue to change as the technology to produce fanzines changes.

2.3 How these examples can help in your assignments

There are two ways in which these examples can help in your assignments:

1 to make sense of the media texts that you are asked to discuss

2 to explain media texts that you have produced.

If you are asked to discuss any work from the media, then you can show a better understanding of that work by focusing on the forms and conventions.

Forms

First, ask yourself what form the work you are studying takes. When studying any media product, always ask: 'What form does the product take?' Do not be afraid of the obvious answer because this is the start of a more detailed explanation which should lead to more marks.

So, for example, if your answer is that the product is a TV situation comedy, you should then examine the product in more detail, identify the particular pieces and begin to explain what they are and why they are there. This may sound a little vague, but when you are asked to do this in an assignment, it will almost certainly be as a result of spending some time in class looking at a particular kind of product. You should therefore be familiar with some of the terms you will need to use. For example, if you are studying newspapers in class, then you will be familiar with some of the terms and ideas used in the tabloid newspaper example in this chapter.

One important point to remember is that media forms are all linked to money in some way. If you ask what advantage there would be for the makers of a certain media product in producing it in a particular form, you should begin to construct a good argument to show an understanding of media form. You can also discuss when and where a media product is used and think about the way that the form of the product helps in this use.

Look at the tabloid newspaper example again and you will see that all of the points above are considered in explaining why *The Sun* is presented as a tabloid. In terms of form it is a tabloid paper. The advantage to the makers of it being a tabloid is that it is easy to carry around, can be read anywhere, etc. In terms of how it is used, you may note that the paper is passed around, read easily on the way to work, etc. All of these are simple points that show an understanding of media form. This brings us back to money because media forms, like tabloid papers, are developed to reach the biggest audience. In the case of *The Sun* we can see how the paper is designed for the way it is used. If it came in any other form – such as a larger broadsheet size – like *The Times* – it would not be suitable for this kind of use.

Conventions

You can make similar points about media conventions and ask similar questions. Once more, the rule to remember is that these conventions have come about as a result of the manufacturers of a media product trying to make money. Consider, the first example in this chapter of the reggae single. The conventions there included the fact that singles are a certain length which makes them suitable for radio play, and that they have a catchy and memorable musical element, which makes them more appealing.

Whatever product you are studying, you can ask the same kind of questions to those you asked about form. What conventions does this product have? Why would the people making this product follow these conventions? You can also ask when and where the product would be used because this will help in understanding conventions.

In the case of the Aswad single, the conventions would include the length of the song, the way the band members are dressed, the style of the lettering, etc. The obvious advantages to the makers of the record are that the song could be played on radio and television. The band might appear as the kind you would trust to make a good song, and the name of the band would be given enough exposure to help it remain successful.

Once again, if this sounds vague, then you should remind yourself that any assignment which involves making sense of a media product will be presented in class and you should be familiar with the product before you need to write about it.

Media texts

When writing about the work of others, what matters is that you understand the difference between forms and conventions. Then you can discuss each one. Do not be afraid of starting by stating the obvious like 'I am studying a television programme'. Build your arguments about forms and conventions upon this.

You can follow similar rules when it comes to talking about your own work. You can identify forms and conventions and discuss why you followed each. The way to do this is exactly the same as the way you can discuss the work of others. Starting with the obvious and gradually building an argument is usually the best way.

It may be that you have produced a product that tries to do something new with forms and conventions, such as a video that makes fun of an existing type of video. If this is the case, then you can still follow the advice for constructing an argument outlined in this section. Simply discuss the forms and conventions in your work and then describe the way that you have set out to make fun of these forms and conventions.

Summary

1 A media form is the type of product.

2 We can describe a media form in terms of the limits of the product, for example, its length in time, size, etc.

3 Media forms have all developed through the needs of the producers to make money.

4 If we consider where and when a media form is used, we can begin to understand how it makes money. For example, a tabloid newspaper is often passed around and carried by people. Its size and shape mean this is easily done and so this form is well designed to appeal to a wide readership.

5 Some media forms such as fanzines are still changing.

6 Media forms are changing for a number of reasons. Most of these reasons are linked to money. For example, the A5 size of many fanzines makes them easy to post and so easier to sell.

7 Another area of change is technology. In practice this is linked closely to reducing the costs of production. Technology is changing the media in two important ways: by giving more people the chance to make their own products; and by allowing continued improvements in the quality of production.

8 The different parts of the media are an industry, and technological changes must be considered in terms of their cost. However, new technology such as desk-top publishing equipment is designed to allow individuals to produce media texts. In the past only companies had any real chance to do this.

9 Media conventions are the 'usual' things that we would find in a media form.

10 Media conventions have also developed as a result of the industry trying to make money.

11 If we ask when and where products are used, we can also understand why their media conventions developed. For example, pop singles are usually $2\frac{1}{2}$–4 minutes long. This is because they fit easily into radio programmes, and air-time on the radio means that they are more likely to sell.

12 Some conventions in the media are still changing.

13 Where conventions are still changing, these changes are linked to money. For example, fanzines are increasingly using graphics and pictures. This is because the technology to allow these to be included is getting cheaper and it is possible to produce a good quality fanzine for very little money.

Self-test questions

1 In three or four sentences explain the meaning of 'media form'.
2 In three or four sentences explain the meaning of 'media convention'.
3 Why do some media forms keep changing? Explain in four or five sentences.
4 Why are the changes in media conventions always linked to money? Explain in five or six sentences.

Chapter 3
Media viewpoints

3.1 What you need to know

Media viewpoints are the views expressed within the media. This is a detailed and complicated area with books devoted to its study. For the purposes of this study guide we need to note only two of the ways in which views may be expressed – **explicit** and **implicit messages**.

Explicit messages

Explicit messages make clear statements. For example, the statement on the cover of a book which says 'over one million copies sold in paperback' is explicit. There is no real doubt about the sales figure once you have read this message.

Implicit messages

Implicit messages are contained within media products, but are not stated openly. Some people object to papers like *The Sun* printing topless photos of women. The newspapers themselves often claim that the photos are simply fun for readers to look at. The captions certainly say this and usually give information about the models. Critics argue that these pictures encourage people to see women as sex objects and that they undervalue women in general.

The newspapers contain no explicit message to say that women should be viewed in this way. However, an implicit study of the pictures might suggest that it is acceptable to consider women only in terms of their attractiveness.

You need to pay particular attention to the idea of implicit meaning because the GCSE boards require candidates to look at meanings and values in the media. The important point to remember about implicit meanings is that they often work because we see our own views and ideas in them. The Kwik Save advert later in this chapter is an example of how we can see our own views in a media text. You should study this as an example of how implicit ideas are put across in the media.

'Reading' media texts

Both examining boards agree that studying media viewpoints is an important part of **'reading' media texts**, which means studying the media to make sense of the way that products work.

Media viewpoints overlap with the idea of media languages (see chapter 1). If you can 'read' and understand a media language you will be able to see that the point of view offered to the audience is carefully put together.

3.2 Three examples of media viewpoints

Song lyrics to 'Multinational Corporations' by Napalm Death, from the album 'Scum', 1987

This example shows a direct and explicit viewpoint being put across in a simple way.

Multinational Corporations

Multinational corporations
Genocide of the starving nations.

Multinational corporations
Genocide of the starving nations.

Multinational corporations
Genocide of the starving nations.

Multinational corporations
Genocide of the starving nations.

Arghhhh.

In terms of musical style or **genre**, this record would probably be classed as thrash metal. That is extremely fast and distorted heavy metal. Napalm Death was one of the first bands to make this style of music popular and the above lyric comes from their first album.

The song is short and loud and the final line is simply a scream. The lyrics are hard to make out because of the growling vocal sound, but they are printed on a lyric sheet included with the album.

The song's explicit message

The message of the song is simple – big international corporations are causing deaths in the developing world. Shortly before this album was released, there was a major industrial accident in India in which many people were killed and many others badly maimed. The company operating the chemical plant was held responsible. Its safety standards would not have been acceptable in many western countries.

The song refers to accidents such as this. It may also be talking about international trade. However, Napalm Death represents one particular viewpoint.

The multinational companies themselves will certainly see the situation differently. Another view might suggest that big companies employ millions of people in the third world and without this work conditions would be much worse.

The message of the lyrics is backed up by the fast and angry sound of the music and the growl of the singer. All of the above points can be classed as explicit.

Identifying the implicit messages

The appearance of the band is very masculine and the image is of classic heavy metal. While this style of dress doesn't make any explicit point about big business, it does have a message contained within it. Heavy metal dress is very different to ways of dressing that may be considered 'smart' or presentable. You would be unlikely to find someone dressed like a member of Napalm Death working in the local branch of a high street bank or supermarket chain. The obvious message we get from the rock band's appearance is that it wishes to set itself apart from the regular working world.

Thrash metal music is fast, loud, aggressive and very different to commercial chart pop. Fans of thrash metal bands value the fact that they have not been pressurised into making the music more commercial.

If we think about the implicit messages here, we could say that the musicians and fans of thrash metal reject the values of big business and regular office jobs. This implicit message backs up the explicit message of the song 'Multinational Corporations'.

In terms of a viewpoint, 'Multinational Corporations' makes a direct statement. This is explicit. When we consider the image of the band and the style of music, we can also see that the implicit messages behind the track support the direct statement.

EXAMPLE ## Ugly Dudley: the hard man of football

This example shows how certain viewpoints are targeted at an audience.

The song by Napalm Death discussed in the first example was clearly aimed at an audience, and the explicit message it contained probably reflected the views of most of the audience.

The important difference between Napalm Death and Ugly Dudley is that most of the message in the Ugly Dudley cartoon (Fig. 3.1) is presented in an implicit way.

The cartoon comes from a magazine called *C'Mon Ref*, which is aimed at teenage boys and young men, and deals with a combination of football and humour. In the same magazine that featured this strip there were items on famous footballers, a one-page pin-up of a girl, adverts for phone lines and a joke advert for a plate that celebrated Kevin Keegan's permed haircuts. The meaning of a magazine like this might seem hard to identify, but when we read the implicit ideas in some of the contents, we can see that it gives a particular viewpoint on football.

Listing the contents of a media product

We have already seen that implicit views are in a product, but are not openly stated. One obvious way of trying to make sense of an implicit viewpoint is to list the contents of a media product and then look for the things that link them. In the case of a magazine this means trying to imagine the person who would be interested in the contents and then deciding how that person would look at life.

The contents of *C'Mon Ref* suggest that they are aimed at young men. The pin-up of the girl is one example. Ugly Dudley is another. In this cartoon strip the explicit content is simply the joke of Dudley's misunderstanding. He is a humorous character. Think about the contents that make him funny – you can do this even if you don't find this particular joke funny. Try to explain the following ideas in two to three sentences:

● Dudley looks comical.

● Dudley is not particularly intelligent.

● Dudley takes things to extremes.

It is likely that you will understand these points quite easily, but it is the quality of your arguments that will gain you marks in your GCSE. It is, therefore, worth putting in the effort to try to explain these simple ideas about Ugly Dudley.

Fig. 3.1

Different viewpoints

Implicitly, this cartoon strip offers a different viewpoint. It suggests that violence doesn't matter too much. This is obvious from the expressions on the faces of Dudley's team-mates in the last frame. Dudley appears to have committed mass murder, but they simply look a little puzzled. The fact that the strip is about 'the hard man of football' also shows that it is centred on violence.

Some people find such cartoon stories offensive. Others simply think they are silly. These are viewpoints which conflict with the viewpoint offered by the story. When we consider the way that this story makes a joke of violence and the way it would offend some people, we can see how it offers a viewpoint that appeals to the audience.

Target audiences

The makers of media products often talk about a **target audience**. This means the people or market to whom they hope to sell their product. Target audiences are usually described in some detail by the makers of products. This is because success depends on a detailed understanding of audiences.

The audience for this magazine comprises teenage boys and it is aimed particularly at young boys who are branching out, making some of their own choices in life and developing different views to those of their parents. This audience often jokes about things like violence and finds humour in swear words. They also take some interest in football and sometimes make heroes of footballers. While the media see some footballers with a past disciplinary record as bad characters, it is often the kind of audience that would read Ugly Dudley who support such footballers.

There are some things in this viewpoint on life that make sense when we consider the audience. For example, finding fun in violence is one way of rebelling against the views of parents and teachers. Young people often find death and injury in comic stories funny because they are unlikely to have come across it in real life. The older you are, the more likely you are to have been affected by death and injury. If you or someone you know have been involved in an accident, it is less likely that you would laugh at such things.

The fact that some people would find the violence in this comic strip offensive could make it more attractive to a young male audience. If older people react in a negative way, it often makes a young audience feel special. This is something that has been observed often in the media. The TV programme 'The Word' managed to keep a steady young audience for years because the regular complaints about it led to publicity that made the young people watching it feel special. So-called 'adult humour' comics like *Viz* have a similar appeal.

In terms of media viewpoints, what matters in the 'Ugly Dudley' strip is that the humour covers the kind of things that the audience jokes about. We can say that the humour shares the viewpoint of the audience. It is also important to the viewpoint that some people would not find the cartoon humorous – they are also stating a viewpoint. This fact is likely to make the cartoon more attractive to regular readers of the magazine.

A 'constructed' media image

Ugly Dudley has been put together to meet the needs of the audience. In that sense it is **constructed**.

List the qualities you find in Dudley and then write down in two to three sentences a basic explanation of why they would appeal to the teenage audience outlined here. To help you look at the example below:

'Not value free'

As we have seen, the values in the strip are those of the audience. Other people might not find them funny. This shows that the story is **not value free**. The fact that people will react to it confirms that there are values in the story.

QUALITY
Dudley is violent.

WHY THIS WOULD APPEAL
The audience for the magazine consists of young people who are starting to make their own way in life. Talking about violence and occasionally getting involved in a fight is often part of the lives of this audience. Dudley is presented as somebody who uses violence as a way of solving problems, like beating opposing football teams.

EXAMPLE **Kwik Save advert**

This example shows how a viewpoint can be presented in a totally implicit way.

The Kwik Save advert (Fig. 3.2) was placed in the *Daily Mirror* in July 1994. The job of the advert is to sell the products that are shown and to encourage people to visit Kwik Save, a chain of discount stores. The chain was running a promotion aimed at people who were looking after young children during the school summer holidays. (This advert also appeared in the GCSE Media Studies written paper set by the Welsh Board in 1995.)

Identifying the advert's explicit message

The advert has an explicit message – that a set of products, like toy guns and pavement chalks, are available at Kwik Save. It makes it clear that these items are at low prices and that the prices are part of a promotion.

What is the advert's viewpoint?

The advert promotes a viewpoint which becomes clear when we start to think about the alternatives to buying the advertised toys. Kwik Save is offering toys at low prices. It makes a profit by selling such items at a price that is lower than the competition. The competition in this case is largely made up of other shops that sell more expensive toys.

Fig. 3.2

They make a profit by selling toys that are more complicated than the ones in this advert and they might argue that their toys are better quality.

The viewpoint is offered by showing all of these toys in one advert and encouraging the reader to think about the possibility, offered by Kwik Save, of being able to buy entertaining toys at bargain prices. It presents one solution to the problem of keeping children occupied during a long holiday, and by displaying the bargain prices, it leaves readers to decide that this is the 'right' solution for them.

Customers deciding between buying toys at Kwik Save or elsewhere are making a decision which represents a viewpoint. Another viewpoint to this advert might involve parents or carers taking children to a local leisure centre. In this case, we might say that they had taken the view that their money was better spent on an event rather than the toys in the Kwik Save advert.

When we consider these different buying decisions we can see that the Kwik Save advert is offering one viewpoint. This viewpoint says that toys for children should be sold at an affordable price and that children should have plenty of simple and straightforward toys. Kwik Save's viewpoint is supported by its shops which sell a range of goods at competitive prices.

Shops reflect customer viewpoints

If you think about other chains of shops, you will realise that most of these sell a particular range of goods aimed at a certain market – for example, clothes shops where the idea of fashion immediately reflects different viewpoints. 'Upmarket' shops sell designer labels at a high price, while major chain stores sell clothes that are still fashionable but tend to be cheaper and less distinctive than the designer labels. There are other shops that only sell discounted goods. Each of these appeals to people with a different viewpoint.

Some people find that they are often put under pressure by magazines, friends, etc. to look good. The choices offered by the different clothing shops present different solutions to this problem. It is likely that the viewpoint of a person would lead to them adopt a certain pattern of clothes' buying.

Viewpoints reflected in the media

In the case of the viewpoints of shops, it is unlikely that any manager would be prepared to state the values of his or her shop. However, we have seen that there are implicit viewpoints and shops provide a good example of this. It is likely that many of the regular customers of a particular shop do share similar points of view and they go to their chosen shop because they see these reflected in the products on sale.

These viewpoints also extend to the media because shops advertise themselves in a range of media texts. The Kwik Save advert is one example of many similar adverts that appear every week in newspapers and magazines.

The Kwik Save advert used in this example shows an implicit viewpoint because it collects the goods on sale in one part of the company's stores and presents them to customers. Anyone sharing the view that a good way to keep children amused during a long holiday is to supply them with toys is likely to be attracted by the advert.

3.3 How these examples can help in your assignments

The examining boards require candidates to be able to 'read' media texts. This means understanding the way that the texts are put together. One important aspect of this is understanding the points of view within media products.

Some of the assignments in your GCSE Media Studies course will ask you to examine media products and make comments on them. Identifying a viewpoint and discussing it in a similar way to the examples in this chapter will help you to get marks. It is important you read and understand such assignments and check any uncertainties with your teacher.

An understanding of the way that explicit and implicit messages work will also help you to make sense of the media. It is easy to identify explicit messages. Implicit messages are much harder to include in assignments and some students find it easier to identify implicit messages than to explain them. It is a good idea therefore to practise looking for implicit messages and trying to explain them in clear sentences before you start an assignment.

If you are preparing for SEG's GCSE, it is also important to explain about 'values' when you are considering a point of view in a media example. SEG requires students to realise that media texts are 'not value free' – you must be able to identify the values in a media text. We have seen examples of values in the three detailed examples in this chapter.

To help you to understand values when looking at a media example, ask yourself: 'What does this example suggest is important?' You could use some of the examples in this chapter as a guide when you are doing this in an assignment. As long as you manage to show an understanding of a media example's viewpoint and briefly discuss the kind of values it is promoting, you should be able to get good marks in assignments that require an understanding of viewpoint.

One way to get a good mark is to bring in some simple examples to compare with the thing you are studying. Consider them in terms of viewpoints and values and make quick points that compare the thing you have been given to study with your own chosen example. This is often useful because it shows that you have a wide understanding of viewpoints.

When you have to put your own practical work together, you will probably have to make some decisions about a viewpoint. At this time you should make sure you understand viewpoints and it is worth looking at the explanations of 'implicit' and 'explicit' in the Glossary at the end of this book. Making clear decisions about the point of view you take and whether you put this over explicitly, implicitly or through a combination of both should gain you practical marks.

If you make a decision before producing your practical work, then it will be easier to put a project together in a way that appeals to the right audience. More importantly, you will be able to argue about why you produced your work in a particular way and how it is intended to appeal. Most practical work in media studies courses involves some written explanation of the work and the decisions that were made. If you follow the outline in this paragraph, you give yourself a good chance of putting together an argument that will gain marks.

You might be able to get some extra marks in your practical work by explaining why you didn't do particular things. For example, if you put an explicit viewpoint into your work, then in an assignment you could discuss the nature of an implicit viewpoint. This makes the point that you had choices and that you used them to find the best way to put your message across to an audience.

To get the best marks with this kind of argument you should use examples to show the kind of thing you could have done. For instance, imagine that you had written the Ugly Dudley story in the second example. You could make the same arguments about viewpoint that are covered in this example. You could explain that some people might find jokes about violence offensive and include an example of a much gentler comic story with a more pleasant point of view – the kind of story that ends with everyone being friends. You could then explain that you had rejected this because your audience actually wanted the kind of approach that was taken in the Ugly Dudley story.

Examiners like to see such comparisons. They are particularly keen on work that compares one media with another because this allows students to compare a range of issues such as form, genre and viewpoint. If we continue with the Ugly Dudley example, you could try thinking about how this character and story would change in other media.

For instance, television would not easily be able to show the violence in this story – it would be disturbing if presented within a programme and expensive to generate the special effects. Radio could suggest this violence in a comical way by using sound effects and including comments like 'Give me my leg back!'. Radio would leave much more of the actual violence to the imagination of a listener. Changing the media that carried this story could also change the viewpoint offered by the story.

It is always advisable to plan these arguments and discuss them with your teacher before submitting them. The points in this chapter are important, but different teachers cover them in different ways and the shortest route to good marks is to make sure you understand what a particular assignment demands before putting your final version together.

Summary

1 The term 'media viewpoint' is used to describe a range of ideas offered by a media text.

2 This 'viewpoint' usually appeals when it reflects ideas and opinions held by members of the audience.

3 Media products are put together with audiences and profits in mind and so the media producers want to reflect the opinions of the likely audience.

4 Because media products are constructed they contain values.

5 Values are opinions and ideas that people have. In real life they make up a point of view. When the media reflect a person's point of view we can say that the media and that person share the same viewpoint.

6 Media viewpoints can be put across in an explicit way. This means a product which contains a message and openly states that message. The first example in this chapter is explicit.

7 Media viewpoints can be put across in an implicit way. This means a product which contains a message but does not state it openly. The third example in this chapter is implicit.

8 Media viewpoints may be expressed in a combination of explicit and implicit messages. This means a combination of the two points above. The second example in this chapter – Ugly Dudley – combines the explicit and implicit.

Self-test questions

1   Explain in four or five sentences why people making media products tend to reflect the views of their audiences.
2   In two or three sentences explain the idea of values in the media.
3   In four or five sentences explain the meaning of putting across a viewpoint in an 'explicit' way and give one example.
4   In four or five sentences explain the meaning of putting across a viewpoint in an 'implicit' way and give one example.

Chapter 4
Narrative

4.1 What you need to know

The term **narrative** describes the way that the media tell stories. It is important in media studies because different media can tell stories in different ways. Narrative can be divided into two parts:

a   **plot** – a simple outline of the story

b   **narration** – the point of view from which the story is told, i.e. whether someone involved in the story is telling it, whether the story is happening now or in the past, etc.

Narrative can be found throughout the media but different media use it in their own ways. For example, pop records tend to have simple narrative structures, leaving much of the story vague. This is done deliberately to allow audiences to put their own meanings into the songs.

Other media choose more complicated forms of narrative. In film and television, the media do a lot of the work for the audience. The opening shot of ITV's 'Coronation Street' shows a view over the roofs of the street. At this point the camera is lowered to street level. This tells us that the programme is set in a modern city, but that the events will revolve around the life of this particular street.

We tend to recognise the different ways used by the media to tell stories because we are familiar with the ways in which stories can be told. The examination boards expect you to be able to describe these various ways. You need also to be able to show an understanding of how different segments of media texts can be constructed into stories and to realise that there are definite patterns in the way that stories are developed within the media.

4.2 Three examples of narrative

EXAMPLE   **Song lyric: 'Horse With No Name'**

This example shows how a media text develops a narrative from a few simple elements.

Horse With No Name

On the first part of the journey, I was looking at all the life.
There were plants and birds and rocks and things.
There was sand and hills and rings.

The first thing I met was a fly with a buzz and the sky with no clouds.
The heat was hot and the ground was dry but the air was full of sounds.

I've been through the desert on a horse with no name.
It was good to be out of the rain.
In the desert you can remember your name, cos there ain't no one for to give you no pain.

La, la, la, la la la la, la la, la la.

After two days in the desert sun, my skin began to turn red.
After three days in the desert sun I was looking at a river bed.
And the story it told of a river that flowed made me sad to think it was dead.

You see, I've been through the desert on a horse with no name.
It felt good to be out of the rain.
In the desert you can remember your name, cos there ain't no one for to give you no pain.

La, la, etc.

After nine days I let the horse run free cos the desert had turned to sea.
There were plants and birds and rocks and things.
There was sand and hills and rings.

The ocean is a desert with its life underground and the perfect disguise above.
Under the cities lies a heart made of ground but the humans will give no love.

You see, I've been through the desert on a horse with no name.
It felt good to be out of the rain.
In the desert you can remember your name, cos there ain't no one for to give you no pain.

La, la, etc.

'Horse With No Name' reached No. 3 in the UK pop charts in 1972. It was also a No. 1 hit in several countries including the USA. By the end of 1972 it had sold several million copies making it one of the biggest hits of the year.

Since then the song has appeared on a number of albums including 'History: America's Greatest Hits' which has sold over 4 million copies worldwide. America has released three other live versions of the song, and the single has been reissued. Several other acts have also recorded this song. Today the song still gets a lot of airplay around the world and is regularly heard on British radio, especially on commercial stations that play old hits.

This song has become a well-known pop classic hit because it has appealed to a wide audience. People of different ages, religions and views, etc have found something of interest in the story it tells.

Our interest lies in the narrative of the song. Most of this is carried by the lyrics which you can see above. Studying this old song will also show you that certain patterns of story-telling in the media have remained the same over a number of years.

On the record the song is sung by a male.

Making a story from different pieces of media text
The examining boards expect you to understand the way that different pieces of media text can be added together to make a story. Our example lyric offers a good place to start because most of the story is told in words. It is easy to identify the important words and look at the way they are used.

The plot
The story tells of a man riding into the desert on a horse. He gradually becomes more aware of the environment and the importance of life, eventually letting go his horse. Finally, he realises how important it is to look after the environment. This is the *plot* of the song.

The narration
The *narration* is from the point of view of the man on the horse. We do not know when the story took place, nor where the desert is. We are left to assume that the man singing the song is telling his own story. On the record he has a young-sounding voice, which gives us some idea of his age, but we don't learn anything else about him.

This lack of information has allowed the song to remain popular because many different people have been able to link or identify themselves with the character in the song.

The importance of a simple narrative structure

In terms of the pieces of information used in telling the story, we need to be aware of some things that happen in this song because they give us a better understanding of how pop lyrics develop narratives.

One simple trick used by lyric writers to achieve a maximum audience for their songs is to give few details of the person singing or the character featured in the story. In 'Horse With No Name' we know very little about the singer, such as his appearance or ethnic background. We can only assume he is male because if we listen to the record, the song is sung by a male voice.

The simple narrative structure – with its deliberate lack of an identifiable central character – allows a wide audience to put their own meanings into the song. Also to the song's advantage, the band America was never strongly identified with a particular image. 'Horse With No Name' has remained popular as a piece of music with a story.

You can probably think of other modern-day examples of hit songs that have been successful because they do not identify the age, gender or other details of the characters mentioned in the story. If these are hits at the moment, it is likely that they will continue to be played on the radio for years to come.

Different elements in narrative

This brief study of one pop song has only touched on a couple of issues in narrative. We haven't even discussed the way that the song sounds. However, you can see from this that narrative is made up of different elements.

In this example, we looked in particular at the way some details are deliberately left out of a song. These elements work to tell a story because the audience understands the way in which the whole product is put together. In this case, the audience expects to have to do some of the work to make sense of the song. Listeners also understand that simple visual images in songs can be used to mean something else.

What makes a classic pop song?

'Horse With No Name' is a **classic** pop song – it is an old hit that has withstood the test of time like old songs by The Beatles or the Rolling Stones.

Now think of a few recent songs that you know. Pick songs with lyrics that tell a story. Try to list all the definite facts that you find out about the person/people in the story of the song.

The likelihood is that you will find the same things that have been outlined above about 'Horse With No Name'.

Write your own lyrics

Try to write your own lyrics. Consider the points made in the above example. You should aim to write individual lines that sum up particular ideas. These should allow listeners to use their own imagination to put themselves into your story.

To help you, think about the following two examples of lyrics:

- The Righteous Brothers' song 'You've Lost That Lovin' Feeling' has been a hit several times around the world. The title sums up the idea that a couple are falling out of love. The song never really explains what a 'Lovin' Feeling' is. If you have ever felt attracted to someone, then you will probably have your own ideas about this. You might also relate to this song if you have ever fallen out with someone you cared about.

- In the song 'Fairground' by Simply Red, which reached No. 1 in the UK pop charts in 1995, singer Mick Hucknall repeats the line 'I love the thought of coming home to you'. Once again, these few simple words sum up a personal feeling. If you have ever looked forward to seeing somebody you care about, you might well relate to this song.

These songs were written 30 years apart. They both show that using easily understood phrases to talk about the kinds of emotion that most of us understand is a way of making audiences feel involved with songs. When lyrics use these ideas and put them into a story that allows the listener to use his or her imagination, the song is often successful.

Write a line of a lyric to describe each of the following situations:

a   feeling jealous

b   feeling attracted to someone

c   not being understood by your friends.

Once you have done this, choose one of the lines you have written and write a verse around it that begins to tell a story about yourself. Mention the events of the story, but don't include details of your appearance, age, where you live, etc.

Why good narrative is essential

From the above exercise, you should see that you can easily develop a narrative in a lyric that could apply to many other people. For example, a 15-year-old might write a line about feeling jealous, an emotion which could also be felt by a much older person.

Good narrative is therefore essential to media products – when many people relate to a narrative, the song becomes successful and can generate huge profits for the recording company. The three songs mentioned in this example each produced large profits for their companies and performers.

All three songs use simple and general statements to suggest ideas and stories. All three records were bought by people of different ages and backgrounds – most of them could relate to something in the stories the songs told.

EXAMPLE   ## Sit-com storyboarding

This example shows the way that narratives develop to include a number of different features.

The **situation comedy** (sit-com) is one of the most successful types of TV programme. Sit-coms usually involve a number of characters who meet in the same place, usually the area where they live, and their day-to-day problems provide the basis for a comedy story.

You will probably be able to think of a few examples. Whichever situation comedy you enjoy, you should be able to recognise some of the basic ideas behind the appeal of these shows.

A strong sense of identity

Most sit-coms revolve around situations, characters and locations that give their shows a strong sense of identity. Like the song lyrics mentioned above, this has been true for decades. Here are four examples of past and present sit-coms:

- 'Dad's Army', a show about members of the Home Guard during the Second World War, was made in the late 1960s and early 1970s. Men of the Home Guard were generally unfit for active military service – some were too young, some too old, etc. The sit-com revolves around a variety of characters of differing ages and occupations. Because the characters are so different, they are bound to react to new situations in their own way. So the show simply needed to present the same group of people with a different problem in each episode to guarantee that there would be some disagreement and confusion, and therefore the potential for comedy.

- 'The Young Ones' was made almost 20 years after 'Dad's Army', and concerns a group of students sharing a flat. Each of the students is a strong character in his own right. They often disagree and, like the earlier sit-com, the show generated humour from presenting the group with a different problem each week.

- 'Desmonds' was made in the early 1990s and focuses on a hairdressing shop run by a West Indian barber in London. The show dealt with many issues facing the Afro-Caribbean community in London.

- 'Rab C Nesbitt', which is still being produced, looks at the lives of a group of unemployed people in a run-down district of Glasgow.

Who? Where? When?

The above examples show that situation comedy can be adapted to cover a range of issues. The appeal of such shows depends very much on three important factors – sometimes called the three 'Ws' by people who study the media:

- **Who?**

- **Where?**

- **When?**

All four shows concerned different people at different times and in different places. They were popular enough to be repeated.

If an audience understands the basic situation and characters, then it is possible to develop the narrative by arranging something to happen that will have an effect on the characters' daily lives. In an episode of 'Rab C Nesbitt', for example, one of the characters gets a job. Since his unemployed friends see this as betrayal, the comedy largely revolves around the man with the job trying to hide the fact that he is working.

Developing the story-line

Once the who/where/when? points of the sit-com have been established and an idea put together that will allow for some comedy, the writers of the show have to think about the events and scenes that will develop the **story-line** and make it funny. Most of the humour will come from the way the audience sees things happen and the way that the characters react.

Media narratives and storyboards

When we consider the way that narrative works, we soon realise that it is the events, the reaction of the characters to those events and our own understanding of these that move the story forward. This last point is very important because the whole idea of **media narrative** depends on the audience.

Media narratives have developed because audiences understand the different ways used by the media to structure stories. To help you find your own evidence of this, complete the two exercises below. Both are based on the way that situation comedies develop stories.

a   Choose an episode from a sit-com that you know well and study one minute of the show which should include one example of humour. (Ideally, you should have a video of the episode.) Make notes about the one-minute excerpt. These should simply describe the action you have seen.

Use the notes as the basis for a **storyboard**. A storyboard looks like a comic strip and provides drawings and some notes to enable the planning of a film or video sequence. Draw one new picture on the storyboard for every new shot that you see. Your drawings do not need to be too detailed but they should show enough to allow somebody else looking at the storyboard to understand the action.

Study your final work and consider the way that the programme actually delivered the joke. Answer the following questions about the storyboard and the joke:

- Does the joke depend on the audience understanding something about the situation before it happens?

- Does the audience get a look at a character doing something that the other characters don't see?

- Is there a shot of one character's face reacting to an event?

In most cases the answer to these questions is 'Yes'. All of the points mentioned in the questions are important parts of the narrative structure of situation comedy. Audiences must understand the basic situation of a comedy programme to make sense of the events.

When audiences know that something funny is going to happen, they can take pleasure in the reactions of the characters who are surprised. Close-up shots of the actors help audiences to understand the humour in a situation. The humour is understood because audiences usually see the characters surprised or shocked but not suffering.

b   Complete the storyboard in Fig. 4.1 as instructed in the assignment below. The storyboard is based on a well-known commercial for Tango drinks. The commercial showed a large orange-coloured man running into shot and slapping a young person drinking Tango. The voice-over on the commercial and the appearance of the large man added an element of humour.

Fig. 4.1

Assignment: You have been employed by Bingo Soft Drinks to advertise its products. The company wants an advert aimed at 14–16-year-olds from different ethnic backgrounds. Your task is to fill in the blank shots with an exciting or memorable experience which can be linked to Bingo drinks. You will also need to invent a catchphrase to appeal to this audience. To help you the storyboard includes close-up shots of a young person with a drink – you should try to do something similar to the Tango advert without copying it.

In terms of understanding media narrative, the above exercise is exactly what the advertisers of Tango did. Audiences made sense of the 'You know you've been Tangoed' commercials because the shots of the boy drinking Tango helped them to understand that the advert was meant to be funny.

EXAMPLE   Rosie and Jim story

This example shows how narrative codes can be changed to meet the needs of a particular audience.

The story shown in Fig. 4.2 comes from the *Rosie and Jim magazine*. This magazine is aimed at young children and contains stories, activities, puzzles and other items which are designed to entertain children and also help them to learn. The purpose of this story is to encourage children to make sense of the sounds of letters and to help them to put the letter sounds into particular words.

This example combines the kind of media studies that we considered in the first two examples because it uses words and some pictures to move the story along. The important point to consider here is the way that the narrative is developed to take account of the needs of young children. This story is written to allow young children to take part in it.

Narrative codes
Study Fig. 4.2. The story is very simple. We can break it down into parts of the **narrative code**:

- **Pictures**. The picture of Rosie is used to show her puzzlement while Jim is painting his picture. The other pictures show the way his painting develops.

- **Questions**. These are used to make children think as the story unfolds so that they come up with answers that will force them to use letter sounds to make words.

The pictures and words in this story are used very simply, although the story uses an unusual writing style to get children involved – the repetition of letter sounds.
The repetition of letter sounds is unusual even in material written for young children. It is certainly normal for the English language to be used in strange ways in material aimed at this age group. However, some people argue that the use of the letter sounds is so unusual that it cannot be accepted as part of a narrative code.

"Oooh, Jim, what are you painting?" asked Rosie.

"It's something beginning with a **b** sound," said Jim. Rosie began to think.

"B... b... b...**boat!**" she said.

"No," said Jim.

"B... b... b... **banana!**" she said.

"No," said Jim.

"B... b... b... **big, bad boogaloo!**" said Rosie.

"No," said Jim. Then Jim folded his paper over, squashing his painting.

"Jim!" shouted Rosie. "What! What! What are you doing?"

Fig. 4.2

Then Jim peeled the paper open again.

Then he drew two little lines like this:

"There!" he said. "Something beginning with a **b** sound - b... b... b... **butterfly!**"

"Ooh, yes, Jim," said Rosie. "And I thought it was something beginning with a **mm** sound!"

"M... m... m... **mouse?**" said Jim.

"No," giggled Rosie. "M for m... m... m... **mess!**"

Understanding why the letter sounds were written in this way helps us to see the purpose of the story – it has been designed to prompt young children to guess at words and also aims to encourage young readers to practise making the sounds.

The narrator

The story is told from the third person, i.e. neither Rosie nor Jim is the story-teller.

This example also shows other important points about the way that narratives develop. The plot has been developed to allow children to become involved. If they start shouting out words, they are taking Rosie's part for most of the story.

In terms of narration there is also some uncertainty as to who is telling the story because it is likely that younger children will have the story read to them. They will know the reader and may talk to him or her as the story unfolds. Because of this, it is possible that the story will not be read word for word, e.g. a parent might stop to look at the picture of Rosie and talk to the child about the puzzled expression on her face.

Audiences affect narratives

This example shows that the way narratives develop is determined by an audience. In some cases it is possible that a media product will bend some of the rules about narrative as outlined in media studies books. Sometimes bending the rules can make a product more successful.

In the case of the Rosie and Jim story, there is certainly some doubt about whether using letter sounds is part of a narrative code that everyone would recognise. There is no real doubt about why this is done or what it means in the story.

4.3 How these examples can help in your assignments

All media use narratives to tell stories. As long as you understand this and also that different media may tell stories in different ways, you should be able to make sense of any examples you are asked to study in class. You should also be able to write about any piece of practical work you have completed.

Many media studies teachers do not set assignments on narrative alone. However, assignments on general topics like stating what a media product – like an advert – is telling us can involve narrative. If you are clear on the definition of narrative, you should be able to use this information in some assignments. It is advisable to check with your teacher to make sure that you are doing this in the right assignments.

The three examples in this chapter make straightforward points. The first two show how particular narratives work and the third pays attention to the way that a narrative code is developed to meet the needs of one particular audience. If you are going to discuss narratives in an assignment, you would probably gain marks by bringing in examples of your own to add to an argument. You could use the examples in this chapter as a starting point and look for other similar examples.

If you looked in the same areas, you would quickly find the examples you wanted. For instance, there are other pop lyrics which assume that audiences will use their own imaginations to put together much of the story. This is also the narrative taken by many adverts, poems and other short written texts. In the case of the second example, the way the story is told through different scenes is typical of most film and television. You would also find the same approach in radio dramas and long comic/graphic novels.

The final example shows a narrative developed for the needs of a particular audience. You would find examples of this in material aimed at young children, very small audiences and 'cult' audiences.

In your own practical work, you could make points about narrative and narrative structure in the same way that has been outlined for assignments on the work of others. An important point here is **planning**. If you want to write about the narrative in your own work, then good planning with clear decisions about how you will tell a story should make a lot of difference. You could probably gain extra marks if you kept notes on ideas you rejected at the planning stage because you could consider these as alternatives in your assignment and explain why they were rejected. You could also make some notes on different ways of developing a narrative and use examples from the real media to show these alternatives when discussing your own practical work.

Summary

1   Narrative is the way that a media product tells a story.

2   Narrative is often split into plot and narration.

3   *Plot* is the basic substance of a story, i.e. the simplest form into which the story can be broken down.

4   *Narration* is the point of view from which the story is told, i.e. whether one of the characters is telling it, whether it is told in the past or present, etc.

5   Media products tend to use familiar forms of narrative to make them easy to understand.

6   Simple media forms – like pop singles – tend to use forms of narrative that allow audiences to use their own imagination to develop some of the story-line.

7   More complicated media texts – like situation comedies – tend to use forms of narrative that do a lot of the work for the audience.

8   A narrative is organised to make a media text appealing to the audience. In some cases there are particular ways of arranging a narrative that take account of the way an audience will use the text. One example of this is the 'Rosie and Jim' story discussed in this chapter.

Self-test questions

1   In three sentences define the meaning of 'plot'.
2   In three sentences define the meaning of 'narration'.
3   In four to five sentences explain why some narratives leave audiences to do much of the work for themselves and give one example.
4   In four to five sentences explain why some narratives do a great deal of work for the audiences and give one example.

Chapter 5
Genre

5.1 What you need to know

A **genre** is a group of media products that show a clear link in terms of their style and content. Some genres exist strongly within one area of the media, e.g. reggae music. Other genres cross over a number of kinds of media, e.g. horror which can be found in films, books and comics.

Genre is a French word meaning 'type'. In media studies it is used to describe the way that products form a set or group – in other words, a **type** of product. Genres grow up because successful products often lead to **imitations**. They also develop because technology used by the media demands that products are made a certain way.

Imitation: an example

An example of imitation involves the most successful pop album of all time – 'Thriller' by Michael Jackson. Before the release of this record there were few acts combining rock and dance. This album combined both in a way that gained it much radio play on rock and pop radio stations and much exposure in discos.

The appeal of music that could combine both markets caused many other acts to copy this style and also led record companies to promote acts that already sounded like Michael Jackson.

'Thriller' was released in 1984, and within the next 10 years Jackson, Madonna and Prince became the world's biggest pop superstars. All of them played a type of pop music with a big dance element. Most chart 'pop' of the early 1990s had a dance beat and, in some cases, special dance mixes of pop records were released.

Before 'Thriller' the chart pop and dance markets were very separate. This example shows how a style or genre of music was clearly influenced by massive success.

Genre and technology

An example of a genre that grew up partly for technical reasons is the 'Western' film. In the early days of the cinema, cameras and sound equipment were very basic. Film companies needed to limit most of their work to locations where their equipment would give good results. This meant that they had to work out of doors in places where the weather was always good. Many film companies working to small budgets found desert locations most suited to their needs. Cowboy stories fitted naturally into these locations.

This does not mean that the requirement for good filming conditions led to the whole genre of Western films. However, it is important to understand that the cost of production of a particular type of media text plays a part in developing a genre.

How audiences understand genres

Both examining boards are looking for arguments to show that you can explain the way that audiences understand genres. Audiences do so because they are familiar with the way the media present things. For example, a picture of 'Thomas the Tank Engine' smiling on the front of a comic tells a young child a great deal – as long as the size and colour of the product are right, the genre of comic is clearly established in the child's mind.

Most products include enough familiar images, sounds and ideas to clearly establish themselves in some kind of genre. For the people making the products it is important to do this because products that can be understood quickly have a better chance of making money.

5.2 Three examples of genre

EXAMPLE **Heavy metal music**

This example shows how the steady success of one genre in the media allows the products in that genre to remain very much the same.

Study the two photographs of the bands Black Sabbath and Metallica (Figs 5.1 and 5.2). Both of these bands were still working at the time this book was written but each represents different eras in the minds of most heavy metal fans.

Sabbath is most famous for its work in the 1970s when this photo was taken. Metallica is best known for its work 20 years later.

In terms of genre, both of these bands fit the standard heavy metal image of long-haired men in guitar-based bands singing loud and fast songs, often about women or subjects related to death.

Fig. 5.1 Black Sabbath

Fig. 5.2 Metallica

Heavy metal as a genre

Heavy metal as a genre has changed very little in the last 25 years compared to other areas of music, such as dance. A major reason for this is that the market, mainly young males, has stayed very much the same and their needs are still met by the same kind of product. From the point of view of record companies, this means that there is a clear advantage in signing new groups that fit into the genre as it stands.

How audiences understand the heavy metal genre

If we consider how audiences understand this genre, then the two photos give some clues.

- The images presented are strong, male and serious. These appeal to audiences who see themselves in the same way.

- The black clothing also adds an important element. Black is often associated with death. The names of many heavy metal bands have references to death, heavy metal music or fantasy.

- Metal bands are often pictured against plain backgrounds or in concert. This suggests that they don't have much to do with 'normal' or everyday life.

Audiences understand these small aspects of the genre and if they recognise them in a new product, then it is likely that they will take some interest. There are other meanings to things within the genre – the colour black is used in other ways, for example – but audiences understand the combination mentioned here as belonging to heavy metal.

This is another important point about the way that audiences understand genres. It shows that we understand genres as a combination of things – like long hair, black clothing, etc in heavy metal. This means that the combination provided by the genre rules out other meanings for these things.

There are differences in the two bands and fans who follow the music closely understand these differences. For example, the cut of the jeans and T-shirts in the two photos is different, and both bands use slightly different guitar sounds and subjects for songs. To people outside of heavy metal these differences wouldn't be obvious, but to fans they mean a lot. Because these little differences have a big impact on the audiences, the genre can still remain very much the same.

EXAMPLE | **'On the Scene'**

This example looks at how the needs of an audience are covered in a media text. It shows how media texts tend to follow certain patterns. Because these patterns help the media texts to remain popular, a genre can emerge.

'On the Scene' is a feature which appears in *Catch*, a monthly magazine for teenage girls. In each issue, 'On the Scene' visits a different town and features photographs of some of its young people. Their comments on the clothes they wear and where they buy them appear alongside the photos.

This feature is typical of the kind of material that is included in such magazines. Such features are laid out in a way that allows them to be read quickly and easily. Much of the information is presented in the photos and any comments give you some idea of the personalities of the people featured.

Appeal

The readers themselves will also have different ideas about the way they dress. They are likely to have different tastes in music, enjoy different subjects at school or college, etc.

The readers of magazines such as *Catch* tend to be in their early- to mid-teens. This tends to be the age when people make some important decisions and changes in their lives. These decisions and changes include growing less dependent on their parents and choosing clothes that make them feel comfortable.

Features such as 'On the Scene' present teenage readers with examples of people near to their own age who are making the same sort of choices. Many readers will be able to get some moral support from seeing the people featured.

© D. C. Thomson & Co. Ltd.

Fig. 5.3

Keeping to a pattern

'On the Scene' is similar to many items that appear in magazines aimed at teenage girls. If you look at some examples, you will see that most tend to include 'problem' pages, items on fashion and articles based on the real–life experiences of readers. For readers of these magazines, such features are important because they tend to deal with the kind of problems and decisions that most teenage girls will face in their lives.

Little has changed over the last 20 years. Teenage girls magazines in the 1970s carried the same kind of features. This is because the problems and choices facing teenagers at that time were very much the same as those with which you may be familiar. If we could look ahead 20 years, we would probably find the same kind of material in magazines like *Catch*.

A genre emerges

Catch is one magazine in this area. You may well be able to name a few others. The fact that many magazines can compete in this market means that there is a genre. This genre has tended to deal with the same subjects for years because these subjects have always been popular.

The audience for these magazines tends to start reading them in their early teens and then stop reading them after two or three years. There is another genre of young women's magazines aimed at readers slightly older than the audience for *Catch*.

This example has given us some insight into the way that a whole genre has developed. The genre will remain until the interests of the audience change or until someone in the media develops an alternative to these magazines which threatens their sales. The next example shows how successful genres can change.

The Elvis Mandible

This example shows how genres can change because of changes that are taking place within the media.

Look at the two pages from a comic book called *The Elvis Mandible* (Fig. 5.4). This was published in 1990 by a company that specialised in 'cult' comic books. The story in this book concerns the fate of Elvis Presley's jawbone after his death and takes in a few unlikely events that link the death of Elvis with huge political changes that really took place in the world.

This is a strange story that would be unlikely to find a huge audience. It may well look different to any comic story that you have ever read.

For years comics were well-known as entertainment for children. They relied heavily on action and simple characters. As computer technology made printing cheaper in the mid-1980s it became possible to make a profit on fewer and fewer sales of a print product. Comics cashed in on these changes and the industry managed to expand by finding new markets that appreciated different kinds of stories to the 'traditional' comic styles.

In fact, these cult types of comics had always been around, but the falling production costs allowed many more to appear and a definite market to develop.

Fig. 5.4

'Typical' parts of the comic genre

The Elvis Mandible shows how a genre can expand in a situation in which the products and the market are changing. We would recognise some 'typical' parts of the comic genre in these pages but there are also some unusual points.

The following items in this example can be regarded as a 'typical' part of a comic:

- the layout

- the use of speech bubbles

- the way the story relies on action

- the use of different views, such as close-ups, to keep the pictures interesting.

'Cult' comics

The strange pictures, such as the carpet with the outline of a body and the close-up of the fibres, make it clear that this comic is aimed at a small, cult audience. This audience appreciates comics as more than entertainment, and a part of their enjoyment of this story is provided by the way that it uses some of the possibilities offered by comics to give unusual visual views.

Another aspect of this comic that shows it is aimed at a cult audience is the detail in the story. It assumes some interest in Elvis Presley and, as the story develops, it also assumes that readers would have some knowledge of politics. Both of these assumptions will rule out some of the audience for comics who have no interest in Elvis or politics.

Sub-genres

This example shows that genres can change. Genres are identified by a similarity of style and content. We have seen in this brief discussion that the style and content of *The Elvis Mandible* are not typical of the vast majority of the comic genre. Comics such as this have only become widespread as the cost of production has dropped in comparison to inflation, and the technology to make comics has become available to more and more people.

There is now a small group of comics which specialise in such stories. They are united by their creative use of the comic format and their interest in exploring unusual story-lines. Media Studies experts refer to small groups of products like these as **sub-genres**.

5.3 How these examples can help in your assignments

Many media products fit into genres. When analysing a media product, you can quickly show an understanding of the product by considering the genre to which it belongs, mentioning some similarities between this product and others and briefly discussing genres. If a product seems to be unusual and does not easily fit a genre, this fact alone may be deliberate. Some products set out to avoid fitting into any existing genre because this makes them seem different.

When you are looking at any media product as part of an assignment, you can consider the points about that product which have come about for financial reasons. If you simply start by listing things about the product, then look for reasons for these things, you will soon be able to think up some answers.

For example, we saw in chapter 2 that most chart records are between 2½ and 4 minutes long. A simple reason for this is that records of this length fit easily into radio and television programmes. This allows people to hear the records, which helps to sell them and so gets them into the charts. Part of the pop record 'genre' is that records are a few minutes in length.

These notes on genre should also be useful if you have to explain your own practical product. You will have made some decisions about things to include and things to leave out and these may well link to what you know about a genre that already exists.

Remember, if you have created a product that doesn't easily fit into a genre, then you should still be able to gain some marks by discussing genres in your evaluation. If you show an understanding of genre and then give good reasons for your product avoiding this, you can show an awareness that should be worth marks. You should discuss this with your teacher before you hand in your work, but there are marks to be gained if this is done well.

Planning is the key to getting as many marks as possible when writing about your own work. If you make decisions ahead of time about genre and note down other suggestions that were rejected, it should be possible to put all of these details into an argument that explains what you did and how you went about your work. A well constructed argument should be worth a lot of marks.

Important note: There are marks to be gained by discussing genre in set assignments and in evaluating your own practical work. However, it is important that you discuss this with your teacher and check that assignments actually ask for this in some way.

Summary

1   Genre is a French word meaning 'type'.

2   In media studies genre is used to describe a group of products which are similar in style and content.

3   Some genres are recognised within a single media, e.g. reggae music.

4   Genres exist for two financial reasons:

   –   People copy successful products.

   –   The cost of making products and the technology used shapes the products that are made. For example, Western films appeared partly because outdoor locations with good weather made cheap film sets.

5   Most media products have some element of genre. Those that deliberately break boundaries can still be discussed in terms of genre for media studies assignments.

Self-test questions

1   In two to three sentences explain the meaning of 'genre'.
2   In three to four sentences explain the meaning of 'sub–genre'.
3   In four to five sentences explain the two main advantages to media producers of genres.

Chapter 6
Representations

6.1 What you need to know

Media representations are the ways in which the media portray particular things. Media representations cover images of people, places, ideas, etc. People who study the media pay particular attention to these representations and also identify the reasons why they appear.

Here are some of the reasons why the media have developed particular images of people, places, and so on.

❶ **Repetition:** Once an image is established, it can be easily understood. Changing this image would involve effort on the part of media producers and audiences.

❷ **Simplicity:** If one image can represent a lot of complicated information, it can easily be used time and time again. This saves audiences having to work to understand new information all the time. It also saves media producers having to find new ways of putting across information.

❸ **For effect:** Media producers constantly compete with each other to make money. New and exciting ways of representing information can have an impact and ensure success.

❹ **To make understanding easier:** A good representation of something can help audiences make sense of a complicated issue.

❺ **As a comment on something:** This is a slightly more complicated use of representations than the first four points above. For this type of representation to work, an audience must understand the first image. To get the point of the message, the audience must also understand the changes that have been made and the reason for these changes. The best examples of these more complicated uses of representations are found in humour and in a particular kind of humour called 'satire'. Satire tends to comment on things by copying them and making fun of them at the same time.

Study the adverts in the 'Shop By Post' section from *Viz* comic (Fig. 6.1). These adverts are based on the kind of handy

Fig. 6.1

devices that are sold through small ads in papers and magazines. *Viz* makes fun of small ads by advertising useless gadgets at very high prices.

The one thing that unites all of the different uses of representations is money. People studying the media cannot escape the fact that they are looking at the work of an industry. Representations are used to attract audiences and to keep media costs low. Both of these uses are designed to increase profits.

This chapter looks at the construction of media representations. The next chapter considers the ideas built around representations.

6.2 Three examples of representations

EXAMPLE ### Dominic Cork photograph from *The Sun*

This example shows the way in which a representation is selected and how it is used to illustrate a particular point. It also provides an exercise in decoding a representation.

The photograph of England cricketer Dominic Cork (Fig. 6.2) appeared in *The Sun* newspaper following his team's victory in a test match against the West Indies in June 1995. The match marked the test debut of Dominic Cork, who played so well that he was named 'Man of the match'. Press coverage following this win gave a lot of attention to Cork. Some papers compared him with former cricketing heroes like Ian Botham while other papers considered his skills.

The photograph was printed alongside two stories that discussed ways in which English cricket could keep a winning formula. Both stories considered things that were good and bad about the national team and the man mainly responsible for selecting the team at the time.

Fig. 6.2

What the photo represents

The picture of Dominic Cork was used to illustrate – or represent – the good qualities of the game of cricket. In terms of understanding representations, you might find it useful to look at the picture and make a list of the things it suggests about cricket before you read the rest of this example. List as many things as you can within two minutes.

The photo shows Dominic Cork after he has bowled a ball. It suggests energy, excitement, action, aggression and the will to win. You may have spotted other points, or used different words to explain the same points. These qualities are usually taken as positive in sports coverage. In this case, the job of the picture is to show that there is something to celebrate in English cricket and to sum up the game's qualities.

Sports stars are often featured in papers, and each new picture that appears adds a little to the image of that star. You will be familiar with pictures of footballers, racing drivers, athletes, etc used in a number of ways.

Because Dominic Cork was not well known before he was an international player, except among knowledgeable cricket supporters, this picture could also be said to have helped his image. If we think about some of the other things that it might represent, we might list words like 'youth', 'clean cut', etc.

Decoding representations

This example shows that even simple pictures can represent a number of qualities. The examining boards expect students to be able to **decode** representations. You can see from this example that it is possible to understand a number of different meanings from one picture. This is decoding.

We can talk about a '**code**' in this representation because many of the things in the picture are familiar from pictures of sports stars in action. You will have seen other action pictures of stars that show aggression, excitement, etc. Because action pictures of sports stars often have the same qualities within them we can say that all of the pictures together show us a 'code'.

Constructing representations

The examining boards also want you to understand the idea that representations are **constructed**. In this case, the construction lies in the way that the picture was used in the feature. The two articles accompanying it both considered how English cricket could go forward and be successful. The picture of Dominic Cork is an image of cricket's success. The representation of the whole feature can be seen as a construction involving some ideas – included in the articles – and an action picture showing the kind of qualities that cricket fans enjoy.

EXAMPLE ## Skin, singer with Skunk Anansie/BROS

This example shows how images can be structured to achieve a particular purpose. These images are examined before some general points are made.

Skin: a carefully created image

Study the photo of the singer Skin (Fig. 6.3). This is an action shot taken from a concert. Like most rock and pop acts, Skin's band, Skunk Anansie, has based part of its appeal on an image – in this case on the image of the lead singer.

First, try to list some of the things that are suggested by the photo. The singer is clearly female, but the image she has developed doesn't appear to be very feminine. The picture suggests aggression, strength, seriousness and even some anger. Because the camera is below the singer, she towers over us and appears a bit threatening.

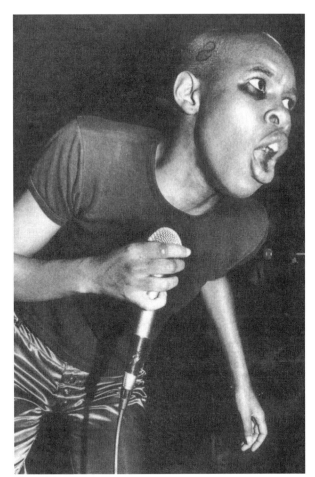

On the other hand, the shiny trousers suggest a pop or rock performer and the backward letter 'S' and mascara show that this image is a carefully created look.

It is a strong and distinctive image and is different to many pop images which make more of an effort to be attractive or pretty.

The band's music also has a hard and aggressive quality. The image of the singer supports the sound of the band.

You may well be familiar with more popular images of singers. This particular image has been chosen as an example because it is so simple and strong that it will not date badly.

BROS: a dated image

Some pop images date very badly. Look at the photo of BROS (Fig. 6.4). About 10 years before this book was published, BROS was the biggest pop act in the UK and the band's records were guaranteed hits. After their career started to struggle the various members of the band tried unsuccessfully to make a comeback.

The BROS image is very stylish in the sense that a lot of time and money was spent on putting it together. The image of BROS was right for its time. The proof of this is the number of records that the band managed to sell. Its success led to the sales of posters, T-shirts and other promotional material. This meant that its look was well established. To have

Fig. 6.3

Fig. 6.4

maintained this success, BROS would have had to update its look and sound. The band didn't succeed in this.

The pop stars that followed BROS included a much greater element of fun in their music, and one problem with the image that BROS had developed was that it was based on a serious look and the idea of financial success being very important. One BROS hit was even called 'When Will I Be Famous?' It was hard for the band to leave this image behind and become more easy-going in the eyes of pop fans.

Reasons behind pop images

This short look at pop images has shown that they are manufactured for reasons. These images matter to a pop audience because they back up the messages in music and lyrics. It would be possible to study a long series of these images and list the things that they 'represent', but the two in this example are enough to make the point.

The picture of Skin from Skunk Anansie shows an image that says a lot about the sound and message of her band. The picture of BROS shows a well-developed image that would not work today, but did work around 10 years ago.

Pop images are some of the best examples of representations that have been carefully put together for a particular purpose. Fans tend to see this purpose as being linked to the message and ideas in the music. We shouldn't forget that these images come from the music industry and this industry's aim is to make money. So the record companies see the purpose behind the images of most pop stars as being to keep them successful and profitable.

EXAMPLE James Dean

This example shows how a representation can be used over a period of time to make a profit.

Both examining boards want you to study the way that the media can portray and represent individuals. The WJEC, in particular, expects students to understand the way that images of stars are constructed. This can be done by:

● building images like those of the two pop acts included in the second example above.

● the careful use of images that the media already have.

Many 'representations' in the media are the result of companies that already own media properties – like films, television programmes, etc – trying to find new ways of selling their material. The problem they face is how to make it appeal to audiences that are too young to remember it from the first time around.

A lasting image

James Dean's image has lasted better than the images of other actors of his generation. One reason for this is that Dean died at the age of 24 and so there are no pictures of him as an old man. Another reason that his image has lasted is that it has been promoted ever since and the people who have sold everything from videos to posters have been able to change Dean's image a little to fit changing fashions.

James Dean died in a car crash in 1955 and this gives his image a tragic quality. The images of other dead stars – like rock singer Kurt Cobain – also have this quality. While the photos of Dean will never change, it is still possible for his image to be constructed through the careful use of these and good marketing.

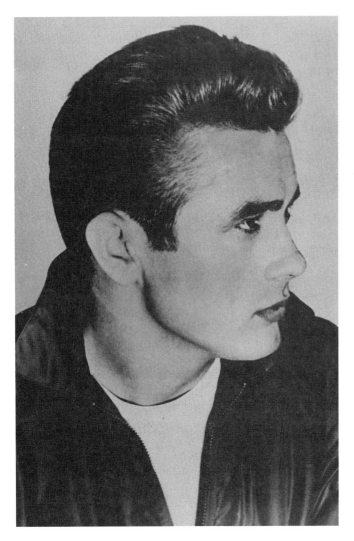

Fig. 6.5

The selection of images

Study the picture of James Dean (Fig. 6.5). It is an example of the way that Dean's image has been kept alive. A similar picture was used on the cover of the book *James Dean – Shooting Star*. 'Shooting Star' suggests something that is brilliant but burns out very quickly. On the cover of this book the title has been written over a black and white picture of Dean wearing a T-shirt and a bomber jacket, the clothes he wore in a film in which he played a teenage rebel.

The people responsible for marketing Dean over 40 years after his death are careful to use pictures in which Dean's clothes resemble those worn today, such as bomber jackets and jeans. In the early 1990s his image was even used in a commercial for Levi jeans.

Editing

The selection of some images and the rejection of others is called **editing**. Editing is the name given to any process in the media in which information is considered for inclusion in some product and only a certain amount is selected. The editors of the book *James Dean – Shooting Star* have decided to 'represent' Dean as a teenage rebel. There are other pictures of Dean that show him as a different kind of character.

How images can be exploited

There is another important point to be considered in this example of representation. Dean died before the age of video and video contracts and so legally he could have no say in the way that his image was used after his death. This means that people can exploit his image more easily than they can exploit living film stars like Brad Pitt or Sharon Stone. People who own negatives of Dean can sell them without having to give the profits away to the star himself.

This tells us something about another kind of pressure on representations, that of the media industry itself. The media industry exists to make money and when it puts together any kind of representation, this is then aimed at a market or audience.

In the case of the book about James Dean, the publishers did their best to make his image appeal to readers in the 1990s and aimed their title and cover photo at a young audience who would not remember Dean. At the same time, this book was intended to make money.

This is typical of the way that many media representations are now constructed. Film companies, record companies and others who produce media products all own increasingly large stockpiles of past products. Some of these are as simple as the photographs of James Dean included in *Shooting Star*. Others are much more complicated, such as entire feature films.

Media producers like to make money from old products because this can save them from investing in new material. They can succeed in making a profit in this way when they manage to update an old image or present it in the right way for a new audience (see chapter 12 for a discussion of this).

The portrayal of images by the media

The James Dean example helps us to understand how the media portray and represent individuals. It shows that people in the media work to select – or edit – material and aim it directly at a particular market. The most important point about portrayal is that the media are always trying to make a profit and any representation of a person, event, etc is aimed at an audience in the hope that it will make an impact and therefore help the media producer to make money.

6.3 How these examples can help in your assignments

The idea of representations is one of the major points in the syllabuses of both examining boards. It is vital that you understand something of the way that the media constructs these representations. In this chapter we have simplified the ideas behind this area of study, but there are still some important points that can help you to get marks.

In assignments that deal with other people's work in the media, it is important that you can use the term 'representations' and show an understanding of its meaning. You can also show an understanding of the fact that representations are put together to hold particular messages and that they are aimed at audiences. If you discuss these points with your teacher you should be able to include this information in a way that will get you some useful coursework marks.

You should also be able to discuss the way that some representations, like the image of BROS, can date badly. Whenever you discuss representations it is important that you consider the fact that you are looking at the work of an industry. There are marks to be gained by pointing out that any representation is aimed at an audience. When you can find pieces of this representation and discuss why an audience would want to see them, you can gain further marks.

You can use the basic points in this chapter to build up arguments that show an understanding of representations. For example, if you are given an assignment to study a picture from a newspaper, you can discuss the contents of the picture and then consider the way these work to appeal to an audience. You could mention the fact that most pictures follow certain conventions and support the way that a written story sees an event. These are the points covered in the first example.

You can use the other examples in studies of representation by pointing out some basic points. The second example shows clearly that representations are constructed to reach an audience. Both syllabuses use the word 'constructed', so it is important that you remember this term and use it in assignments. You can also find similar uses of old images like the one of James Dean in the third example. Discussing any example of an old product being relaunched allows you to show an understanding of the way that the media makes money as a result of owning material.

It is important that you discuss these points with a teacher before attempting an assignment. The issues in representation are complicated — that is why it has two chapters in this book. So long as you grasp the basic points about the issues you should be able to find your own examples and use them to get marks in assignments.

In your own practical work the same rules apply. You will put some kind of product together that will 'represent' something. This could be as simple as a leaflet that makes a particular point or as complicated as a video that uses a popular style and makes fun of it.

If you want to get the maximum possible marks for understanding representation in this work, then you should list the points from the chapters on this subject and discuss with your teacher in advance how you can use these to put arguments together. This is especially important in the case of practical work because the practical assignments from teachers vary a great deal, but most ask students to explain the work that they did.

The key to getting good marks in a practical assignment is good planning. If you keep a careful record of the work you did and the decisions you made, you can always get marks for discussing ideas that were rejected. This will depend on you keeping notes on the rejected ideas and developing a good explanation for your selection decisions.

Summary

1 'Representations' is the term used to describe the way that the media portray things such as people, events, etc.

2   The various sections of the media together form an industry. The main aim of this industry is to make a profit. Because of this the media construct 'representations' which are likely to appeal to an audience.

3   All of the representations that we see within the media can be said to be 'constructed'.

4   Constructed representations have been planned in some way to make an impact and reach an audience.

5   Constructed representations are the result of selection decisions. These decisions involve choosing material to be included in a media product.

6   There are certain codes which regularly occur in representations. A simple example of this is the use of exciting action shots of people involved in sports – such as the picture of Dominic Cork used in the first example in this chapter.

7   It is possible to **deconstruct** representations. All of the examples in this chapter deconstruct media images.

Self-test questions

1   In two to three sentences explain the concept of representations.
2   In three to four sentences explain the idea of 'constructed' images.
3   In three to four sentences explain the meaning of 'editing'.
4   In three to four sentences explain the meaning of 'deconstruction'.

Chapter 7
Issues in representation

7.1 What you need to know

This chapter is slightly different to others in this book.

- It should be read alongside another chapter – chapter 6 on representations.
- It deals with three different points rather than one topic.

The topic of representation is a complicated one. The previous chapter was designed to help you to understand representations. This chapter explains three issues linked to representations:

- bias and impartiality
- mediation
- audience placement within a text.

Bias and impartiality

This means the extent to which any representation in the media is free from opinions.
  Bias occurs when a media text takes sides in its coverage of any subject.
  Impartiality is the other extreme – an impartial product takes no sides and allows the audience to make up its own mind on any particular topic.

Mediation

Mediation is the process of constructing meaning through the media. The idea behind this is that the media present things through their various products – films, comics, etc. When they do this they are said to 'mediate' the message that they present. This means, in effect, putting it into a particular form. The word 'media' actually comes from the word 'mediation'.

Audience placement within a text

This refers to the way that media products address audiences in different ways. For example, some products actually encourage audiences to become involved while others assume that the audience will be happy to watch/read/listen and be entertained.

- Children's cartoons are designed to be watched and enjoyed. They present constant action for a few minutes.
- Phone-in shows on radio depend on some members of the audience having opinions and deciding to get involved in the show.

Important note: If you have just turned to this chapter and the idea of representations is unfamiliar, you should read 'What you need to know' on pages 54–5 before studying the examples below.

7.2 Three examples of issues in representation

Each of these examples deals with one of the issues mentioned above. The issues – or concepts – are complicated and to make them easier to understand, two of the examples are very simple. They have been taken from children's comics. If you want to make more sense of the concepts after reading the examples, you could use the summary at the end of this chapter to help you consider other examples in this book. This should give you a more detailed knowledge of the three concepts discussed below.

EXAMPLE **Bias and impartiality: 'My guilty secret'**

Study the article 'My guilty secret' (Fig. 7.1) which appeared in *Just Seventeen* magazine. This magazine is aimed at teenage girls, probably about the same age as Paula, the girl with the 'guilty secret'.

My guilty secret

Paula, 16, has a new boyfriend – the trouble is, he's 26 …

Up until about six months ago my life was pretty ordinary. I went to school and hung out with my friends at weekends. If we went out to a disco, it was the under-18s one held by the local youth club. And, as you can imagine, that got pretty boring.

So when one of my mates, Carly, suggested we all go into town one Saturday night and go to a proper club, we thought it was a fab idea. The only thing that worried us was getting served; we didn't think we'd look old enough. But we thought we'd give it a try anyway. Saturday night came around, and we put on our best gear and headed off into town. Needless to say, none of our parents knew what we were up to – they'd have gone mad.

Out on the town

We were all a bit nervous, and on the way into the pub I bumped into one of the bouncers. I thought my number was up and he'd throw me out, but he just smiled and said, "Hello, love!" I giggled and walked

past him, but I couldn't help noticing now cute he was. He was tall, with dark hair and a great tan. Later that night, he came over and spoke to me – I was so nervous I could barely say a word back. He told me his name was Adam, and as we left, he said he hoped to see me next week, and winked at me!

I couldn't wait until the next Saturday. Luckily Adam was there again and we soon got chatting. He asked me what I did, and that's when I started lying – I told him I was 19 and reading English at university.

Hot date

We talked for ages and he told me he was 26 and had his own flat near the pub. Then he asked if he could take me out. I was thrilled and said yes straight away. I gave him my phone number and he said he'd call the next day.

When he called I pounced on the phone! We arranged to meet at the pub. When I put the phone down, my mum asked who I was meeting. I couldn't tell her the truth, so I just said I was meeting a boy from the youth group. Adam and I had a brilliant time; he was so grown up and a great laugh. I had to

keep up my lie about being at university, so whenever he asked me about that, I had to rack my brains for something to say. At the end of the evening, he took me home in a cab, kissed me goodnight and said he'd ring me.

Secret lover

Since then, we've been seeing each other regularly, which is great, but as we get to know each other better, it's getting harder to hide my secret. For example, Adam has his own car and said he'd pick me up from university one Friday, so I had to get out of school early, change and get a bus to the campus! Also my parents keep saying they want to meet my new boyfriend.

As I've been seeing Adam for a few months now, our relationship is getting quite intense. I don't know if I'm ready for a full-blown sexual relationship with him, and it scares me. Plus, I can't do with all this lying – I've got important exams coming up and can't concentrate because of it. If I tell Adam the truth, he's bound to finish with me; but I'm going to be found out sooner or later. I just don't know what to do.

ADVICE

First things first: besides the fact that alcohol can be a health risk, under-age drinking is illegal. You have to be at least 18 to drink alcohol in a pub. Remember, you don't need booze to have a laugh.

Lying to impress people never works, and nobody deserves to be lied to. Plus, there's all the stress involved in having to tell more and more lies to cover up the old ones. Paula could try to keep up the charade, but it's bound to backfire in a big way. Her best option is to own up to Adam and deal with the consequences.

● Older guys can seem way more attractive than boys your own age, but those extra years count for an awful lot – including the possibility of sexual intimacy you may not be ready for. So if, like Paula, you find yourself in this predicament, remember: don't do anything you don't want to do. It's your body and your choice. (And if you're under 16, sex is illegal.)

Fig 7.1

Paula's guilty secret concerns the lies she has told to a number of people. She has lied to her parents about going to the pub and her boyfriend. She has lied to her boyfriend about her age and where she is studying. On the surface, this is simply a story about a girl with problems who is now sharing her experiences with the readers of the magazine.

Is the story biased?

The story does not appear to be biased. It certainly does not insult Paula or even say that the things she did were wrong. It allows her to talk and presents a character to whom the readers should respond. The story accepts that Paula made some choices about her own life and even mentions that she 'couldn't wait' until she saw Adam again after their first meeting.

However, the conclusions that come from the whole piece do definitely take a particular side. The advice at the bottom of the story clearly warns about the dangers of under-age drinking, telling lies and teenage girls going out with older males. In this advice, the feature takes a **responsible line**. There is also a responsible line in the story because it shows that Paula's lies got her into trouble.

This feature highlights some important points about the issues of bias and impartiality.

A responsible line

Media producers are often obliged to take a responsible line in the way they tell stories. For example, most action films pit good characters against bad characters, and the good characters win in the end.

On a much smaller scale, 'My guilty secret' suggests that the solutions to problems like Paula's are found in following a code of conduct that involves honesty and observing the law.

There are a number of reasons why media producers follow the responsible line much of the time. Mostly these are financial. It is easier to get funding for products – like magazines, films, etc – that follow a responsible line.

Content and comment

Like all magazine features 'My guilty secret' has been through a process of editing – decisions have been made about what to include and what to leave out. Although such features are based on material sent to the magazine by readers – and therefore based on reader's real experiences – they are prepared by members of the magazine's staff to fit a certain length and style.

This raises another issue of bias or impartiality because decisions have been made about the content of the story that also make comments on Paula and her actions.

Consider Paula's situation for a minute and ask yourself some questions about this story:

- Do you know people who buy alcoholic drinks even though they are under age?

- Have you ever lied to get something you wanted?

- Would Paula get the same advice from her friends, her parents and her boyfriend's mates?

The chances are that the answers you give to these questions will show that there are a number of ways of looking at Paula's problem. Some people feel proud of the fact that there is an age gap between themselves and their boyfriend or girlfriend, or that they can get served in pubs before they are legally old enough. The magazine is right to point out that there are problems in these situations.

Teenage magazines like *Just Seventeen* do not openly tell readers they must do things a certain way. They present a friendly image and deal with typical readers' problems – many other girls have had the same experiences as Paula. At the same time, the magazines are under pressure to suggest responsible solutions to these problems, including giving information and advice that involves being honest, following the law, getting on with parents, etc.

A mix of bias and impartiality

This story shows some of the problems with bias and impartiality. We can see bias in the advice given to Paula and impartiality in the way that she is allowed to tell her story to other readers. Bias and impartiality are opposites. This story is not totally biased or totally impartial. In the end it is hard to conclude how much of each – bias and impartiality – there are. It is likely that different people would reach different conclusions on this point.

The examining boards are aware of the difficulty of making definite conclusions about bias and impartiality. Their main concern is that you understand the ideas and the way that bias and impartiality can affect the media.

Bias in TV and radio news?

The same is true of many media products. Television and radio news is legally supposed to be impartial in political coverage but people still argue about bias. As you can see, this problem is hard to solve and the examining boards do not expect you to know exactly how much bias there is in any media product. They do expect you to know what the words 'bias' and 'impartiality' mean. They also expect you to be able to spot both and produce arguments on paper to show you understand something about them. Some ideas for this are included in section 7.3.

Develop your skills

To develop your skills in arguing bias and impartiality try the following exercises:

❶ Look through a newspaper and select one story that is given extensive coverage. Note down the main conclusion of the story.

    (a) Who would want to read this story? Why would they be interested?

    (b) Who would have a different view of the story? What would this different view be?

    (c) If you were working in the media, where could you present a different view of the story?

❷ If you find the above exercise difficult first try asking yourself the same questions about 'My guilty secret'.

In this case, the main conclusion is that Paula should be doing things differently and that her actions got her into trouble. A different view might come from Paula's boyfriend. It is possible that he might care about her and forgive her if he found out. This different view could be presented in a TV soap opera like 'Eastenders' or 'Coronation Street'. These programmes tend to explore issues and see them from more than one side.

EXAMPLE # Mediation at work: 'Pingu's world'

We have already seen that mediation is the process of taking information and putting it into a media concept to reach an audience. 'Pingu's world' (Fig. 7.2) provides an insight into this, although the process is very complicated. This example gives us the opportunity to identify mediation at work and discuss it.

'Pingu's world' comes from *Pingu magazine* which is aimed at 2–6-year-olds. The comic is based on Pingu the penguin, a popular children's TV character.

Pingu offers the usual features of magazines for this age group and includes pages with an educational theme. One example is 'Pingu's world', in which Pingu presents information on different countries.

In this issue, 'Pingu's world' looks at Egypt but the country is presented in a very simple way to suit the age group of the audience. Many important points about Egypt are deliberately left out of the feature – it includes only basic information like the type of houses, animals and the national flag.

Definitions of mediation

A dictionary definition:

    'The act of intervening between two parties.'

This is a good description of how mediation works in the media. In the case of this example, the two parties are:

● young children with no real knowledge of the wide world

● the writer who knows about Egypt but needs to present his or her message in a way that the audience will understand.

Fig. 7.2

Another definition of mediation – this time from a dictionary on media studies:

'The act of channelling' information to an audience.

We can see this **channelling** in the example because the comic is acting as the channel. Young children expect to get information and entertainment from their comics.

Both of these definitions show us that the media are in the middle ground between an audience and the information that this audience wants. The media 'mediate' this information. In doing this, they fill in the gap between the audience and information and also channel this information to an audience.

Choosing a suitable 'channel'

All media products channel information and every type of media has its own way of channelling. Some types of media are more suitable than others for particular messages. For example, if you wanted to put across a serious political point, it would be a bad idea to sample a speech and put it into a hard–core dance record. The audience would be wrong and listeners would be more interested in the beats than the words. By contrast, *Pingu magazine* is a good place to teach children something about Egypt because the pictures and information fit the format of the comic very well.

Practise your understanding of mediation

Every example in this book is an example of mediation. The process itself is easy enough to explain but it becomes a problem in media studies because the examples you can quote are so varied. In terms of your own work as a student what matters is that you can explain this process and discuss examples from the media and from your own practical work.

Here is a useful exercise to practice your understanding of mediation.

Take the information on Egypt in this example. Present this as part of three different media products from the list below and try to find something interesting to say in each case:

- a dance record

- a pop record

- scene in a major film

- scene in a soap opera

- leaflet on your local area

- article for a local newspaper

- comic story.

Aim each product for an audience of your own age.

If you spend around 15 minutes planning this, you should begin to get some ideas. What you are looking for is a way of making this information appeal to an audience. For example:

- In a film the use of close-ups, the chance to use music, etc can add atmosphere.

- In a local newspaper readers expect to find information that is easy to read – perhaps a comparison of life in your home town and life in Egypt would be interesting if you kept it short.

- A dance record might seem an odd place to put information about Egypt, but if you think about such records for a while you will realise that they often use unusual sounds to make themselves different from other records. You could sample some Egyptian sounds or simply use some information as a phrase that gets repeated over and over again.

At the end of this exercise you should find that the same event will appear differently because each media has different strengths and weaknesses. This should give you some insight into the way that putting information into the media changes it in some way. The term used to describe this process of change is 'mediation'.

EXAMPLE   Audience placement within a text: Dennis the Menace

Audience placement within a text means the way that a media text talks to an audience and the kind of involvement that it demands from them. This concept – like mediation in the example above – can be explained easily. Studying the concept can present problems. This is because, like mediation, the examples of audience placement vary so much. They also tend to vary from media to media. For example, dance records are designed to accompany an activity while comics are designed to provide quick laughs and entertainment.

This example should explain the concept. Study the single page from the Dennis the Menace story (Fig. 7.3). This is the final frame of the story but it has been blown up to a full page to give readers of the comic their own cut-out mask of Dennis the Menace. The story involved Dennis having his own cut-out mask and using it to play jokes on people in his local area. Study Fig. 7.4 for an example of one of these jokes.

Dennis the Menace is a popular character from the children's comic *The Beano*. The jokes in Dennis stories often revolve around Dennis tricking other people in some way. Dennis is popular partly because he tries the kind of tricking and mischief that other children enjoy. This makes him something of a **role model**. In other words, he presents children with advice on how to behave, etc.

Because of this Dennis the Menace stories place the audience in a particular position. They tend to suggest that Dennis is the same kind of character as, for example, the cheekiest kid in their gang. Dennis appears braver and more resourceful than other children, although he sometimes loses in the stories.

In our example there is a clear placement for the audience which involves readers cutting out the mask from their own copy of the comic and using it in a trick. The audience is being told to have fun, and play a trick.

This is unusual even for a children's comic because most stories in such comics tend to encourage children to appreciate and admire the characters. In this final frame, the

Fig. 7.3   © D. C. Thomson & Co. Ltd.

audience is placed in the position of being Dennis's friends or his gang and he is suggesting to them that they can do the same things he has done in the story.

Other examples of audience placement
This is one example of audience placement. In most cases such placement is harder to pin down but some thinking on your part could help you to recognise this as it happens. Look for obvious examples to start with. In adverts, for instance, audiences are often placed in the situation of lacking something or needing the help of a particular product or service.

Look at a few adverts and write down in two or three sentences how they place an audience:

● What do they say about this audience?

● What do they suggest might be wrong with the audience to make them need the product or service on offer?

Audience placement in other media products
At this point, it is worth considering other media products. Many media products have an appeal because they give us a close look at the way other people live their lives. This is certainly true of programmes like soap operas in which domestic issues are the main story ideas.

Briefly, think about this in another way. If a house near where you live had a solid wall replaced with a glass wall, wouldn't you be interested in seeing how the people inside actually lived? You might get some answers to things you had wondered about the people inside.

The audience placement within the text of a soap opera works because it appeals to the curiosity within people. The same curiosity that would make it interesting to look into a friend or neighbour's house and see what they were doing at any given time of the day.

The more you think about the media in this way, the more obvious it becomes that most media products offer you a look at something from a viewpoint that is important to you. You can be given a chance to see something that you have wondered about, you can find a role model that thinks the things you do, you may simply admire somebody. All of these are examples of a text placing an audience in some way.

Fig. 7.4   © D. C. Thomson & Co. Ltd.

Complete the grid

To get you familiar with this idea, the grid below asks you to find examples of audience placement and to give reasons for each. Completing this grid would be a short but useful exercise to help you to spot different types of placement and to argue about how they work.

Simply note down further examples of each type of audience placement in each category of the grid and give reasons for your answer. These are not the only categories of audience placement, but they have been selected to show some of the different ways in which this concept can work.

Example	Category	How do we know this is true?
1 Soap powder adverts	Audience placed at disadvantage – they lack something	The adverts present people who can't wash cleanly enough or who are spending too much money on the powder they usually use.
2 Fan magazine on great football team	Audience invited to admire – audience don't have same level of skill	Such magazines emphasise skill and success. The idea behind them is that the teams involved are in a position to deliver these qualities. Most teams do not qualify for such publications to be sold nationally and this alone places the team and the audience in a rare relationship. The audience for such products are, basically, buying into success.
3 Comedy video	Audience sees someone else saying things that members of the audience feel but lack the courage to say	Comedy has proven over decades that certain themes, such as making fun of people who are successful, are popular. Comedians often say outrageous things about sex, politics, etc. They make money from doing this because many people in their audience probably think such things but wouldn't have the courage or the opportunity to say them in the same way.
4		
5		
6		

7.3 How these examples can help in your assignments

These examples are likely to be of more use in helping you to make sense of other media products than they are in discussing your own work. However, there are marks to be picked up in both areas and if you use the details in this chapter properly, the understanding of representation that it offers should help you.

It is unlikely that you will be given a whole assignment on just one of the three issues discussed above. It is more likely that a whole assignment will deal with the wider topic of representation. Because of this you are most likely to get good marks by including details of the issues covered in chapters 6 and 7 in a short and well-argued way.

Bearing this in mind, the most useful thing you can do is to read and understand the definitions included here and then practise spotting bias/impartiality, mediation and audience placement. You can then put short paragraphs into assignments that show an understanding of these issues, which will get you marks. It is always worth discussing this with a teacher beforehand for two reasons:

❶ Because you must check if doing this is likely to get you marks in the particular assignment.

❷ Because the teacher can give you feedback on your own understanding of these issues and check that you have properly understood the points.

The same is true in your practical work. You produce representations which are the result of your own ideas and opinions. When you produce practical work you are bound to show some bias. This could be in the form of using your own ideas and aiming them at people with the same kind of outlook on life.

On the other hand, you could show impartiality if you make a real effort to present things in an even and fair way. The point here is that there will be some bias because you are bound to make decisions on a personal basis and choose things that you think are entertaining, fair, etc.

You also mediate:

● Your idea will be mediated by the kind of media you are using. For example, a newspaper and a video might have a similar idea about a local story, but each would present this in a slightly different way because each has different strengths and weaknesses.

● Your idea will be mediated by the way that you decide to treat and present it.

Finally, all practical projects place an audience in some way. If you are writing about mediation in your evaluation it is probably useful to discuss it with a teacher.

Before you do so, ask yourself how you expect an audience to react to your work, what kind of audience you think will be interested and what you are telling them that they want to know. Try to write down a sentence or two that explains how you place your audience within your practical work. You might get some ideas on placement from the third example in unit 7.2.

It is particularly important that you discuss the audience placement aspect with your teacher because this concept is quite complicated and you will get the best possible marks if your explanation and reasoning are very clear. Your teacher may well be able to help you put your own ideas into the best words possible to get a good mark.

Summary

1   Issues in representation are the important ideas and pieces of theory behind the wider idea of representations.

2 Bias is distorting or changing a message in some way.

3 Impartiality is the act of not taking sides in a debate.

4 In the media, impartiality is usually understood as presenting things in the most accurate way possible.

5 Bias and impartiality are opposites.

6 Mediation is the act of channelling a message through the media.

7 Mediation concentrates on the way that messages are changed and shaped as they are channelled.

8 The media themselves are channels for messages and the word 'media' comes from the word 'mediation'.

9 It is generally understood within the media that different media have their own particular strengths and weaknesses and this means that they tend to mediate messages in their own ways.

10 Audience placement within a text means the way in which that text – or media product – addresses the audience and the way it expects them to react.

11 Texts can place audiences in many different ways, e.g. telling them to do things, asking them to admire people, giving them a look at something they would like to see, etc.

12 There are a number of different examples of audience placement explained in the Dennis the Menace example.

Self-test questions

You should close the book at this point and make note answers to these questions.
1   In two or three sentences give an example of bias in the media.
2   In two or three sentences give an example of impartiality in the media.
3   In two or three sentences give an example of mediation.
4   In two or three sentences describe an example of audience placement within the media.

Chapter 8
Stereotyping

8.1 What you need to know

Stereotyping refers to the way that the media create simplified images and then regularly use these images. Both examining boards insist that this is covered within the coursework.

A **stereotype** is a simplified image of something – usually a person, group of people, place or event. People often use these stereotypes to help them understand the world and the media frequently feature such stereotypes.

Stereotypes are useful to the media because they mean that stories and other media products can be quickly understood. Stereotypes tend to occur where the quick understanding of something is important.

An example of stereotyping

Stereotyping is often found in humour. Characters in situation comedy shows have to be easily understood. This allows audiences to make sense of the programme and to follow the story without needing to make much effort. A good example of the use of a stereotype is the character Victor Meldrew from the popular TV sit-com 'One Foot in the Grave'. He is based on the stereotypical idea of a 'grumpy old man'. His character is more than just a stereotype, but an understanding of Victor Meldrew depends on an understanding of the stereotype concerning old men.

This example highlights some other points about stereotypes. They tend to back up ideas that people already have. This means that audiences do not have to make much effort to understand stereotypes and that the media can use the same stereotypes over a period of years.

Criticism of stereotypes

The use of stereotypes has been much criticised and groups of people who dislike the way they are presented often complain about this. It is true that using stereotypes means that we don't get the full facts about the person, group, etc that is stereotyped.

Financial reasons for the use of stereotypes

The media keep using stereotypes for good financial reasons. Because stereotypes are understood by a wide group of people, they give a media product – like a film or a television programme – the chance of appealing to a large audience.

Another good financial reason for using stereotypes is that they reflect the way that some people see the world. For example, in films aimed at a teenage audience, middle-aged characters are often stereotypes in the way that they try to stop younger characters enjoying themselves. This is often how teenagers view older people.

In films aimed at older audiences, it is often younger characters that behave in a stereotypical way for the same reasons. The link with making money is obvious. If these films back up the ideas of their audiences, then the audiences are likely to feel better about the film, enjoy it and recommend others to see it.

8.2 Three examples of stereotyping

EXAMPLE **'Dumb blonde' stereotype**

This example shows a well-tried and tested stereotype and explains how it has come about.

Study the photo of actress Marilyn Monroe (Fig. 8.1). She is quoted in books on film as an example of the 'dumb blonde stereotype'. A number of characters in films fit into this category.

Fig. 8.1

The creation of 'dumb blonde' images came at a time when the world was dominated by men much more than it is today. Dumb blonde images were designed to appeal to men. They were images of women who fitted the ideas of their time. Dumb blonde characters were good-looking, tended to lack intelligence and in films, often needed men to look after them. This backed up the current ideas about the way men and women should be together.

One important thing about dumb blonde images was that they didn't present a threat to men being in charge of the world.

The dumb blonde stereotype was based on a kind of fantasy idea. Marilyn Monroe is one good example of this. In the photo you can see her eyes and teeth are striking features. People who study the way we are attracted to the opposite sex note that eyes and teeth are the features of the face that we look at first. Marilyn's image used her sexual attractiveness.

At the height of the dumb blonde stereotype, men tended to make decisions about which films they went to see with girlfriends. They also tended to pay.

The dumb blonde stereotype helped to get men into cinemas and to make films profitable. This example shows how a stereotypical image can be carefully made for a particular reason.

EXAMPLE **Northern characters in a radio script**

This example shows the way that stereotypes are used within the media and explains how this process occurs.

The script from the radio comedy programme 'Week Ending' (Fig. 8.2) was written following the relegation of football club Halifax Town from the Football League after it finished at the very bottom. It uses stereotypical images of Northern people and mentions things like 'cloth caps' and 'Websters' beer which are linked with the North of England in a stereotypical way.

The script is intended to be funny. It contrasts the North with other places and shows how out of touch with fashion Northern people are supposed to be by mentioning 'fashionable curly perms' which went out of style years ago. The jokes in the script work because the stereotype of Northern people as out of touch, poor, beer drinkers and wearing cloth caps is still understood.

HALIFAX TOWN

[*All voices with heavy Yorkshire accents*]

[*Noises of meeting settling down followed by gavel being banged on a table*]

CHAIRMAN Give order, give order yer buggers.

[*They give order*]

CHAIRMAN Now then, I declare this meeting of Halifax Town open. Lets 'ave t' reports from t'officials. Manager, owz t' season gone?

MANAGER Aye well, we started season wi' high hopes but fifteen minutes in it were obvious that we were as bad as the last ten years. By t' end we got chucked out and we'll be playing in a lower league next season.

CHAIRMAN Lower league! Lower bloody league! By heck, you mean there's teams worse than us? That's handy to know. Treasurer's report.

TREASURER Well we started t' season wi' nowt and at t' moment we've got...

[*sound of paper being rustled*] ...nowt.

CHAIRMAN Aye well, there's many a bigger club would give their fashionable curly perms for our consistency. Is there owt else before we put us cloth caps on and have a right tasty pint of Websters?

[*Murmuring*]

TREASURER I've just got a letter from London.

CHAIRMAN London is it, you flash sod. So what's it say?

TREASURER It's t' cheque for us share of t' first season's profits on t' new football TV deal.

[*Murmur gets loud*]

CHAIRMAN By heck, give it here.

[*Rustle of paper*]

CHAIRMAN Bugger me, we can strengthen t' squad wi this.

MANAGER I've never bought a player before.

CHAIRMAN Buy a player, divvent be so daft. This'll put some meat in't half time sandwiches for t' lads. Howay, let's get down t' pub. By heck, great days for football these.

(ENDS)

Fig. 8.2

In this example it is fair to say that the characters are being used in a stereotypical way. The stereotypes are the Northern men. The script does not present stereotypes of their jobs – like football chairman.

This is a very short script designed to fit into a radio show that is full of short comedy sketches. It might upset some Northern people, but the reason for using stereotypes is that this sketch has to be quickly understood if people are going to find the comedy funny. Using stereotypes quickly sets the scene in terms of location and the kind of people who appear.

EXAMPLE ## SCHWA merchandise advert

This example shows how and why stereotypes are developed. It is also an example of a stereotype that is still developing.

Study the advert for SCHWA merchandise (Fig. 8.3). This merchandise is sold as a joke item. It reproduces pictures of the face of an alien. There have been many representations of aliens in media history. You are probably familiar with Mr Bean and possibly Mork from the TV series 'Mork and Mindy'. These are human representations of aliens.

Some science fiction films – like the *Star Wars* and *Alien* series of films have used expensive make-up and special effects to represent aliens. None of these images listed have become stereotypes, but there are a growing number of alien-related products that use a similar image to the face featured on the SCHWA merchandise.

ALIEN TROUBLE? NO TROUBLE!

Hounded by space aliens? Abducted and subjected to stringent medical examinations on a regular basis? You need SCHWA. Earth's most complete range of alien defence equipment, exclusively manufactured for Fortean Times by the SCHWA Corp. of Reno, Nevada.

BLACK GLOW-IN-THE-DARK SCHWA T-SHIRT
100% cotton heavyweight T-shirt will keep you safe at all times. Alien detector on front glows in the dark, flashes red in the presence of aliens. Available in large or XL sizes – **£10.99**

WHITE GLOW-IN-THE-DARK SCHWA T-SHIRT
100% cotton heavyweight shirt bears glow-in-the-dark alien head on front, Bomb Squad logo on rear.
Available in size XL – **£10.99**

COUNTER SCHWA KIT
An all-new complete SCHWA kit. Features Emergency Personal Life TV card, Xenon-coated warning stickers, time travel sticker (good for one second per year), new SCHWA book, crazy meter and lots of other cards and surprises. Replaces old Complete Kit as the definitive all-you-need defence pack. T-shirt not included – **£9.99**

SCHWA STICKER & CARD PACK Things you need! Includes alien invasion survival card, repellent patches, "Defended by SCHWA" car stickers and other cards and surprises – **£4.99**

CAR STICKER CONVERSION PACK
Turn your car into a SCHWA corporate vehicle with this comprehensive sticker pack. Includes over 18 stickers, two 8in alien heads, two "For Unofficial Use Only" stickers and invasion mirror dangler - **£6.99**

Fig. 8.3

Use of truth in stereotypes

Representing aliens presents a problem to the media because nobody knows what they look like and there is debate about whether aliens have ever visited our planet. Despite this, the media have invented stereotypes of aliens in the same way that they develop stereotypes of other things. This is an important point. It shows that the media are not limited by truth in their development of stereotypes.

In the first two examples above there might have been some truth to the stereotypes. In the case of the dumb blonde image the 'truth' is that this has been a kind of fantasy figure for some men. In the case of the Northern characters in the radio script, the truth is in the accents and the fact that there has been some tradition of beer drinking and cloth cap wearing in the North of England.

The 'truth' with aliens is very suspect and it is possible that the creatures on the SCHWA merchandise do not exist in reality. The faces have been based on reports of contact with aliens but they have also been developed by the media industry. SCHWA is a company that has taken advantage of a developing stereotype.

Inferential reading of the media

The examining boards want students to learn the technique of **inferential reading** of the media. This means that you should be able to make sense of media texts in a way that shows some understanding of their meaning and purpose.

The idea behind inferential reading is that you can study media texts and make 'inferences' or conclusions about why they work in the way that they do. The examples in this book make inferences in this way.

The developing stereotype of the alien provides a good example of how meanings are built up. This point about the truth is crucial to the idea of inferential reading because there is no doubt that the alien image is at least partly the result of a media construction.

If you study the image of the 'alien' face, you can infer some meanings and find good reasons for these inferences. For example, you might infer – conclude – that aliens are cold and unfeeling. This inference can easily be linked to the black eyes with no details. It might also lead to another conclusion: that aliens present some kind of threat. This conclusion can be based on the idea of the aliens being unfeeling, the fact that they must be here if we are wearing T-shirts, etc and the fact that some of the products are designed to warn us about them.

The advantages of a simplified image

These meanings have been constructed by people making products with alien images on them. There is another side to this alien stereotype – like all stereotypes, it is a simplified image.

Because the 'truth' behind the image is controversial, the media have had more freedom than usual in developing the stereotype. We can see this in the image itself which suggests the qualities outlined above.

We can also see the advantage to the media of such a simple stereotype. The black and white face is easy to reproduce and to understand. It is as simple as most road signs and the lack of colour in the figure will further cut costs.

There is some demand for this stereotype but it is also clear that the industry behind the making of products with such a simple image has an interest in keeping the stereotype in this form.

A developing stereotype

We saw above that there are other examples of alien images. The SCHWA image looks nothing like Mr Bean or the Klingon characters in the *Star Trek* films and television shows. This stereotype is still evolving and at the moment, its development is being helped by a few reports of people actually meeting aliens.

Its development is also being encouraged by media producers who want to use simple alien images in everything from comic-strip stories to films. If all of the media producers can keep the image simple and maintain the meanings that were listed in the section on inferential reading above, they will be able to exploit this stereotype.

8.3 How these examples can help in your assignments

There are two obvious ways in which these examples can help you:

❶ They should be useful if you are doing any work linked to studying media images.

❷ They can help if you are putting your own images and ideas together.

a Work linked to media images

The first example shows a visual image that was carefully put together for a reason. Any work you might be doing on images should consider how they are aimed at an audience and how the media simplify images to make them appeal to bigger audiences. Simplifying images and using them over and over again is the way that stereotypes are created – the WJEC's syllabus refers to this as 'production and reproduction'.

This does not mean that every media image is a stereotype. But, mentioning the creation of stereotypes and the way they continue does show an understanding of how the media make images. Ask yourself the following questions when you are studying images for an assignment:

- Where does the image come from?

- Who is the audience for this image?

- Does the image reflect the way that this audience sees the world?

- Has the image been simplified to allow for easy understanding?

By answering these questions and using the summary at the end of the chapter, you should be able to include some arguments about stereotypes. These can help with assignments on media images. Remember, even if the image you are studying isn't a stereotype, there may still be some bits of stereotype within it. For example, the image may have been simplified.

b Producing your own work

Anyone involved in producing images and ideas has to make some choices about their work. These choices usually involve thinking about the audience to make sure that it will understand and like the images and ideas. If you are doing this, ask yourself these questions:

- Am I using a type of image or idea that is common in the media?

- Have I deliberately simplified this work?

- Am I using some simple thing to stand for something else that is more complicated? For example, have I invented a character to represent a particular type of person?

- Will the images and ideas I am using reflect opinions that my audience will already have?

Summary

1 Stereotypes are simplified images or ideas that are understood by a large number of people.

2 They are based on truth, but this truth may be badly distorted by the stereotype.

3 The advantage of stereotypes to the media is that they are easily understood by a large number of people.

4 Media products use stereotypes to allow the whole product to be understood and to reflect the opinions that the audience already holds.

5 Stereotypes can be simple visual images, e.g. Marilyn Monroe.

6 They can also be ideas, like the image of Northern people in the radio script in the second example.

7 The use of stereotypes has been criticised. Some people object to the way that stereotypes simplify complicated ideas.

8 Creating stereotypes within productions – like characters within a television programme – is an easy way of getting across a lot of information to an audience.

9 The media industry makes money working in this way, so it is likely that it will always create and keep reproducing stereotypes.

10 Stereotypes are developing all the time and the pressures to make money and reach audiences are pushing this development along. An example of a developing stereotype is the alien face on SCHWA's merchandise.

Self-test questions

1 In three to four sentences explain the idea of stereotypes.
2 Why do some people object to the use of stereotypes?
3 Why would media products be more expensive to make without the use of stereotypes?

Self-test activity

You work for a company that makes comics for young children. You have been commissioned to produce a comic story based on a grandmother character. The idea of the character is to present a positive image of old people to the readers of the comic. You should aim to use some elements of stereotype in this character.

Create a character and draw a sketch to illustrate your creation. Write a short description – about half a side of A4 paper – of your character. List the elements of your character that you consider are stereotypical of images of old people.

Chapter 9
Working practices in the media

9.1 What you need to know

Working practices are the ways in which people within an industry or service do their jobs. The media industry, like any other, is an employer of people. The jobs that these people currently do are the result of the demands from the audience for their work. They are also the result of changing technologies. All of these things will be investigated within this chapter.

Before we explore working practices in detail, it is worth considering two other points. Both of these are good news for students of media studies.

❶ Once you fully understand the fact that the media is an industry, you should get a much clearer understanding of all of the theory you need for your course. This is because almost all important media theory is firmly linked to finance. For example, the idea of a genre as a group of products makes sense when you see that these products are made time and again because that is the best way for the media to make money. Look at other examples of products, like cars. These tend to fall into categories with a similarity of style and content.

❷ If you intend to follow up your GCSE Media Studies with a BTEC National Diploma in the same subject, this chapter is of particular importance. The BTEC National Course has modules on Working Practices.

Working practices in GCSE Media Studies will involve you in finding out about and understanding the ways in which jobs are done in the media, the kind of jobs that exist and the ways in which the media use the skills of different people to produce finished work.

One important point that should be remembered here is that GCSE Media Studies also requires you to produce some practical media work. This work will involve working practices of your own although you are very unlikely to have the use of any top of the range media production equipment.

Bearing this in mind, your own discussions of working practices within your assignments will probably concentrate on the ways in which decisions are made, methods of organisation, etc. You will of course also have to discuss what you actually did in terms of using equipment.

9.2 Three examples of working practices in the media

The area of working practices is so vast within the media that each of the examples below has been chosen as a case study of one particular area. Each example makes clear what it is intended to teach you.

EXAMPLE | **'The Smell of Reeves and Mortimer', BBC Television, 1995**

This example discusses changing working practices within the 'mainstream' parts of the media. It also looks at an 'autocratic' decision-making process.

The programme 'The Smell of Reeves and Mortimer', screened by BBC 2 in 1995, was produced by an independent company for the BBC and sold to the corporation for screening.

The BBC has a great tradition of producing comedy and an international reputation for producing new and innovative comedies. Comedies that broke new ground in television such as 'Monty Python's Flying Circus', 'Not the Nine O'Clock News' and 'The Young Ones' were BBC productions.

Vic Reeves and Bob Mortimer appeared on BBC having left Channel 4. But their show was produced in a different way to the other successes from the past.

The consequences of a change in working practices

By the time Reeves and Mortimer appeared on BBC 2, there had been an important change within the BBC – a scheme called the 'producer choice' had been introduced. This scheme saw the BBC scale down its staff and use many more independent production companies to provide programmes for the network.

The scheme was controversial within the BBC and there was some resistance from people who felt that their jobs and career prospects were under threat. The other financial side of the argument was that the cost of producing programmes was falling as new technology became available and this meant that independent producers could make programmes much more cheaply than a heavily staffed operation like the BBC.

To further add to the threat to the BBC, the rise of satellite and cable broadcasting meant that there was more competition in the market for television audiences.

The BBC had been a stable employer for years and the trade unions within the BBC had been strong enough to make deals that gave their members reasonable rates for specific jobs – for example, the BBC employed many sound recordists and provided some of the best work in the country for people in this type of job.

As new television companies and independent producers became better established, many of the new operations didn't work in the same way. They took advantage of the new technology to save money. For example, sound recording could be combined with another job and in some cases small operations used one person to film pictures, record sound and present information to a camera.

With 'producer choice', the BBC allowed itself to use these independent companies and also to get programmes at the most competitive price. In terms of cutting costs, there were some obvious advantages. If a company offered the BBC three hours of comedy – like 'The Smell of Reeves and Mortimer' – it could agree a price and this price would include the profit for the company. If the production ran up to budget or even over it, then the likelihood was that the company making the programme would carry the loss.

Even if companies stand to make a loss in a situation which involves them producing a programme for a bigger company, they are still likely to deliver the programme. If they don't their chances of getting further work are reduced.

All of this has had a major effect on the way that big media companies work. The things that have made the most difference are:

- the expansion of markets
- new technology.

All media areas have seen their markets expand. In the case of television, we have already mentioned satellite and cable TV, but radio, the music industry, comics, newspapers and magazines have all taken advantage of new technology to expand what they do. This has sometimes led to new products, as we will see in the next example. However, in the case of 'The Smell of Reeves and Mortimer', the product hasn't changed a great deal.

This television comedy is in the tradition of BBC comedy that takes a few chances and breaks some new ground. It is likely that most of the audience watching the show will not have realised that it was not a BBC production. To the audience the show seemed very similar to BBC productions. It clearly uses a studio, outside locations, costumes and many props.

In terms of working practices, the show presents a fairly typical picture of the kind of changes that are having an effect on big companies. The show is produced on an agreed contract between a big company and an independent producer. The number of people involved in producing it is less than it would have taken to make the show 20 years ago. Some of the jobs now done in production by one person would have been the jobs of two or more people under the old agreements.

Everyone involved in decision-making within the show will be aware of the need to make a profit. In the case of the BBC the 'profit' is the money that it can save against the cost of producing the same show. In the case of the company that made the show all of the deals agreed on delivery of the show, the cost of filming, etc will have been worked out against the likely amount of profit from screening, video sales and any other exploitation of the series.

An autocratic structure

Because the BBC is still a huge operation, it operates a particular structure for making decisions. This might be called **autocratic** or **hierarchical**. These terms mean that decisions are made at a higher level and passed down a chain of command.

The existence of 'producer choice' was imposed in this way and while some people inside the BBC didn't like it, the management saw very good economic reasons for introducing the scheme.

This example has shown the way an autocratic structure works. The main point in terms of decision-making is that the system in use in an autocratic structure makes some logical sense and that this system works to organise everyone within it.

EXAMPLE ## Tilted Tim album: 'Fate Made A Mess Of My Jeans'

This example discusses the current expansion of media production for performers with a small following. This expansion has been made possible by the falling costs of production and the growing market for work. The laissez-faire *decision-making process is explained.*

A BRIEF HISTORY OF TIM

1980–1981 THE NOTLEYS
Founder member, lead vocalist and main writer. Made a cassette album entitled, 'Bring Down the Trough' in 1981. Received a fair amount of airplay on Nicky Horne's Radio Rock Show. Did a session for Nicky, broadcast in late 1981. Played c50 gigs in and around London.

1983–1984 TOOTH 'N' NAIL
Duo with guitarist (Glen Baker) from the Notleys. Supported pomp-rock dinosaur cult The Enid on a British tour of Universities, Colleges and Civic Halls. Video of gig at Brighton Pavillion in December 1983. Unmixed but quite entertaining!

1985
Penniless. Recorded solo album, 'Sucking In The Wind', using cheapo Casio keyboard and borrowed four-track. Completed TOPS course in computing and concentrated on earning money to pay off debts and buy some decent equipment.

1987–1992 TILTED TIM
Bought modest home studio. Wrote and produced, 'Fate Made A Mess Of My Jeans' in my spare time.

Fig. 9.1

Even if you are a music fan with a wide knowledge of the industry, you probably won't have heard of Tilted Tim. Tim has a full-time job and writing and recording his own brand of music is a hobby that also brings in some money.

As you can see from the 'Brief History of Tim' (Fig. 9.1), he has been working at his hobby for over 15 years including some periods when he was, in effect, a professional musician. In this time he has bought a home studio and made his own album.

Trying to categorise Tim's music is difficult but 'Fate Made A Mess Of My Jeans' is made up of songs that are put together in the normal way with verses and a chorus. The lyrics and ideas behind some of the songs are odd and humorous – Tim is unique to the point that his style doesn't copy anyone else's. The recording quality is exceptionally good.

New technology reduces costs

A review from *Recording Musician* points out that musically and lyrically the album is eccentric. So eccentric in fact that Tim's chances of getting signed by a big record company would be very slim. In the past, this would have been an impossible problem for a musician wanting to make his or her own album but the kind of technology available today has made a real difference to performers like Tim.

The most obvious example of technology from which Tim has benefited is the 'modest' home studio that allowed him to record in his own home and in his own time. This kind of equipment has revolutionised some sections of the music industry, in particular, the dance area. Many successful writers and composers of dance records work almost exclusively from home.

The cost of making 'Fate Made A Mess of My Jeans' includes a charge for the facilities of a professional studio, but this bill was a fraction of the amount a major act would spend. In fact, this sum wouldn't come close to paying off the costs of a single for most acts.

The rise of the non-mainstream musician

The kind of home studio used by acts like Tilted Tim has made a significant difference to the music industry. In Tim's case, it meant that much of the work that could have been done in the recording studio at great cost to him was done at home.

Home studios have become cheaper because the electronic and computer technology that they use has become cheaper to make and more readily available. This industry now depends on the existence of many working musicians who are not by any means in the 'mainstream' of music.

Bands that play at weddings and parties often use home-studio technology to record extra instrumental parts which they use to fill out their sound on stage. Many other musicians use studios to make their own recordings, hoping that one day they will be signed to a record label.

Recording for a small following

Tim's total bill − exclusive of VAT − is £7,077.50. While this seems like a lot, you should remember that this paid for 1000 CD copies of his album, 1000 tape copies and 1000 promotional flexi discs.

An unusual act like Tim is more likely to make money nationally because the small audience that collects 'weird and wonderful' recordings of all kinds is scattered around the country.

Tim could have produced his recording much more cheaply − in chapter 13 Rancid Hell Spawn is another act that records for a fraction of these costs − but the gamble he made was that a good quality recording would find a specific market which was looking for interesting and unusual music.

Tim did some national promotion for the album which included spending around £13 to get his album into the *Viz* comic top ten chart. This chart has now been scrapped, but it used to allow artistes to 'hype' themselves by paying the comic for a chart place. This was an obvious joke at the expense of the national charts which have often faced allegations of hyping.

Tim's small investment got his picture into *Viz* and a short write-up about his album. The *Viz* audience, like the audience for strange records in general, are scattered nationally and tend to appreciate humour in the things they read and listen to. *Viz* readers are obvious Tilted Tim fans and this investment − coupled with the chance to get a free flexi record before buying the album − helped sales.

On a local basis, Tim still has copies of the album to sell if and when he plays gigs.

If all of the tapes and CDs sold at full price, Tim would earn £15,480 − leaving him with a reasonable profit on his investment. If there was demand for even more copies, then the profits would increase because the recording costs of the album have already been paid off.

Tilted Tim is an odd act in musical terms and his realistic ambitions are unlikely to include hit singles and albums. However, in the present climate in the music industry acts like Tim can survive and make a profit so long as they can find a small and loyal audience.

Such acts and audiences do exist and the costs from the recording of Tilted Tim's album show the economics of this business. Allowing for some extra costs − postage, use of the phone, etc − Tim could still make a profit on around 700 CD sales alone, less than 50 per cent of the albums actually made.

A change in working practices leads to expansion

In terms of working practices, Tilted Tim reveals another expanding side of the media industry. As a professional person with a full-time job, he can treat his musical career as a hobby and he is not tied to the demands of record companies, promoters, etc. There is the possibility of profit for musicians who do what they like and aim it at a small audience of people with a similar outlook to themselves. The media now employs many people like Tim on a part-time basis as they use cheaper and cheaper technology to make their own media products.

The existence of people working in this way has helped many small companies involved in producing equipment, distributing work, and so on to make a profit. Acts like Tilted Tim provide work for recording studios, manufacturers of recording equipment, small mail-order record companies which advertise in music publications, etc.

Cheaper technology in the media industry as a whole has led to a massive expansion of work at this end of the market and there are now many people involved in the music industry who work part-time in some area.

This pattern is not limited to the music industry and we will see some other examples of cheaply produced products in this section.

Laissez-faire decision-making

Laissez-faire decision-making involves making decisions in response to particular conditions and working without a set structure.

Tilted Tim is typical of a new breed of people working within the media who can operate in this way. His musical career is driven by his own wish to make records and by the response he gets to things he does. If someone running a club heard Tim's album and wanted to book him for a one-off date, Tim could agree it himself. He does not need to consult his manager. He also decides when and where he records or does anything else linked to his musical career.

There are some strengths in this like being in charge of your own work. There are also weaknesses in this system, for example, not being able to make accurate predictions of earnings over a long period of time. However, this type of working makes sense for many people who treat their media careers as a well-paid hobby.

EXAMPLE **The European Satellite User Group**

This example shows the types of company and job that are developing as a result of technical changes in the media.

The European Satellite User Group (TESUG) is a small company based in Kent. Its main work is to keep in touch with changes in satellite broadcasting and to provide information to others in the field. The company publishes a regular newsletter containing all this information. It also has interests in radio and broadcasting. Fig. 9.2 shows one member of the company, Eric Wilshire, relaxing in a radio studio. Note the food and drink beside him. This picture was taken during a meeting with a colleague from another company. It shows that in small media companies many things go on at once. This meeting to discuss work took place over a snack. The office pictured here also serves as a record library. Twenty minutes later Eric was on the air doing a radio show along with the colleague, and the author of this book. In a situation like this many deals are done through contacts and there are often no clear breaks between work and relaxation.

Effect of the pace of change

Twenty years ago a company like TESUG could not have existed because the industry it serves did not exist. Most of the technology that has made the satellite and cable television industry possible has been invented in the last 10 years and new technology is being produced all the time. Developments in new technology are one of the items featured in the TESUG newsletter.

One obvious change in working practices in the media is obvious from these facts alone. The pace of change in the media is now so fast that in some areas there are careers for people who are employed to keep everyone else in touch with the changes.

The existence of TESUG also shows us a few other important changes. The offices of the group are in a small industrial unit, but its contacts cover the UK and most of

Fig. 9.2

continental Europe. This has been made possible by the extensive use of technology linked to computers and satellite television.

The company employs a small staff and has links with many other operations of the same size. In this it is typical of the kind of small company that is now setting up within the media.

More flexible working practices
The growing number of small companies has had a major impact on the kind of work that people do in the media. If we compare TESUG to a huge operation like the BBC, it is obvious that TESUG could not compete in most areas with the resources of a big corporation. On the other hand, the BBC is not very well placed to be as responsive as a company like TESUG.

The differences are mainly seen in the type of work that people do. A company like TESUG provides an excellent training for people starting a media career because the work is so varied and any good project will be accepted. This means that while the main work of the company is producing the newsletter, the contacts that it makes with other companies sometimes lead to chances to be involved in television and radio broadcasts and a whole range of other activities.

A big company with a large staff couldn't respond in this way without consulting managers, agreeing strategies and asking some staff to do jobs outside of their contracts. A company like TESUG cannot afford to be bound by contracts and staffing systems.

In its working practices, a company like TESUG represents the future of media employment. As the media continue to expand, it is certain that many more small markets for products will be created. As this happens, small operations will grow up to produce the products that these markets need. With technology and communications improving all the time such companies can work for people in other countries whom they will never meet.

Survival for a small company like this means seizing any useful opportunity for work and making it count. Many of these opportunities come as a result of contact with other small companies working in the same area.

A democratic decision-making process
When job adverts ask for people who are 'flexible', they are looking for the kind of individuals employed by a company like TESUG.

TESUG is an example of a company with a **democratic** decision-making process. This means that everyone involved in a job gets a say in the things that are done and in the end, decisions are made by a majority of employees.

There are obvious advantages to this, for example, everyone feels more involved because their opinions are being considered. One of the main disadvantages is the time it can take to consult people and consider all opinions. In the media this is less of a problem in small companies than it is in other industries. This is because most of these small companies are under permanent pressure from time and money and so everyone is aware that they must discuss points and make decisions quickly.

9.3 How these examples can help in your assignments

The examining boards require you to understand something about working practices in the media, but they do not go into very much detail about what they expect to see included in assignments.

After reading the above examples, you should use the summary below and the sections headed 'An autocratic structure', '*Laissez-faire* decision-making' and 'A democratic decision-making process' to give you a framework for understanding working practices on the media. It is likely that you can bring some argument about decision-making into the discussion of your practical work.

Unless you are set a specific assignment on an area like working practices or the impact of new technologies on the media, it is advisable to ask your teacher before you include much material on the issues raised in this chapter in one of your assignments. In assignments that look at the work of others, you should be able to use information from the summary as points to back up arguments in your assignments.

When discussing and evaluating your own practical work, it is useful to consider the decision-making strategy that you use. All decision-making strategies have strengths and weaknesses, and some of these have been outlined in the examples. If you plan your practical work properly you can gain marks by noting down the way you made decisions and considering how these might have been made differently had you used a different strategy.

Summary

1 Working practices in the media means the ways in which people do their jobs to produce media products.

2 These practices are changing because of changes in the industry.

3 These industrial changes include the introduction of new technology and the expansion of markets for work.

4 Working practices vary from one employer to another, but the major changes in the industry have brought about some patterns of change.

5 One steady change at the moment involves big employers – like the BBC – using independent producers to provide programmes.

6 Another change is the steady growth of small companies that deal with particular markets.

7 A further major change is the increasing presence in the media of people who take advantage of cheap technology to make their own products and are not employed on a full-time basis within the media. Tilted Tim is one example of this.

8 The changes as a whole in the media mean that the industry is now looking for people with skills who can be flexible enough to change the jobs that they do as required.

9 There are a number of ways of making decisions within a working environment. These include autocratic, democratic and *laissez-faire* decision-making.

10 An **autocratic** structure involves decisions being made at the top of an organisation and passed down the line. This usually happens in a large organisation like the BBC – see 'The Smell of Reeves and Mortimer' example.

11 A **democratic** structure usually involves the people within an organisation sharing their opinions and making a decision based on a majority view. This usually happens in very small companies like The European Satellite User Group.

12 A *laissez-faire* decision-making structure usually involves people making decisions without a set structure and in response to events. This usually happens when very few people – possibly just one person – are involved. Tilted Tim is one example.

Self-test questions

1 What do you understand by the term 'working practices in the media'.
2 List three ways in which the introduction of new technology has changed the ways in which people work in the media.
3 Define 'autocratic' decision-making and note one good example.
4 Define 'democratic' decision-making and note one good example.
5 Define '*laissez-faire*' decision-making and note one good example.

Important note: GCSE Media Studies is not intended as a training course for the media industry, but if you are serious about wanting a media career, there are some important points in this chapter to note. Careers teachers can help you with details of jobs that you might want to do, but it should be obvious from the examples here that people working in the industry use a range of skills and tend to have a number of different jobs throughout their career.

Successful media careers are built on skills and an awareness of how to use them. If you want to work in the media it is worth considering the kind(s) of skill you have. For example do you come up with your own ideas quickly? Are you good at research? Do you solve problems quickly?

The media will employ you on the strength of your skills and you will develop your career as you add to these skills and understand ways in which they can be used within the media.

Chapter 10
Markets

10.1 What you need to know

A **market** in media terms is the complete potential audience for a product. For example, satellite broadcasters often talk in terms of markets of millions of people when their products are only watched by a few thousand. What they mean in this case is that millions of people have access to their products even if many of those people do not choose to watch.

Markets matter in media studies because an industry depends on the existence of markets. In fact, no one ever seriously questions the existence of markets for the media. The whole subject of media studies involves studying the workings of this industry. There is a clear assumption from everyone involved that the media will continue.

Some other industries have struggled in recent years and once great British industries like steel-making and coal-mining have been cut to a fraction of their former size. Some of this has been due to a fall in demand for the things that these industries make. This is called a **declining market**. Some of it has been due to competition which involved other countries making the same goods at a cheaper price. This is called **competition**.

No one seriously suggests that the media will face a sudden drop in demand for what they make. Some industries – like food manufacture – involve the production of 'essential' items. In other words, they make things we must have if we are to survive. The media do not make essential items, but this industry seems as safe as the food industry. This suggests that the media have found **dependable markets**.

The British media are well placed within the international industry. Because English is an international language, it is possible for us to export products without working to translate them. Our industry is also one of the best established in the world and there are several major media companies based in the UK.

There are some obvious overlaps between the subject of markets and the material in other chapters. All of the discussion on audiences considers people – including yourself – who make up markets. The chapters on representations and stereotypes consider the way that the market receives images.

10.2 Three examples of markets

This chapter takes a slightly different approach to the examples in the other chapters in this book. All three examples are from the same area of the media – popular music. This is to allow you to make clear comparisons between them. The point is to show you that within any one area of the media there are different markets and different ways of reaching these markets. The considerations in every case are exactly the same – media producers are trying to make a profit by selling their product to as many people as possible.

EXAMPLE **Boyzone/David Cassidy**

This example shows the way that the market for young attractive male pop stars has been sustained over a number of years.

a Boyzone
Boyzone is an Irish band which made a major impact on the UK singles market starting at the end of 1994. There are five members of the band who all sing and dance. Boyzone's fans are mainly young girls. The band has been aimed at this market in Ireland and, more recently, in the UK.

The marketing of Boyzone
The marketing of Boyzone has included all of the usual areas – posters, T-shirts, records, and a carefully managed campaign using the band to promote these items. As a part of this campaign, the band makes appearances and gives interviews such as the exclusive interview given to the magazine *Live & Kicking* in summer, 1995. Part of this feature is included here (Fig. 10.1).

The responses given to the interviewer's questions present the band as thoughtful, caring and generally the kind of people that most teenage girls are supposed to want as boyfriends.

In terms of their music, Boyzone tends to play memorable melodic songs with catchy lyrics about love. Its first British hit 'Love Me For a Reason' had been a No. 1 record 20 years before for The Osmonds, a good-looking five-piece American band aimed at the same market.

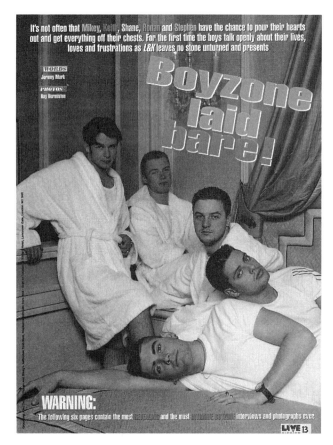

Fig. 10.1

An established market

Boyzone was launched into a market that had been established for years. The Osmonds had proven that 'Love Me For a Reason' was a good song to aim at this market, and many other acts had found success with the teenage girls audience.

Boyzone did not have to create its market or sustain it. Had the band failed to have British hits, the market would have continued to exist and found other stars. Boyzone did have to create a demand for itself within this market – a brief look at the magazine feature shows some of the ways that this was achieved.

The magazine feature: points to look for

- The name of the band is an obvious pun on the words 'Boys own' but putting the words together and adding a 'z' gives it another meaning. The suggestion is that there is an area or zone full of boys – the boys in the band. This is a trick that has been employed by pop bands for years.

  Try listing as many pop names as you can that play on the sound and meaning of words to make another meaning. The most successful pop group of all time – The Beatles – had a name based on a pun.

- The photo of Boyzone suggest meeting the band in an intimate way. It is taken in a hotel bedroom and features the members of the band dressed in bathrobes. The picture manages to suggest a sexual quality about the band without really being explicit.

  Once again, it is useful to examine posed pictures of pop stars of both sexes. If you look at the clothes they are wearing and the poses that they strike, it is worth asking how often people really dress and stand like that. It is also worth asking what these pictures are saying about the pop stars they feature.

- Finally we need to look at the responses that the band gives to the interview questions. These show the band as caring characters who think about other people's feelings. In the extract shown here, Ronan says he felt bad about telling a lie to his mother and that he is very close to her. The thing that hurts Ronan the most is people who deceive him. These answers are mixed in with other answers that give an intimate look at the band members and tell readers things like the favourite sleeping position of members of Boyzone.

Sustaining success

Boyzone's success in sustaining the market for their own records depends very much on how well interviews such as this actually work. Like most pop acts, the band's members want to continue to have success and attract an audience that will stay with them. This has proven very hard for most pop stars coming from the teenage pop market. Ten years before Boyzone, Wham! was the biggest teen pop sensation in Britain. George Michael did manage to become a respected artiste in the adult rock market after Wham! split, but many people who remember Wham! have forgotten Andrew Ridgeley who was the other half of the band.

b David Cassidy

David Cassidy was the biggest teen idol in the UK market in the early 1970s. If you are taking GCSE Media Studies in the mid- to late 1990s, you may well be the son or daughter of a David Cassidy fan!

Despite record company backing and the help of many respected musicians, David Cassidy's musical career suffered for many years after his success as a teen idol. If you look at 'The Secret of David's Success' (Fig. 10.2) from the 1975 David Cassidy annual, you will see that many of the same kind of qualities that are contained in the Boyzone interview are also present here. For example, David is 'just as beautiful inside as he is outside!', he has a wonderful personality and he is really grateful to the fans who made him such a success.

A comparison of the two pop acts

This short study of two pop acts 20 years apart provides a useful look at some of the important issues at this end of the market. Both of these acts have sold millions of records and made a great impact on audiences of young girls.

The secret of David's success

Why has David Cassidy become the biggest superstar on today's pop scene? What is the secret of his remarkable success?

It's not really much of a secret why our David is first in the hearts of millions of fans – just look what he's got going for him:

Looks: That gorgeous smile, that lovely hair, that twinkle in his eyes, and that slim, trim, just-right build … let's face it, when they made David, they threw away the mould!

Kindness: And he's just as beautiful inside as he is outside! Some people make it to the top, by ruthlessly treading on anyone who stands in their way on the road to success. Not so, David. He's a kind human being who genuinely cares about others. When he meets someone who wants to become a pop star, David does what he can to help. And most of his kindnesses are eventually repaid, too.

Talent: David's got a double store of talent … not only is he a fabulous singer, but he's a super actor as well. (He's even studied dancing too!)

Ambition: All the talent in the world isn't enough to turn a pop artist into a superstar. What's needed is drive, ambition, stick-to-itiveness and a commitment to working hard in order to achieve success. David has all those qualities and they've taken him right to the top.

Laughter: Though he's worked very hard to get where he is, and though he's had his own fair share of hard knocks, David has never lost his sense of humour. You can always get a giggle out of him no matter how tired or involved with his work he may be. And when David laughs, it's catching!

Courage: The glamorous side of show business seems very appealing to most people, but it takes a lot of courage to plunge into the turmoil of the entertainment world … and to hang in there when times get rough. It took David a long while to get his first break – a part in a Broadway show. Then he thought he was made – until the show closed down just four days after it opened! It was quite a blow to David, but he was determined to stay in show-biz. Little did he know that a talent scout had spotted him and lots of good parts were just around the corner!

Personality: David is a guy who makes other people feel good – so naturally they like to have him around. Whether it's with a little joke, a kind word, or just a smile, he knows how to make people feel completely at ease. He knows when to be the life of the party and when to let the other guy be the centre of attention. He's confident but at the same time sensitive to another's needs … and that's an unbeatable combination.

You: Yes, you're the best thing David's got going for him … Because you appreciate his music and because you show your devotion to him in lots of ways. Knowing that you're there, knowing that you want him to go on making records and personal appearances, is what has given David the strength to climb to the top. He's depending on *you* …

Fig. 10.2

We can see from comparing the two examples that creating and sustaining the market for each act depends to some extent on selling the acts themselves as the kind of attractive, thoughtful and sensitive boys that many teenage girls want as boyfriends. Acts in this market usually have these qualities. This is because the market itself is sustained by the demands of teenage girls.

This audience tends to want young and attractive boy pop stars. The reasons for this include the fact that the girls in the audience are taking their first serious interest in boys and these pop stars provide an ideal model. They certainly seem better balanced, more mature, etc than most boys that the same girls would meet at school or college or local discos. The proof of this last point is found on the problem pages of magazines like *Live & Kicking* where girls often write in to say that boys ignore them, make fun of them, etc.

For as long as this situation remains unchanged, the market for young male pop stars is likely to stay the same. It is quite likely that in 10 years' time students of media studies will be considering this topic but with a different example of a pop star or group.

Marketing strategies

Because the stakes are so high in this area, **marketing strategies** can be very complicated, but we can see here that one part of the overall strategy has stayed the same for years. Pop stars like Boyzone and David Cassidy have always been part of a strategy that tried to present them as the ideal boys so that teenage girls would find them attractive to look at and as personalities. This would make these fans more loyal and more likely to keep buying records.

EXAMPLE ## T. Rex reissues

This example shows the way that a company worked to target and sustain a market that already existed. It also explains how a particular strategy was adopted to keep this market alive.

T. Rex was popular in the 1970s alongside David Cassidy and if you are taking GCSE Media Studies in the mid- to late 1990s, you may be the son or daughter of a T. Rex fan.

T. Rex and its leader Marc Bolan enjoyed four No. 1 singles, three No. 1 albums and many more top ten hits in both charts. The band still had a following when Bolan was killed in a car crash in 1977.

Since then there have been sporadic hits and the old recordings have stayed available. The last top ten hit came in 1992 when an old T. Rex single was used in a jeans commercial. In 1994 Demon records began a major programme to reissue most of Bolan's work on CD.

Demon specialises in reissues of old material and the company's catalogue – the music it has available at any one time – is usually around 75 per cent reissues. Record collectors know the label well and, over the years, have come to trust its ability to release good work from the past.

A guaranteed market

Chapter 12 looks at ownership and control, but it is worth considering here the value of Marc Bolan and T. Rex's back catalogue to a new owner. Although the band cannot promote its old material, there is still a guaranteed market among old fans and a few new fans curious about Marc Bolan.

The recording costs of these albums were paid off years ago and, as we see below, Demon is in a position to issue several 'new' albums. In this sense, an act like Marc Bolan and T. Rex represent less of a risk to a label like Demon than signing an unknown band like the one featured in the last example.

T. Rex already has an established fan base. This is made up of many people who remember the group from the first time around. Many of these fans still buy records and want to update their old vinyl recordings. The newer fans of the band are people who take an active interest in rock music to the point that they would go out and buy recordings by older acts who might have inspired some of the present generation of bands. This second audience see Bolan as a 'cult' hero, similar in some ways to other dead rock stars like Kurt Cobain, Jimi Hendrix and Jim Morrison.

The advantage of a limited market

Demon's major problem in issuing this material is the fact that the market is limited. There is a distinct advantage in a limited market to a company in that it can **target** any campaign at the right audience. Demon gave out few review copies, mostly to magazines like *Record Collector* and *Vox* which are read by mature rock fans and the kind of younger fans who would be likely to buy some of the Bolan back catalogue.

The only adverts for the reissues appeared in these magazines and much of the other marketing activities were concerned with creating the right kind of product for the market.

A standard marketing tactic

Demon has reissued the 1972 vinyl album, 'The Slider', on CD with extra tracks – mainly B-sides of singles from around the same time as the album. This is a standard marketing tactic in the music business to make older recordings more attractive to record buyers when they are reissued on a new format.

A carefully planned marketing strategy

However, Demon has also carefully planned its reissue strategy to keep T. Rex fans loyal to the whole programme. There are a series of 'unchained' albums, all of which feature previously unissued recordings from specific years and a compilation album of the best of these unissued cuts. The compilation of the best of the unissued tracks – 'Messing With The Mystic' – came out in advance of the other recordings to give fans a taste of what was coming.

In addition to these albums of previously unissued songs, there are also other 'new' albums which feature demo versions and alternative takes of the songs on the well-known albums from the past. 'Rabbit Fighter' is the alternative version of 'The Slider'.

The covers for these alternative albums use the same pictures as the original covers but give them a different treatment so that old fans will recognise the pictures but also notice that there is something different about them.

Finally, Demon employed two Bolan experts including the biographer of the singer to provide detailed notes about every track issued. This made the whole reissue package very tempting, even to people who already owned much of the catalogue.

Sustaining an existing market

When all of these things are added together we can see how an existing market has been sustained. The old fans stand to gain a lot. They get good quality recordings of the old tracks including several old B-sides which have been hard to find for years. They also purchase a lot of material that has never been heard and a massive amount of detail on the old tracks, which means every CD contains new information for even the most dedicated fan.

For new fans still finding their way into the Bolan catalogue, the chance to hear classic albums on CD is useful and the sheer amount of detail in the notes is likely to give them a greater sense of knowledge and involvement with Marc Bolan and T. Rex. It will also direct them to further recordings and hopefully keep them buying Bolan's music for years.

The importance of a limited campaign

This example shows how much can be achieved with a limited campaign. In terms of advertising and even giving out review copies, Demon's promotion of the T. Rex back catalogue was very low key. Having bought the catalogue, Demon concentrated on making it work by planning to issue anything of interest and making the products as attractive as possible to the audience that was already there. The packaging of each CD with notes and extra tracks adds quality to the product, an important point if Demon wants to sustain the market.

Marketing: some important points

The T. Rex example makes some important points about marketing and the way that the GCSE courses intend students to study the subject.

- A well-planned campaign can sustain a market. Sustaining a market is vital to companies which own material, like back catalogues of music. You can check this out for yourself in any major record shop by looking at the number of old records available from performers like Marc Bolan and Jimi Hendrix, who have been dead for years.

- Well-planned marketing needs more than advertising to make it succeed. In the case of Demon's Bolan promotion, most of the work went into packaging and planning the releases. Good marketing is about getting the right product as well as advertising.

- Targeting the right market is vital. There are many record buyers who would not be interested in T. Rex reissues. For this reason Demon did not waste money advertising the albums in general magazines that would have a wide readership. Its adverts appeared in magazines aimed at people with a serious and informed interest in rock. Most of the readership would have been aware of Marc Bolan and T. Rex and many of the readers would already be familiar with the music.

A low-cost strategy

Demon's campaign is a good example of marketing that set clear targets and kept to a **low-cost strategy** which was likely to give a good return in sales. The company could have spent money on promoting Bolan to new markets, possibly grunge fans who would find something of interest in his music. This other strategy would probably have increased record sales, but it would have cost a lot more and the return on such a big investment would have been harder to predict.

EXAMPLE ## The Twiggs – cover-mounted cassette promoting first album

This is an example of a targeted piece of marketing designed to create a national market.

Although the band featured here was launched into a national music market and its music was most likely to appeal to 'indie' music fans, there is a difference between the intention of this campaign and the promotion of Boyzone in the first example.

Boyzone was launched into an existing pop market and there was no attempt in its marketing to change the nature of the market or the tastes of the market. Boyzone was trying to be the best in an existing market. In the case of bands like The Twiggs there is a definite attempt to change the nature of the market because most indie bands have to offer some new musical ideas before they find an audience.

The Twiggs is a three-piece band which plays music influenced by acts from the 1960s but with its own sound and style. One thing it offered to the indie scene in terms of creating a new market was a chance to appeal strongly to fans who had been around for the first wave of psychedelic music in the 1960s. It was also likely to appeal to people who liked this 1960s style of music and had bought it whether or not it was fashionable at any time.

The Twiggs' first album, '20,000 Leaves Under the Tree' was released in 1994.

The cassette box shown in Fig. 10.3 was mounted on the front cover of the magazine

Fig. 10.3

Sun, Zoom, Spark. The magazine looks at the music scene, in particular at independent bands and labels. The readership of the magazine is younger than the readership of the bigger selling music magazines and has a greater interest in new and unknown bands than most music fans.

The band is on a very small record company label and has a loyal following in the north of England, particularly around Cumbria where its members live. This kind of following is usually called a 'cult' or 'underground' following. It certainly didn't have the power to get the band noticed on a large scale when the album was released. A band like The Twiggs experiences problems getting its records into shops nationally.

The idea of the cover-mounted cassette was to create an interest in the band and to sell copies of the album by mail order. Although *Sun, Zoom, Spark* is available throughout the UK, there are many outlets that do not stock it. It is the kind of magazine that sells to dedicated fans of particular types of music. If music fans are motivated to seek out copies of *Sun, Zoom, Spark*, then they are also likely to be the kind of people who would go to the trouble of listening to a cover-mounted cassette and, if they like the music, to order a CD by post.

In fact, this audience often takes great satisfaction in discovering new acts and new sounds in the music business, and the fact that The Twiggs is not particularly well known among music fans means that the readership of a magazine like *Sun, Zoom, Spark* would feel special for 'discovering' it.

We can see from this example that marketing can be targeted and that, in some cases, it is possible to use the behaviour of people in the target market to plan the campaign. Bands like The Twiggs that fall into the indie market are often launched in this way. Their popularity builds slowly as music fans discover them and then take some pride in telling friends about them.

10.3 An exercise

All of the examples in this chapter have concerned the music industry. Whatever your taste in music, try the following exercise to check on the points that have been made in these examples and to give yourself a greater understanding of marketing in the media.

a Note down four or five of your favourite musical performers and try to put them into a category of music – dance, indie, rap, for example.

b Choose one and then write down when and how you first learned about this act and the first thing you found out about it – for example, did you find out what the act looked like before hearing any records?

c Consider how the marketing of this act led to you finding out about it and therefore becoming a fan. You need also to consider whether your discovery of this act was accidental or whether some aspect of the marketing was at work.

When answering **c**, you should think about the points made in this chapter. For example:

● If your first contact with a pop act was through a photo and interview in a magazine, then it was no accident that these appeared – the record company and the management of the band agreed to the feature for a reason.

● If an advert sparked your interest, then this again was placed with a particular purpose in mind.

● If you heard a dance record at a dance event, then it is quite possible that the copy of the record you heard was given free to the DJ playing it.

- If your first contact was through a display of records in a shop or just finding a particular record cover in the stock, then this was also the result of marketing.

In all of these cases the marketing was trying to reach the right kind of fans for the music and to make particular points to them.

10.4 How these examples can help in your assignments

The examples in this chapter show different aspects of the important points about marketing outlined by the examining boards. It is unlikely that you will get a specific assignment about marketing, but it is likely that you will have to discuss marketing within a larger assignment.

The examples can help you by giving you an insight into the way that markets are created and sustained. They show certain strategies in action. All strategies aim to find the right market for the product and to maximise sales for as long as possible.

You are most likely to get marks in an assignment by showing a good understanding of these points. You should make sure that you can produce arguments that show how a market can be created and sustained. You should also make sure that you can explain a strategy.

When you are given an assignment that includes some aspect of considering the appeal of a product or, possibly, the audience for a product, it is likely that you will be able to use the points in this chapter to get marks.

You should always discuss this with your teacher because it is likely that he or she will have a strategy of his or her own for completing the coursework. This will include a plan of when marketing will be dealt with and how it will be covered.

In terms of your own practical work, it is likely that any evaluation you have to write will include a consideration of who would want your product, why it would appeal to them, etc. Even if your practical work leaves out any direct planning of an advertising campaign, there is still plenty of scope for you to consider the way your own product might work to sustain a market.

Summary

1 Marketing is the act of making an audience aware of the existence of a product.

2 Marketing is usually planned to give the best possible chance of success within a given budget. This planning is called a marketing strategy.

3 Some marketing is designed to 'create' a market for a product. This means finding a group of people likely to be interested in the product and presenting the product to them in a way that is likely to make them buy it.

4 A case of creating a market appeared in the example of The Twiggs.

5 Some marketing is designed to sustain an existing market. This may mean changing a product or reinforcing its strengths in some way.

6 A case of sustaining an existing market appeared in the T. Rex example.

7 Marketing can involve changes in the product as well as advertising and promotion. In the T. Rex example, a great deal of attention was given to the product and the advertising was very low key.

Self-test questions

1 In two or three sentences define marketing.
2 What does the phrase 'sustain a market' mean?
3 What does the phrase 'create a market' mean?
4 In four or five sentences explain the meaning of the term 'marketing strategy'.

Chapter 11
Media technologies

11.1 What you need to know

Media technologies refers to the equipment used to produce media products. Both examining boards expect students to understand something about these technologies and about the way that media technology is changing. These technologies and technical changes occur in a number of areas but can be divided into four groups:

❶ *Technologies for making media products.* These include any equipment used in the manufacture of media products. For example, desktop publishing systems allow anyone with the money and an idea to make a magazine or publication.

❷ *Technologies for using media products.* These include any equipment used in the enjoyment or other use of media products. A good example of changing technology here is the way that equipment to play recorded music has changed. CDs are a fairly recent development. Your parents probably remember LP records and your grandparents may well remember 78 RPM records.

❸ *Technologies used to distribute media products.* This refers to any equipment not directly used in making the product that is used to help it reach an audience. An example of this is the way that broadcasting systems for television and radio have developed. With the use of increasingly sophisticated satellite and cable technology, it is now possible to move television pictures around the world and offer people a wide choice of channels in their homes.

❹ *Technologies to own and control media products.* This refers to any equipment used in the ownership and control of media products such as the increasingly sophisticated scanning equipment available to those policing pirate radio broadcasters. In the past people had to turn dials by hand and listen in for illegal radio broadcasts. Today some of the routine work can be done by a computer attached to a radio receiver.

Media technology is sometimes seen as a separate subject, but it does overlap areas like markets and working practices. This is because technology has a direct effect on the type of media products available and their cost to the consumer. These issues will be explored in the examples in this chapter.

11.2 Three examples of media technologies

EXAMPLE ## Television technology

This example shows the way that new media technology is developing around existing technology.

Study Fig. 11.1 which shows some of the equipment that can be connected to a standard TV set.

Television has been a feature of most British households for decades. You will probably have grown up with a TV set in your home and today it is hard to find anyone under the age of 40 who can remember living without one.

Before the coronation of Queen Elizabeth II in 1953 many households did not have a TV set, but this one event is widely credited with starting the trend in virtually every household to own one.

Because TV sets are so widely used, the media industry has gradually invented more and more machines to attach to them. This is hardly surprising when we consider that the industry making media technology is just as competitive as the industry that makes the products.

Satellite, cable and multi-media technology

TV sets themselves have greatly improved in quality in the last 20 years and one area of pressure on television consumers comes from television manufacturers who want people to buy newer and better sets.

Satellite and cable companies are increasing their share of the television market all the time and many other companies – such as the makers of video games – are launching products that also use the television.

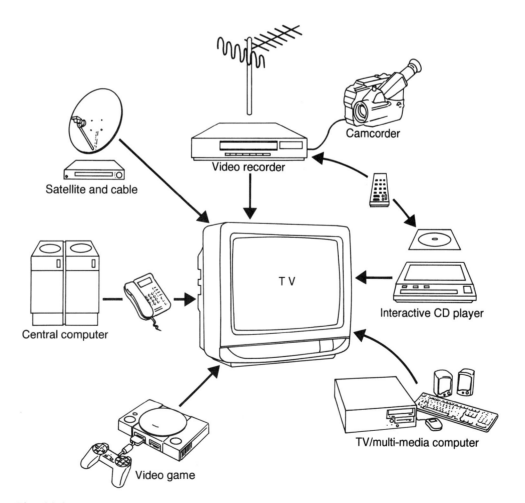

Fig. 11.1

The development of multi-media systems and fibre optic technology is likely to further change the way we use television. Within the next few years we will be able to link televisions to computers for a range of activities from shopping to editing our own home movies.

Developments from existing technology

All of these developments are being made on the back of existing technology, the technology that has given us the TV set. This shows us an important aspect of the way that media technologies develop. They often grow out of things that are already in place. The reason for this is that it is easier to sell people technology to add to their existing equipment than it is to sell them a complete new system.

Competition

Another factor driving this market forward is competition and many companies are competing in every area of media technology. Each one wants to become a market leader and to get their own systems and software into as many homes as possible. There are a number of instances of this happening to such an extent that the name of the company has become used as the name of a product.

One of the best-known examples of this comes from outside the media – many people call the vacuum cleaner a 'Hoover' because there was a time when the Hoover company sold so many cleaners that the name became stuck in people's minds. In the media many people still call a personal stereo a 'Walkman'. This was actually the name of a very successful personal stereo marketed by the Sony company.

Profiting from inventions

The pattern we can see in television technology is repeated in all areas of the media. Developments in new technology are pioneered by companies who want to make money from their inventions. Their best chance of this comes from selling systems that will allow people to update, expand or improve the quality of machines they already have. People gradually get used to the new machines and once they are using them regularly, the market builds up a clear demand for these machines and the other products that go with them.

You can check this by asking people of different ages about the pieces of technology shown in Fig. 11.1. Ask anyone over 25 if he or she can remember not having a video recorder at home; the answer will probably be 'Yes'. If you ask your classmates the same question, you will find that many of them say 'No'. Future generations may well grow up in a world in which the technology linked to TV sets and telephones will organise every aspect of their lives.

EXAMPLE ## Zombic News

This example shows how new technology affects media products at all levels. It also describes the way that improving technology has opened up small markets in the media.

Fig. 11.2

This odd publication – see Fig. 11.2 – is presented in a comic style. It is something of a joke and claims to be written as a newspaper for Zombies. The artwork is very complicated and if you study it, this soon becomes obvious as some of the symbols turn out to be detailed drawings.

Zombic News costs about £2.50 from mail-order outlets. Twenty years ago a publication such as this would have been very expensive to produce because of the complicated printing techniques involved. With its limited market *Zombic News* would have been unlikely to make a profit, so no one would have wanted to publish it.

Today's computer technology can generate images like these quite easily and scan in drawings that can then be turned into books and magazines. This has led to a drop in production costs so that almost anyone with a good idea has a chance of turning it into a publication and making a profit. *Zombic News* will never be a best seller. However, it has found a market and it does sell.

Although publications like *Zombie News* are now appearing in greater numbers than before, new products in the media still operate within the other rules outlined in this book. The ability to make a profit is still the most important factor in deciding whether or not a media product is made and most products are aimed at a definite audience.

Because changing technology has reduced the time and cost of making media products, it has brought about an expansion in the number of markets and products. This trend is continuing and the size of an audience required to make a media product profitable gets smaller and smaller.

You may well get the chance to test this yourself if your practical project involves you in making something that will also be sold. If you choose a print product, you should be able to use computers and photocopiers to produce something that will cost very little to make and may sell for less than the cost of a bar of chocolate.

EXAMPLE James Pond 2 computer game

This example shows the way that the media are expanding as technical changes make new products possible.

Fig. 11.3

The job of industry is to forge ahead to make more profit. The media industry is no exception. We have already seen that new developments, like the television hardware spin-offs in the first example, tend to be based on familiar products. A study of the cover of this computer game (Fig. 11.3) shows that these rules about the media also apply to newer forms of media-based entertainment, like computer games.

James Pond is one game in a massive industry that has developed within the last decade. As home computers and games consoles have become commonplace, the software packages aimed at this market have increased in number. Large companies, like Sega, have become leaders in the market.

The success of computer games is based on the excitement and entertainment that they offer to their audience. Much of this comes from seeing hero characters being threatened and fighting their way through tests. This is similar to the plots of most action and adventure movies, but in the case of computer games there are a few different features. These include:

- the direct involvement of the audience in the action – the audience can control the action and master the game

- heroes can be killed time and time again but still come back for more action.

Use of media technologies

There are several important points to consider here in terms of the way that media technologies are used.

- Computer games like James Pond 2 use similar shots, plot lines and ideas to children's animated cartoons and more adult action and adventure films. The tension and excitement comes from the same kinds of situation. The planning and make-up of these products is similar.

- The physical make-up of these products is, of course, different. Action and adventure films are generated by actors and film cameras while James Pond exists totally within a computer. However, the making of both of these products is coming closer together as technology and markets change. Computer games are now overlapping with the film industry. There are already films based on characters in computer games and an increasing number of effects and action sequences in films are generated by computer.

- Computer technology is being used to generate images and ideas that have a wide appeal. In some cases, this is opening up new possibilities. The fact that characters can die hundreds of times in a game and still come back for more is one example of a new possibility that computer games have introduced to media products.

Limitations of media products

We can see from this short example that media products are made within certain limits, styles, etc. Technology has dictated some of these – for example, the limitations of camera lenses have led to most of the familiar kinds of shots in films.

Products are limited by what is possible and what an audience will pay for. Computer games and computer technology have pushed back some of these limits. They have offered us new shots, for example, shots of characters being totally blown apart. They have also offered a new kind of narrative in which the audience can play a part by operating a character and making decisions. All these things have been made possible by computer technology that uses memory and the programming of a package to generate images.

New products follow rules of media

As the demand for these products has continued to grow, they have followed all the rules laid out in this book for media products. Computer games mediate ideas, fit into genres, have their own narrative codes and visual languages and behave in a market in the same way as other types of products.

Expansion and modification of existing products

This shows us that one vital use of technology in the media is to expand the types of product on the market and to extend the possibilities of existing products. If you had been taking GCSE Media Studies 20 years ago, you would not have been asked to study video tapes because the market for home video recorders was very small. If you were to study the subject in 20 years' time, you would almost certainly find yourself considering computer-generated media.

Because the media are driven by profit, this process of expansion and modifying existing products will continue.

11.3 How these examples can help in your assignments

It is unlikely that you will be set an assignment that asks you simply to study media technology. It is likely that you will be given assignment work that asks you to consider the make-up of a media product, possibly a product that you have put together yourself. The best possible marks in this work are likely to come from you putting forward a clear argument that talks about the technical side of making a media product and discusses the way that technologies are used in the media.

You should also get some marks if you can add the extra information that has appeared throughout this chapter pointing out that the media industry is profit-driven and the technology of the media is used to make products more profitable. The summary at the end of this chapter will help you to focus on these issues. You can also use some of the self-test questions to practise the kind of arguments you will need for the assignment.

Neither of the examining boards demands that you know about any one particular technology, so you are just as likely to get a good mark talking about the use of photocopiers to produce fanzines as you are talking about the way that computer technology has changed the film industry. The thing that really matters here is the planning and quality of your argument. It is important that you discuss these points with your teacher before tackling an assignment.

Summary

1 Media technology is a term that covers all the technical means used to put together media products.

2 This technology ranges from photocopiers to powerful computer systems capable of creating entire products.

3 Most media products are limited in some way by technology – for example, familiar shots in films and television have developed because the cameras have made these possible.

4 The cost of technology has limited the media products that have been made because people have usually decided against making products that would not make a profit.

5 The cost of the hardware to make media products is falling and it is now possible to make many products for a very small audience – see the *Zombic News* example in this chapter.

6 Most technical developments in the media are used to try to generate a profit, either through selling new types of equipment or adding something to existing media products.

7 The first example – on television technology – in this chapter showed the pattern of development for most new types of equipment.

8 The third example in this chapter shows the pattern of development for a new area of media products – computer games.

9 Technologies are used within the media to shape and produce media products as efficiently as possible.

10 The examining boards in GCSE Media Studies specify that students should know products are made and how technologies are used. They do not demand that students should be experts in any one area of media technology.

Self-test questions

1 In three or four sentences summarise the meaning of the term 'media technologies'.

2 In two or three sentences say why it was possible to publish *Zombic News* in 1995, but not in 1975.

3 Why are new pieces of media equipment usually developed to fit existing systems, such as TV sets?

4 Find one example from this chapter of a development in media technology that enabled a media product to be made more cheaply.

5 Find one example from this chapter of a development in media technology that changed some aspect of the making of a media product.

Chapter 12
Ownership and control

12.1 What you need to know

This chapter deals with the patterns of ownership of the media. This area is important because the people who own and control the media shape the products that we see. Some of the points here are extremely obvious. For example, someone who owns a magazine or newspaper can use it to put across their own view. There are also forms of ownership and control that change the nature of media products in ways that are harder to detect.

The subject of ownership and control is very complicated. The examples in this chapter are included to show how the issues of ownership and control have an effect on the media.

Both examining boards expect students to understand the connections between ownership and control and the way that these have an effect on the media itself. You also need to be aware of the effects that media ownership can have on audiences.

The issues in this chapter overlap with areas like representation and working practices. All of these areas explore the way that decisions make a difference to the content and nature of media products. The issue of access is mentioned in this chapter but is dealt with in more detail in chapter 13.

12.2 Three examples of ownership and control

As this is a vast area, the examples below have been chosen to provide a range of case studies that will give you some insight into the workings of ownership and control on the media.

Because there is so much overlap in the areas of ownership and control, the first example is extremely detailed and includes diagrams of the overall structure of some media controls. Since the same kind of controls apply to each example, the other two case studies are briefer.

EXAMPLE TV/video comedy: Roy 'Chubby' Brown/BBC 2 TV schedule

This example shows a range of 'controls' operating on one popular area – comedy.

Roy 'Chubby' Brown is currently one of the most successful stand-up comedians working in Britain. His material uses a lot of sexual detail and swear words, and when released on video is guaranteed an 18 certificate. To expand his appeal and the type of work he did, Chubby Brown produced a feature film called *UFO*. Although this had a science-fiction-style plot line, it still contained plenty of his popular themes for humour and was full of sexual jokes and swearing.

The popularity of humour is a complicated subject. Although it is not a GCSE Media Studies topic, you should be aware that a lot of humour comes from things that people worry or feel guilty about. This is one reason for many jokes about sex – humour about this deals with some of the worry. Comedians like Roy Chubby Brown understand this well and the proof that Chubby Brown in particular is talking about things that matter to people is found in the scale of his success.

Legal controls

The problem with material that deals explicitly with sex and contains a lot of swear words is that it can also offend. Chubby Brown's videos could certainly do so.

One area of media control set up to prevent this involves a number of laws, including one on the publication of obscene material. Videos rarely break this law because to do so would damage their chances of making a profit. Another example of legal regulation is the age bands of video censorship. In this case, the imposing of a minimum age at which people are allowed to see certain films and videos is designed to protect the audience.

The regulation and control of the media is more complicated than the few laws mentioned above might suggest. Study the BBC 2 TV schedule for the evening of Friday 14 July 1995 (Fig. 12.1). The channel broadcast 1½ hours of comedy made up of three programmes, all of which were BBC productions.

The BBC is controlled by a charter that specifies it is a **public-service channel**. This means that it exists to serve the general public by producing a range of programmes that should inform, entertain and offer a range of other views of the world.

Because the BBC is obliged to try different types of programming and develop new talent, it has gained a reputation for comedy that pushes back some barriers. All three programmes could be classed in this way. 'Rab C Nesbitt' is a gritty and tough comedy about life among the unemployed in Glasgow. Alexei Sayle's brand of comedy is often angry and ranting and attacks many sections of the community. 'Monty Python' is famous for rejecting existing styles of genre and narrative.

Much of the comedy produced by the BBC deals with general themes like sex and is based on worries that people have in their everyday lives. There are jokes about such themes in the comedy programmes featured in this schedule. None of the programmes contains material that would need an 18 certificate on video release. In the past, videos from these comedies have had a 15 certificate.

It is also noticeable that these programmes start at 9.00 pm. The **9 o'clock watershed** is a time observed by both BBC and ITV before which they will not show material that might offend.

Fig. 12.1

The differing video certificates given to Roy 'Chubby' Brown's material (18) and to the BBC productions (15) shows that the content of these videos is different. At the same time, we have seen that some of the themes, like sex, are the same. We have also seen that the reason for the same themes occurring in comedy time and time again is that people find these things funny.

Institutional controls

There are a number of reasons for the different treatment of the same subjects in television and video comedy. These lead us into another area of control of the media – **institutional controls**. Both the BBC and ITV are controlled to some extent by conditions governing their operation laid down by the government. These conditions do not state exactly what the TV companies may or may not do, but they ensure that 'quality' is maintained and that a certain amount of programming is aimed at minority audiences, the production of drama, etc.

Both the BBC and ITV want to avoid offending the government or TV audiences. Sometimes programmes do offend and 'Monty Python' which is featured in the schedule in this example has caused some offence over the years. If the companies regularly produced material that offended and upset large numbers of people, they would find that the controls on them imposed by the government would be tightened. They would also find that they were allowed less control over their own affairs.

This does not mean that the government is involved in the day-to-day running of television. But it does show that large TV organisations still have to be careful about causing offence. It is very hard to find the exact point at which television comedy becomes unacceptable because this varies from person to person. What matters in terms of understanding the controls here is that you realise that major TV companies are under pressure to avoid offending people.

Market controls

They are also under pressure to keep their finances in order. If the BBC constantly screened unacceptable comedy, the complaints from some viewers might eventually lead to pressure to keep the licence fee down. In the case of ITV, some advertisers would refuse to put their commercials into programmes that were attracting too much criticism. These financial controls can be called **market controls** because they have an effect on the profitability of programmes.

Conclusion

We can see from the examples included here that there are a number of different controls that affect the screening of comedy. We can also see that there are people involved throughout this process who have some interest in the way that these controls operate. Figs 12.2 and 12.3 should give you a quick understanding of the main points.

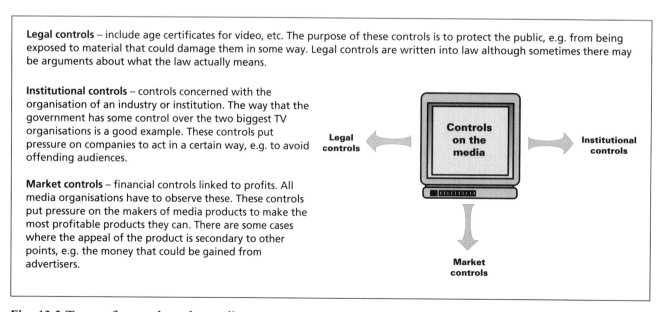

Legal controls – include age certificates for video, etc. The purpose of these controls is to protect the public, e.g. from being exposed to material that could damage them in some way. Legal controls are written into law although sometimes there may be arguments about what the law actually means.

Institutional controls – controls concerned with the organisation of an industry or institution. The way that the government has some control over the two biggest TV organisations is a good example. These controls put pressure on companies to act in a certain way, e.g. to avoid offending audiences.

Market controls – financial controls linked to profits. All media organisations have to observe these. These controls put pressure on the makers of media products to make the most profitable products they can. There are some cases where the appeal of the product is secondary to other points, e.g. the money that could be gained from advertisers.

Fig. 12.2 Types of control on the media

Roy Chubby Brown could attract a huge television audience, but any uncut show would have problems getting adverts and avoiding complaints. Alexei Sayle sells less tickets as a live comedian than Roy Chubby Brown, but he does have material that is acceptable to television.

Writers
(provide comedy ideas and scripts)

Might have range of good ideas unsuitable for broadcast. Tamer ideas which are more suitable for wider markets are likely to make more money in the long run.

Producers
(put money into development of ideas)

Usually employed by a company. Must deliver material that satisfies the company – extreme material may cause problems. Extreme material may also get noticed but many producers are more interested in regular work than brief fame for one of their products.

Performers
(perform material)

Usually employed by production company. Their work is under pressure to fit existing patterns in terms of length, etc and to fit existing markets.

Companies
(own and sell the work)

Their profit comes from selling the work for as much money as possible to the biggest possible audience. Anything limiting this appeal – like offensive contents leading to an 18 certificate – can be a problem. In some cases, this can be turned to the advantage of the company because controversial material can generate its own publicity. In practice, it is usually easier to sell less extreme material.

Legislators
(those making laws and rules of control)

Their interest is in protecting the public and making sure that things run in the public interest. They would rather see things run smoothly than have to get involved all the time to sort them out.

Audiences
(those using the products)

Have clear needs and ideas about what they like. Will find this and enjoy it.

Pressure groups
(particular groups within the audience with certain views)

Normally get together to put pressure on media producers and legislators to make sure their interests represented.

Fig. 12.3 People and organisations involved in both TV/video comedy and their interests in the work

The Family Channel schedules

This example shows the way that ownership and control of media products is a major part of the media business. It explains how financial considerations and the demands of specific markets play a role in controlling and regulating the media.

Study the schedule from The Family Channel (Fig. 12.4). At first glance, it seems to have a great deal in common with the BBC schedule from the first example. Both contain reruns of programmes. But there is one crucial difference – the BBC is repeating its own productions while The Family Channel is basing its schedule around programmes that it has bought in.

The American-owned Family Channel was launched in September 1993, after some of the programmes it shows had been made. It is available via cable and satellite and it holds a vast library of programmes.

The British operation of The Family Channel is based in Maidstone, Kent, on a site that the channel bought from the old ITV company TVS. TVS lost out to Meridian in a franchise battle and when TVS sold its old television centre, it also sold around 800 hours of programmes to The Family Channel.

By buying in the ready-made programmes and having access to an even bigger library of programmes from its parent company in the USA, The Family Channel had enough material to start its own operation. The channel is aimed at a family audience and provides programmes that do not contain excessive amounts of violence or bad language.

Because the channel is marketed directly to a specific audience, it does not have the wide brief to entertain, inform and innovate as does the BBC – see the previous

Fig 12.4

	Monday	Tuesday	Wednesday	Thursday	Friday	Saturday	Sunday
17.00	ANIMATION THE ADVENTURES OF TIN TIN					GAME SHOW TEEN WIN LOSE OR DRAW	ADVENTURE OCEAN ODYSSEY
17.30	INTERNATIONAL GAME SHOW EXTRAVAGANZA JEUX SANS FRONTIERES	SITUATION COMEDY BOOGIES DINER			ENTERTAINMENT MOTORMOUTH (Sept) BLADE WARRIORS (Oct–Dec)	COMEDY DRAMA RAGS TO RICHES	ENTERTAINMENT MOTORMOUTH (Sept) BLADE WARRIORS (Oct–Dec)
18.00		ADVENTURE THE NEW ADVENTURES OF BLACK BEAUTY	ADVENTURE OCEAN ODYSSEY	ADVENTURE THE NEW ADVENTURES OF BLACK BEAUTY			
18.30	GAME SHOW THROUGH THE KEYHOLE					COMEDY THE WONDER YEARS	
19.00	GAME SHOW TRIVIAL PURSUIT					GAME SHOW SECOND GUESS	
19.30	SITUATION COMEDY THE MIGHTY JUNGLE					FAMILY COMEDY DRAMA HARTS OF THE WEST	
20.00	FAMILY DRAMA ROAD TO AVONLEA	FAMILY COMEDY DRAMA DARLING BUDS OF MAY	FAMILY DRAMA ROAD TO AVONLEA	FAMILY DRAMA SNOWY RIVER THE McGREGOR SAGA	FAMILY DRAMA ROAD TO AVONLEA		
20.30						SITUATION COMEDY EVENING SHADE	
21.00	COMEDY ADVENTURE MOONLIGHTING		DRAMA THE RUTH RENDELL MYSTERY MOVIE	COMEDY ADVENTURE MOONLIGHTING		ACTION DRAMA SIRENS	
21.30							
22.00	GAME SHOW CATCHPHRASE			GAME SHOW CATCHPHRASE		THE FAMILY CHANNEL MOVIE	
22.30	SOAP G.P.			SOAP G.P.			
23.00	DRAMA LOU GRANT						
23.30							
24.00	SITUATION COMEDY RHODA						
24.30	SITUATION COMEDY BIG BROTHER JAKE						

example. By putting together a schedule of tried and tested favourite programmes that meet the demands of its audience and by adding programmes of its own, The Family Channel has found itself a market. The investment in past programmes helped the channel to deliver a quality service to its market from the start.

The channel is controlled by its market in the way that we saw in the previous example. It can only continue if it makes a profit. By aiming for a definite section of the market, the channel has ruled out many viewers. At the same time it has allowed advertisers to 'target' their adverts to the specific family audience of the channel. Larger ITV companies might offer the chance for advertisers to reach more viewers, but their audiences are much more varied and their advertising slots more expensive. If the channel can gain a regular group of advertisers and a steady audience, it can build a profitable operation.

We can see from this example that there are advantages in having an operation targeted at a specific audience. These advantages are multiplied when the channel is part of a larger operation, which can limit the financial risks all round. In the case of The Family Channel, it shares programmes with its US parent company and so both companies cut the costs of putting together their schedules.

A successful parent company can also absorb the financial loss of a new operation until the new company is in a position to make a profit on its own.

The example of the UK's Family Channel and its American parent company is typical of a **media ownership structure** in which one company shares an organisation and some resources with several others.

EXAMPLE *Daily Mirror*, 17 July 1995

This example shows the way that ownership and control can influence the messages contained within media products.

The daily press exists to report the news. If you have already read chapter 7 on issues in representation, you will know that television and radio news is legally obliged to be impartial while newspapers do not have to be.

The papers have to find markets and keep them if they want to stay in business. In the case of most of the daily newspapers this leads to profits. Another reason why some businesspeople wish to acquire newspaper organisations is that ownership gives them the chance to put their own views across to an audience.

All the daily papers have editorial pages in which they state their own opinions of news stories. The example of an editorial shown here (Fig. 12.5) deals with the story that appeared on the front page of the *Daily Mirror* about executive pay and perks.

However, the owner of a newspaper can also put his or her own opinions across in other ways. Some obvious examples of this include the stories selected for inclusion, the amount of coverage given to each story, the positioning of this coverage (for example, on the front page) and the facts chosen to be included in the story.

The *Daily Mirror* is well known for supporting the Labour Party and for backing the values of working people rather than the rich and successful. This story is viewed from a typical *Daily Mirror* standpoint when dealing with people who appear to have become rich and successful in an unfair way.

There are many other people involved in the media who get the chance to put their own views across. Songwriters, comic magazine writers, etc can all choose their own stories and angles. The main difference between a newspaper owner and other writers in the media is that audiences tend to view songs and comics as entertainment while they look on newspapers as containing facts. Because of this people involved in studying and controlling the media are concerned about the whole issue of ownership.

One area of concern relates to businesspeople who own a number of different media outlets. In the UK, Rupert Murdoch's media empire, News International, includes huge interests in television, newspapers, book publishing and smaller interests in other media. Because News International owns two national daily newspapers (*The Times* and *The Sun*), some observers are concerned that Rupert Murdoch's views on politics and other issues might get too much coverage. There is, of course, an argument on the other side that suggests that Rupert Murdoch and others like him are just going about their business in a successful way.

We can see from this example that one reason for owning media products, like newspapers, is to put your own views and ideas across.

Fig. 12.5

12.3 How these examples can help in your assignments

Ownership and control is an area that runs throughout the media and so you may get an assignment on it. If so, use the summary at the end of this chapter to build your arguments. As long as you are familiar with the types of control on the media and some of the patterns of ownership, you should be able to build arguments that will get marks. Given the length of GCSE courses and the amount of work students have to produce within a course to get pass grades, both boards will be satisfied with good case studies and good points about ownership and control written into assignments.

The whole pattern of ownership and control in the media is so vast that the examining boards do not expect you to know everything, but you should be familiar with the main points and some of the terminology.

One way to get marks in this area is to discuss issues of ownership and control using an example you have studied. You can then compare this case study with another that follows a different pattern.

For instance, the brief understanding you will have gained from the example of The Family Channel may well help you to understand the appeal and business sense behind other satellite and cable channels. It will also help you to understand the work of radio stations and other media outlets that aim at specific audiences and survive on advertising.

In your own practical work, there is likely to be less need for a full understanding of ownership and control. The examining boards do not encourage practical work that would be likely to encounter problems of control, such as material containing swear words.

You may also be able to gain some marks by thinking about the likely profits your practical project would make if it were available in the market. You could compare it to other products that are already in the market and discuss some issues of ownership and control relating to these real products.

Before trying any of this, you should discuss your ideas with your teacher to make sure that you have understood the points of any given assignment properly and that your planning is likely to get the maximum possible marks.

Summary

1   Ownership within the media can mean ownership of a company or organisation capable of producing something. It can also refer to ownership of media properties such as television programmes.

2   Ownership is an important issue in media studies because people involved in media ownership play a very significant part in the work and development of the media.

3   Ownership of media products is usually motivated by profit. A good example of this is The Family Channel's acquisition of several hundred hours of television programmes.

4   Another motive for acquiring media products is to put across particular ideas and opinions. The ownership of newspapers is sometimes motivated by this.

5   Media controls fall into a number of categories. These include legal, institutional and market controls.

6   Legal controls occur when the law sets out to protect the public in some way and puts a control on the media. One example of this is the certification of video by age.

7 Institutional controls occur when organisational frameworks are placed on the media. For example, the controls that oblige BBC and ITV to produce programmes that inform, etc.

8 Market or financial controls are imposed by the likely profits to be gained from products. These controls limit the money that can be put into the making of a media product. The example of The Family Channel in the UK gives some insight into the way that finances operate. It is also worth examining the examples from chapter 10 on marketing.

9 A variety of people and organisations are involved in the making of media products. Each has different responsibilities and different choices. Some of these are outlined in the first example on TV/video comedy.

10 The organisation of companies and people is called a **framework**. Frameworks involve a number of people or companies all working together to make a product.

Self-test questions

1 In three or four sentences outline the meaning of 'ownership' within the media.
2 What are institutional controls within the media? Give an example.
3 What are legal controls within the media? Give an example.
4 What are market controls within the media? Give an example.
5 Ownership of media companies is usually motivated by profit. Explain one other reason for someone wanting to own a media company and give an example to support this.

Chapter 13
Alternative forms and access

13.1 What you need to know

This chapter considers two issues although, in practice, there is a lot of overlap between them.

Alternative forms

The term **alternative forms** refers to media products that appear in a different form to popular and well-known types of media text. This is a very hard area to define. It is easy to find examples of alternative media products. Most of these can be compared with other media texts. These comparisons allow people studying the media to list the differences between **alternative** and **mainstream** products. In this chapter a 'mainstream' football magazine is compared with an 'alternative' publication.

The difficulty in defining 'alternative' comes from three separate sources:

a   There is an argument that states that something successful cannot be considered alternative. It is thought that by being successful a person or group of people is 'selling out'. This is disputed by others within the media.

   You should think this through for yourself. Consider the kind of examples that could be considered as successful alternatives – a rock band like The Cure is one. This band has made hit albums and singles since the 1970s and its record sales outstrip those of many better known bands. On the other hand, its appearance, sound and style hasn't changed much with fashion. The band could be considered 'alternative' for its attitude and ideas and 'mainstream' for its success.

   You can probably think of other pop acts, television shows, magazines, etc that could be considered in this way. Your own opinion on whether or not they were alternative might not be shared by other people.

b   Some 'alternative' products were never meant to be seen in this way. They find different audiences to those initially intended. The example of *Plan Nine From Outer Space*, which appears in chapter 1 on media languages, shows how this can happen. The film is now valued by people who love bad movies because it is so amateurish. At the time (1959), it was aimed at a young teenage audience who often went to cinemas just to be together and get romantic. A lot of the bad acting, moving scenery, etc was probably missed by the audience. The film now has a 'cult' audience and forms part of 'alternative' movie festivals and publications.

c   The term 'alternative' has some different meanings. This is because it has become linked to some performers and styles and is still used to describe them whether they are successful or not. A good example of this is 'alternative' comedy. In the late 1970s and early 1980s a generation of 'alternative' comedians became well known.

Lenny Henry, Ben Elton, Rik Mayall and many others were branded as 'alternative' because they were an alternative – or different – form of comedy to show-business figures like Bob Monkhouse or Ken Dodd.

One opinion shared by some of the alternative comedians and their audience was that the older generation of comedians made a lot of fuss about raising money for charity when they were really helping their own careers along. Almost 20 years on from the start of alternative comedy, we can now see many of the first generation of alternative comedians taking part in public charity events, presenting quiz shows, appearing in their own situation comedies and presenting their own TV shows. There isn't much difference between the things the older generation of comedians in the 1970s were doing and the things the 'alternative' comedians are now doing.

The examples and the summary in this chapter will help you make sense of this difficult topic.

Access

Access in media studies refers to the opportunity that some people have to make their own media products and get their views represented in the media. This is an important issue in media studies because it is understood that people can have an influence when they get their views included in media products – see the *Daily Mirror* example in chapter 12.

The important point to note about access is that access to the media does not have to mean making your own products. There are people in organised groups who work hard to make their views known.

The availability of access to the media and the controls on this interest many people who study the media. Most of this attention occurs in courses beyond GCSE, but the issue of access is considered at this level.

13.2 Three examples of alternative forms and access

EXAMPLE *Shoot* **magazine and Carlisle United fanzine**

This example gives an insight into an area of alternative media production.

We have seen that there are some difficulties in defining the term 'alternative'. Despite this, it is possible to find alternative media products and explain with some certainty why they deserve the title 'alternative'. One area full of such products is the fanzine end of the publications industry. There are fanzines for many things now. Most popular pop and rock acts have unofficial fanzines devoted to them and all league football teams in England and Wales have such publications.

The purpose of this example is to help you to understand the workings of the 'alternative' sector of the media and so the discussion below focuses on general points that arise from the covers of *Shoot* (Fig. 13.1) and the Carlisle United fanzine (Fig. 13.2).

A positive image
Shoot magazine is well known to football fans throughout the UK. It promoses a positive image of the game and concentrates on big names, big competitions and famous clubs. The names of footballers on the front of this issue will be familiar to football fans and the announcement that the magazine had signed Paul Gascoigne as a columnist was a major coup for *Shoot*.

The advertisers in this issue included Sega computer games, Sky Sports and Umbro football boots. All of these advertisers know they can reach an audience of young to teenage boys through the magazine. Since this audience is being given a positive view of

Fig. 13.1

the game, the products advertised within *Shoot* tend to support this image. *Shoot* is a best-selling mainstream football magazine.

The alternative angle

By complete contrast 'So Jack Ashurst, Where's My Shirt' sells a few hundred copies per issue. This is a fanzine written mainly by fans of Carlisle United for other fans of the team. It provides a complete contrast to *Shoot*. The 'Blue Nightmare' mentioned in the front-page headline concerns the start of Carlisle's championship winning season in Division Three of the Endsleigh League from 1994–5. The team actually finished the season with the best record of any club in the English league, but the cover of the fanzine still puts a different angle on success to the *Shoot* cover – the suggestion is that it must all be a dream.

This shows an alternative view of football success and it is possible to see from this that football fanzines are deliberately intended as an alternative to the mainstream football magazines.

Development of alternative media products

There is a reason for this which gives us an insight into the development of alternative media products in general. For a long time, the cost of producing products in the media meant that the only products made were those that found a reasonably large market, for example *Shoot*. There has always been a large number of boys with a keen interest in successful football teams and by covering a range of top clubs and players the magazine has survived for over 20 years.

Throughout this time there has been a feeling among many regular fans of football clubs that the media do not really cover their experience and views. By the mid-1980s particular groups of fans at certain clubs came to share these views and with the fall in the cost of printing and publishing brought about by the use of computers, a football fanzine industry started. One angle taken by many of the fanzines was to run features that made fun of the view of football presented by magazines like *Shoot* and TV programmes like 'Match of the Day'.

The alternative view of football varies from magazine to magazine – grumbling Manchester United fans have completely different problems to the fans of part-time clubs in the lower leagues – but the focus on the views and experiences of fans is the main theme of the alternative football press. There are also frequent attacks on players and club officials who are seen to be doing a bad job. Some magazines step over the line in terms of libel but this area is, to some extent, outside the law because the magazines do not have enough money to be worth taking to court.

The Carlisle magazine here illustrates these points well. Although it comes from a season in which the team out-performed every other in the league, the team and fans had experienced very unsuccessful times only a few seasons before – once finishing bottom of the entire league – and the cover of the magazine reflects the experiences shared by long-suffering Cumbrian fans.

Important points

This example shows us some important points about alternative media products.

- They are often set up as a type of opposition to mainstream and successful products.

- To be successful they require an audience with some kind of shared view that can be reflected in the alternative product.

Fig. 13.2

● They tend to reflect the experiences of their audience rather than trying to put a particular view across to this group of people.

EXAMPLE ## Alternative music

This example shows products that are deliberately aimed at the alternative market. It explores the products, the forms and some aspects of alternative practice.

Rancid Hell Spawn is, in fact, a recording project made up entirely of one man – Charlie Chainsaw.

By the time that 'Teenage Lard', an EP, was issued in 1995, Rancid Hell Spawn had released four albums and four singles/EPs since 1988. Charlie Chainsaw has a day job and Rancid Hell Spawn is a combination of job and hobby. It is an alternative operation because the person involved has no intention of depending on this work for his main source of income.

Most Hell Spawn song titles can cause offence and humour. Most of the songs are flat-out bursts of grinding punk riffs with heavy distortion. Most come to an abrupt halt within two minutes. Chainsaw Studios mentioned on the back of the cover is in fact a portable studio in Charlie Chainsaw's home.

Alternative elements in 'Teenage Lard'
'Teenage Lard' is still a record release and the music contained would probably fit the definition of songs, but there are alternative elements.

● The presentation and attitude show that this music is not trying to sell a great many copies.

● It uses vinyl, a form rapidly being phased out by the music industry.

● His home recording studio allows Charlie Chainsaw complete creative control over his work and the budgets for his releases are tiny. One album actually cost £40 to record.

This way of working runs against most of the music industry which is concerned with making products that appeal to wide audiences, radio stations, etc. Rancid Hell Spawn records are hardly ever played on radio.

An alternative form of distribution
Charlie Chainsaw also follows an alternative form of distribution for his music. He sells most of his records via mail order. In some cases people like Charlie Chainsaw who record at home exchange a few dozen records with other people who do the same. This allows a number of home recording artistes to build up mail-order lists. There is now a whole network of small mail-order lists operating in the UK. Most of these attract customers by placing small adverts in magazines. This network represents an alternative form of distribution for musicians.

EXAMPLE ## The National Viewers and Listeners Association

This example explores the issue of access to the media.

As we have seen in unit 13.1, the issue of access to the media is easier to explain than alternative products. This example shows one side of the problem of media access. Other examples in this book show people who have had access to the media to put their views across (see page 105). It is worth considering how you can compare this example of the National Viewers and Listeners Association with other examples in the book to get a complete understanding of the issue of access.

Access through ownership
One type of access to the media is the ownership of the means to make media products. We have seen this in other examples, most notably in the final example in chapter 12 on ownership and control.

Access through influence

Another form of access relates to those people in a position of influence in terms of a particular job. In this case the media may approach people for specific reasons. The endless interviews with politicians that appear on news and current affairs programmes are one example; Paul Gascoigne's regular column in *Shoot* is another.

Access through opportunity

A third type of access involves ordinary people taking advantage of opportunities to make programmes, write in magazines, etc. This can vary from a small comment made by a reader of a magazine to an entire programme made by a particular person or organisation.

Access through pressure groups

A fourth kind of access involves groups organising themselves to make points and put pressure on media producers to change the way they do things. Most such campaigns are concerned with more than the media. For example, the pressure group Greenpeace has lobbied politicians, industry and the public in its campaign to protect the environment. One successful part of this has been the group's readiness to stage events for the news media and provide speakers for news programmes, etc. The group has organised its campaigning to be media friendly and this gives it regular access to the media.

A media pressure group

There are some groups that regularly campaign on media issues and one of the best known is the National Viewers and Listeners Association. This group has been campaigning about standards in the media for over 30 years.

The association's major campaigns have concerned the presence of too much violence, swearing and blasphemy in the media and the need for more positive and family-oriented work. Members of the association would probably be horrified if they heard some of the records in the previous example. They would be likely to support the aims and programmes of The Family Channel featured in chapter 12.

The members of the association are not elected and have no legal power, but they are well organised and their campaigning has had a high profile since 1964. In that time they have taken part in many debates about standards, often providing speakers for meetings and news programmes. They also campaign through contact with others, like politicians, who are in positions of power. Because the association's views are well known and it has a high profile, the group can attract support and new members to continue its work.

The National Viewers and Listeners Association is not a media producer in its own right, but its views have made a difference to the way that other media producers do their work. It has also had regular opportunities to state its opinions in the media.

From this example of a pressure group we can see several important points about access to the media for people with a particular view:

● Well-organised groups with clear aims can make a difference to the way that the media work.

● Good organisation can also help groups to get their own people and their own message included in media products.

● Clear and well-stated aims are easy for others to understand and this helps pressure groups to recruit members and continue their work.

The importance of access to the media

The points discussed in this example show that access to the media is regarded as important. People who have this access also have some influence over others. It is not certain how much influence a group like the National Viewers and Listeners Association might have at any one time, but its constant presence and ability to attract people to rally around causes gives it a permanent influence.

13.3 How these examples can help in your assignments

It is extremely unlikely that you will be given a major assignment that counts towards your final mark based on one of these areas alone. The reason for this is that, as we have seen, there is some vagueness about the meaning of 'alternative' products.

There is also some difficulty with the area of alternative media because a student needs a reasonable understanding of the idea of mainstream media before the alternative side makes much sense.

If you think back to the first two examples in this chapter, you will realise that both included some explanation of mainstream ideas to explain why the football fanzine and the Hell Spawn record were 'alternative'.

A final problem with using alternative products as an assignment is that they are often so little known that class time is used up explaining them.

It is much more likely that issues of alternative media and access to the media will occur in a detailed discussion or assignment that looks at one area of the media, like the music industry. In this case you might be able to score marks by using short and punchy arguments that define and consider the concepts of 'alternative' and 'access'.

Before including these points in any coursework or an assignment discuss them with your teacher. Short and well-placed arguments on issues like this are the kind of things that get assignments into the top grades because they show a real understanding. But these arguments must be used appropriately.

In the case of your own practical work there are some clear marks available for the issues of access and alternative media, but getting these marks will need careful planning. When you are set a practical assignment you could plan to produce a product including some kind of alternative slant. The potential advantage of doing this is that your written evaluation can then explain the alternative angle. A good explanation which compares your product with some example from the popular media will gain very good marks because it will show a range of knowledge and understanding.

Before you plan to do this you should be aware that it can be a risky strategy. The difficulty is that your argument has to be good to be worth anything and a good argument about an alternative product has to show an understanding of the mainstream competition and make sharp comparisons between the mainstream and alternative media.

One of the biggest losers of marks in GCSE Media Studies practical work is projects that set out to be funny and send up well-known media products, but end up running out of ideas and being accompanied by practical logs or evaluations that don't include enough explanation to allow someone else to make sense of the work. This kind of work is frustrating all round because students, teachers, moderators and examiners can all see what the original idea might have been, but the work doesn't allow the student to get much credit for the idea or the way it was developed.

If you want to try anything like this, you should plan carefully, discuss things in advance and start mapping out your evaluation well ahead of the deadline. This should make sure that there is time to sort out any problems and avoid you losing marks.

Summary

Alternative forms and practices

1   There are problems in defining what is 'alternative' within the media.

2   What we can say for certain about alternative products is that they are likely to exist outside the mainstream of the media.

3 Alternative products are often produced for a very small profit by people who treat the venture as a hobby. Rancid Hell Spawn in the second example shows this.

4 Alternative products often use similar styles and ideas to popular products but present them in a different way. The football fanzine in the first example shows this.

5 Alternative working practices often involve people taking on similar roles to media professionals on a much smaller scale, for example, recording in their own homes.

6 Alternative working practices can also involve people developing organisations to meet their own particular needs, for example distributing records only by mail order.

7 Alternative working practices often involve people doing jobs themselves rather than employing professionals.

8 Many people involved in alternative media work do so because they really believe in what they are doing and don't want their work changed by business-minded people.

9 Many people involved in alternative media work want their operations to remain small because an increase in size would take up too much of their time.

Access to the media

10 Access to the media is seen as an important issue because people who have such access are in positions of influence.

11 People who own the means to make their own media products have access to the media.

12 The media allow access to others to put across their views – often because they know that these people will provide interesting and useful inputs.

13 A good example of a group allowed such access is Greenpeace.

14 Some groups organise and plan around a certain issue and work hard to make sure their views are considered within the media. A good example of this is the National Viewers and Listeners Association in the third example.

15 Good access to the media for groups like this depends on good planning, clear aims and a good track record of work.

Self-test questions

1   In four or five sentences outline your understanding of 'alternative' media.
2   In four or five sentences describe one problem with defining the term 'alternative'.
3   List three features an 'alternative' media product is likely to have.
4   Explain one point about working practices that is different for people involved in mainstream and alternative media.
5   Why is access to the media seen as so important by people who study the industry?
6   List three points that have made the National Viewers and Listeners Association successful in gaining access to the media.

Chapter 14
Media audiences

14.1 What you need to know

Audiences are a vital part of media studies. Without an audience the media industry could not exist. The audience keeps the media alive, but the study of audiences and the role they play in media studies is much more complicated than this.

Definitions

The term **audience** means the people to whom media products are directed. These people are said to **consume** the products.

There are other definitions of the media – for example, the term **mass audience** is used to describe a huge group of people consuming one product. A soap opera like 'Eastenders' or a national daily tabloid newspaper could be said to appeal to a mass audience.

How this chapter is set out

This chapter is different to all of the other subject-based chapters in this book because it does not concentrate simply on the criteria laid down in the two examination syllabuses. Its purpose is to explain something about audiences and provide you with some ideas that will help you to understand the points in the next three chapters.

The likelihood is that you opted for GCSE Media Studies because you had some interest in the subject. So you are a **media consumer**. This means that the theories, ideas and studies about the media include you.

If you are thinking about a career working in the media, then the ability to understand your own use of the media is an advantage. People who get a real insight into the appeal of media products are much better producers of media work. For this reason, chapters 14–17 replace the third example with a set of exercises using yourself as an example. Hopefully, these should make the theory much easier to understand.

14.2 Three examples of media audiences

EXAMPLE   **Chart organisations**

This example shows how the presence of an audience is recorded and how this information is used.

What are chart organisations?
A number of charts are published which list the success of all the major media. Some of the main organisations and the media they research are shown below.

- **British Audience Research Board (BARB)** – TV viewing and recording of programmes on video to be watched later
- **Radio Joint Audience Research (RAJAR)** – radio listeners
- **Audit Bureau of Circulation (ABC)** – circulation of periodical publications
- **Market Research Information Bureau (MRIB)** – film box office returns (ticket sales)

The information gathered by these organisations is used by the industry. It is also published in a variety of places – TV viewing figures are printed in most national newspapers, for example. The *Guardian* has a weekly special feature on the media which regularly contains viewing figures. Find out if your school or college library stocks this newspaper – if not, your local library will – it will help you to keep up to date with this information.

Record sales charts
The record sales charts are published weekly. One chart, currently compiled by Chart Information Network (CIN), is featured in the regular Sunday night chart shows on Radio 1. This 'official' BBC chart is compiled by a polling organisation and used within the industry.

Study the record charts which were printed in *New Musical Express* in July 1995 (Fig. 14.1). They reflect the behaviour of audiences within a given week. The US charts and the UK charts show some similarities and some differences. A comparison of the week's sales is provided by publishing the five UK singles charts from previous years.

Every one of the charts listed reflects audiences buying records. The industry takes note of this behaviour and it is studied in detail.

The chart used to be compiled from handwritten lists of record sales. It is now compiled by computer.

The importance of audience behaviour
We need to briefly consider the importance of audience behaviour and the way it is used by the music industry. The chart computer is fed with information from the checkouts of record shops throughout the UK. The 25-year-old British chart was compiled from many fewer shops with staff having to give up their own time to file written returns on the sales of records.

Computer information on record sales is also fed directly back to the warehouses that provide record shops with their stock. These warehouses can then order stock, again by computer, from record companies. In business terms, sales returns are the information that really matters. Shops and all of the companies that supply them depend on this information.

Because the information on record sales is so important to the music industry, a lot of effort goes into ensuring that records continue to sell. Acts climbing or staying still in the charts can be asked to appear on 'Top of the Pops' – an appearance on this show is still the most powerful way of boosting singles sales in the UK. 'Top of the Pops' rarely plays records that are falling down the charts.

The importance of the audience's purchase of singles is obvious when you go into any large record shop and look at the singles on sale. There are often four or five

NME CHARTS

INDIE 45s

1	1	DAYDREAMER	Menswear (Laurel)
2	2	A GIRL LIKE YOU	Edwyn Collins (Setanta)
3	(—)	LIES & DECEPTION	The Stranglers (When!)
4	(—)	FREE YOUR MIND	Space Baby (Hooj Choons)
5	3	INTO THE BLUE	Moby (Mute)
6	(—)	WORK TO DOO	Roach Motel (Junior Boys Own)
7	(—)	MY MAGESTIC SUSAN	Sharkboy (Nude)
8	15	SOME MIGHT SAY	Oasis (Creation)
9	11	LIVE FOREVER	Oasis (Creation)
10	(—)	LAST DAY ON EARTH	Oasis (Creation)
11	10	CIGARETTES & ALCOHOL	Oasis (Creation)
12	9	SHAKERMAKER	Oasis (Creation)
13	4	ARE YOU BLUE OR ARE YOU BLIND?	The Bluetones (Superior Quality)
14	8	SUPERSONIC	Oasis (Creation)
15	(—)	SAFETY NET	Apes, Pigs & Spacemen (Music For Nations)
16	12	WHATEVER	Oasis (Creation)
17	6	VICTROLA	Veruca Salt (Hi-Rise Recordings)
18	7	FATHER TO A SISTER OF THOUGHT	Pavement (Big Cat)
19	(—)	I LOVE U	Shut Up & Dance/Ray Davis (Pulse-8)
20	(—)	BRING YOU DOWN	The Real People (Egg)
21	5	SUMMER	Buffalo Tom (Beggars Banquet)
22	(—)	JOURNEY	Gentle People (Rephlex)
23	(—)	ARE FRIENDS ELECTRIC?	Nancy Boy (Equator)
24	14	AFRODISIAC	Powder (Parkway)
25	16	FRIENDLY PRESSURE	Jhelisa (Dorado)
26	(—)	FIND ANOTHER WAY	Captain Hollywood Project (Pulse-8)
27	19	OUT OF MIND	Innersphere (Sabrettes Of Paradise)
28	13	CHECKING IN CHECKING OUT	High Llamas (Alpaca Park)
29	(—)	PARTY ALL NIGHT	Kreuz (Diesel)
30	(—)	SPIRIT	Kitachi (Dope On Plastic)

CIN

INDIE LPs

1	1	POST	Bjork (One Little Indian)
2	(—)	MAKESARACKET	Jake Slazenger (Clear)
3	(—)	REELED & SKINNED	Red Snapper (Warp)
4	13	DEFINITELY MAYBE	Oasis (Creation)
5	2	DEMANUFACTURE	Fear Factory (Roadrunner)
6	4	GRAND PRIX	Teenage Fanclub (Creation)
7	18	SMASH	Offspring (Epitaph)
8	17	ELASTICA	Elastica (Deceptive)
9	8	THE COMPLETE	The Stone Roses (Silvertone)
10	10	HOMEGROWN FANTASY	Zion Train (China)
11	3	BITE IT	Whiteout (Silvertone)
12	5	DRACONIAN TIMES	Paradise Lost (Music For Nations)
13	(—)	AMBIENT DUB – VOLUME 4 – JELLYFISH	Various (Beyond)
14	12	FANTAZIA – THE FOURTH DIMENSION	Various (Fantazia)
15	(—)	UNITED DANCE – 4 BEAT AT ITS BEST	Various (4 Beat)
16	19	WAKE UP!	The Boo Radleys (Creation)
17	11	ABOUT TIME	Pennywise (Epitaph)
18	(—)	TRANSLUCENT FLASHBACKS	Spacemen 3 (Fire)
19	(—)	AMERICAN THIGHS	Veruca Salt (Hi-Rise Recordings)
20	(—)	THE FUTILITY OF A WELL ORDERED LIFE	Various (Alternative Tentacles)
21	(—)	THE REAL SHIT – VOLUME 2	Fried Funk Food (Blunted Vinyl)
22	21	FRESKA! 2	Various (React)
23	(—)	TELEPATHY – JUNGLE DONS	Various (Break Down)
24	RE	SMART	Sleeper (Indolent)
25	RE	CARL COX – FACT	Various (React)
26	RE	HED PHONE SEX	Funki Porcini (Ninja Tune)
27	(—)	LIVE AT THE BBC	Dire Straits (Windsong)
28	(—)	ELLIPSIS	Scorn (Earache)
29	RE	SNIVILISATION	Orbital (Internal)
30	(—)	WHAT'S THAT SOUND?	Sam Severs (Mo Wax)

CIN

PICTURE: STEVE DOUBLE

Noise R us: the incredibly loud Jake Slazenger

FILM BOX OFFICE

1	BAD BOYS (18)	(Columbia Tristar)
2	JACK & SARAH (15)	(Polygram)
3	TANK GIRL (15)	(UIP)
4	THE BRADY BUNCH MOVIE (12)	(UIP)
5	MURIEL'S WEDDING (15)	(Buena Vista)
6	ROB ROY (15)	(UIP)
7	RICHIE RICH (PG)	(Warner)
8	STREET FIGHTER (12)	(Columbia Tristar)
9	IN THE MOUTH OF MADNESS (15)	(Entertainment)
10	CIRCLE OF FRIENDS (15)	(Rank)

MRIB

UK TOP 50 45s

1	2	BOOM BOOM BOOM	Outhere Brothers (Eternal)
2	1	UNCHAINED MELODY/THE WHITE CLIFFS OF DOVER	Robson Green & Jerome Flynn (RCA)
3	(—)	I'M A BELIEVER	EMF/Reeves and Mortimer (Parlophone)
4	(—)	SHY GUY	Diana King (Columbia)
5	4	WHOOMPH! (THERE IT IS)	Clock (Media)
6	3	HOLD ME, THRILL ME, KISS ME, KILL ME	U2 (Atlantic/Island)
7	(—)	SHOOT ME WITH YOUR LOVE	D:ream (Magnet)
8	(—)	HUMPIN' AROUND	Bobby Brown (MCA)
9	10	A GIRL LIKE YOU	Edwyn Collins (Setanta)
10	(—)	IN THE SUMMERTIME	Shaggy Featuring Rayvon (Virgin)
11	7	THINK OF YOU	Whigfield (Systematic)
12	6	I NEED YOUR LOVING (EVERYBODY'S GOT TO)	Baby D (Systematic)
13	11	COMMON PEOPLE	Pulp (Island)
14	(—)	SWEET HARMONY/ONE LOVE FAMILY	Liquid (XL Recordings)
15	(—)	HEART OF GLASS	Blondie (Chrysalis)
16	9	STILLNESS IN TIME	Jamiroquai (Sony S2)
17	12	SEARCH FOR THE HERO	M People (deConstruction)
18	16	ZOMBIE	A.D.A.M. featuring Amy (Eternal)
19	8	SCREAM	Michael Jackson/Janet Jackson (Epic)
20	13	RIGHT IN THE NIGHT (FALL IN LOVE WITH . . .)	Jam & Spoon featuring Plavka (Epic)
21	5	THIS IS A CALL	Foo Fighters (Roswell)
22	(—)	ROLL TO ME	Del Amitri (A&M)
23	(—)	CANDY RAIN	Soul For Real (Uptown)
24	(—)	WATER RUNS DRY	Boyz II Men (Motown)
25	14	DAYDREAMER	Menswear (Laurel)
26	17	WHITE LINES (DON'T DO IT)	Duran Duran (Parlophone)
27	27	BIG YELLOW TAXI	Amy Grant (A&M)
28	15	DON'T WANT TO FORGIVE ME NOW	Wet Wet Wet (Precious Organisation)
29	19	SCATMAN (SKI-BA-BOP-BA-DOP-BOP)	Scatman John (RCA)
30	24	THIS AIN'T A LOVE SONG	Bon Jovi (Mercury)
31	23	GUAGLIONE	Perez 'Prez' Prado & His Orchestra (RCA)
32	29	THAT LOOK IN YOUR EYE	Ali Campbell (Kuff)
33	22	HOLD MY BODY TIGHT	East 17 (London)
34	18	RIGHT HERE	Ultimate Kaos (Wild Card)
35	26	YOUR LOVING ARMS	Billie Ray Martin (Magnet)
36	21	HANDS UP! HANDS UP!	Zig and Zag (RCA)
37	20	OVER THERE (I DON'T CARE)	House Of Pain (Ruffness)
38	(—)	JJ TRIBUTE	Asha (Ffrreedom)
39	(—)	MILKMAN'S SON	Ugly Kid Joe (Mercury)
40	(—)	STARS	Dubstar (Food)
41	(—)	HOW DEEP IS YOUR LOVE	Portrait (Capitol)
42	36	I'LL BE AROUND	Rappin' 4-Tay (Cooltempo)
43	25	SWING LOW SWEET CHARIOT	Ladysmith Black Mambazo/China Black (Polygram TV)
44	30	SELLING THE DRAMA	Live (Radioactive)
45	37	YES	McAlmont & Butler (Hut)
46	35	A BEGGAR ON A BEACH OF GOLD	Mike & The Mechanics (Virgin)
47	33	WE'VE ONLY JUST BEGUN	Bitty McLean (Brilliant)
48	(—)	STAYING ALIVE '95	Fever Featuring Tippa Irie (Telstar)
49	32	FREEK 'N YOU	Jodeci (Uptown)
50	(—)	IL ADORE	Boy George (Virgin)

CIN

You wouldn't Believe it! Out the back, EMF with Reeves & Mortimer

UK TOP 50 LPs

1	1	THESE DAYS	Bon Jovi (Mercury)
2	2	HISTORY: PAST PRESENT AND FUTURE BOOK 1	Michael Jackson (Epic)
3	(—)	FOO FIGHTERS	Foo Fighters (Roswell)
4	(—)	MIRROR BALL	Neil Young (Reprise)
5	5	THE COLOUR OF MY LOVE	Celine Dion (Epic)
6	4	SINGLES	Alison Moyet (Columbia)
7	3	POST	Bjork (One Little Indian)
8	6	PICTURE THIS	Wet Wet Wet (Precious Organisation)
9	(—)	EXIT PLANET DUST	Chemical Brothers (Junior Boy's Own)
10	7	PULSE	Pink Floyd (EMI)
11	12	STANLEY ROAD	Paul Weller (Go! Discs)
12	10	MEDUSA	Annie Lennox (RCA)
13	29	I SHOULD COCO	Supergrass (Parlopohne)
14	8	DAYS LIKE THIS	Van Morrison (Exile)
15	15	BIZARRE FRUIT	M People (deConstruction)
16	(—)	AFRAID OF SUNLIGHT	Marillion (EMI)
17	9	REPLENISH	Reef (Sony S2)
18	23	DEFINITELY MAYBE	Oasis (Creation)
19	13	WHIGFIELD	Whigfield (Systematic)
20	21	ENCORE	Elaine Paige (WEA)
21	28	CROSS ROAD – THE BEST OF	Bon Jovi (Mercury)
22	19	GALORE – THE BEST OF	Kirsty MacColl (Virgin)
23	18	NO NEED TO ARGUE	Cranberries (Island)
24	17	NOBODY ELSE	Take That (RCA)
25	26	THE BEST OF	The Beach Boys (Capitol)
26	11	A SPANNER IN THE WORKS	Rod Stewart (Warner Bros)
27	14	BIG LOVE	Ali Campbell (Kuff)
28	31	HOMEGROWN	Dodgy (A&M)
29	20	THE VIOLIN PLAYER	Vanessa-Mae (EMI Classics)
30	35	DUMMY	Portishead (Go! Beat)
31	42	MUSIC FROM THE RIVERDANCE SHOW	Bill Whelan (Celtic Heartbeat)
32	51	SMASH	Offspring (Epitaph)
33	24	NATURAL MYSTIC	Bob Marley And The Wailers (Tuff Gong)
34	16	PERMANENT: JOY DIVISION 1995	Joy Division (London)
35	30	LOVE UNCHAINED	Englebert Humperdinck (EMI)
36	32	BEGGAR ON A BEACH OF GOLD	Mike And The Mechanics (Virgin)
37	40	DOOKIE	Green Day (Reprise)
38	25	INFERNAL LOVE	Therapy? (A&M)
39	33	CARRY ON UP THE CHARTS – THE BEST OF . . .	The Beautiful South (Go! Discs)
40	22	LET YOUR DIM LIGHT SHINE	Soul Asylum (Columbia)
41	38	PARKLIFE	Blur (Food)
42	RE	HIS 'N' HERS	Pulp (Island)
43	(—)	A VERY FINE LOVE	Dusty Springfield (Columbia)
44	37	GREATEST HITS	Bruce Springsteen (Columbia)
45	36	TUESDAY NIGHT MUSIC CLUB	Sheryl Crow (A&M)
46	RE	ELASTICA	Elastica (Deceptive)
47	41	100 DEGREES AND RISING	Incognito (Talkin Loud)
48	49	MONSTER	REM (Warner Bros)
49	RE	MUSIC FOR THE JILTED GENERATION	Prodigy (XL Recordings)
50	RE	THE RETURN OF THE SPACE COWBOY	Jamiroquai (Sony S2)

CIN

V for Vedder: Uncle Neil havin' another 'Ball

US 45s

1	HAVE YOU EVER REALLY LOVED A WOMAN?	Bryan Adams (A&M)
2	DON'T TAKE IT PERSONAL	Monica (Rowdy)
3	ONE MORE CHANCE	The Notorious BIG (Bad Boy)
4	TOTAL ECLIPSE OF THE HEART	Nicki French (Critique)
5	SCREAM/CHILDHOOD	Michael Jackson (Epic)
6	WATER RUNS DRY	Boyz II Men (Motown)
7	WATERFALLS	TLC (LaFace)
8	I'LL BE THERE FOR YOU	Method Man (Def Jam)
9	FREAK LIKE ME	Adina Howard (Mecca Don)
10	THIS IS HOW WE DO IT	Montell Jordan (PMP)
11	LET HER CRY	Hootie & The Blowfish (Atlantic)
12	I CAN LOVE YOU LIKE THAT	All-4-One (Blitzz)
13	I BELIEVE	Blessed Union Of Souls (EMI)
14	SOMEONE TO LOVE	Jon B featuring (Yab Yum)
15	RUN-AROUND	Blues Traveler (A&M)

Billboard

US LPs

1	CRACKED REAR VIEW	Hootie & The Blowfish (Atlantic)
2	POCAHANTAS (OST)	Various (Walt Disney)
3	PULSE	Pink Floyd (Columbia)
4	CRAZYSEXYCOOL	TLC (LaFace)
5	THROWING COPPER	Live (Radioactive)
6	BATMAN FOREVER (OST)	Various (Atlantic)
7	JOHN MICHAEL MONTGOMERY	John Michael Montgomery (Atlantic)
8	LET YOUR DIM LIGHT SHINE	Soul Asylum (Columbia)
9	II	Boyz II Men (Motown)
10	FOUR	Blues Traveler (A&M)
11	THE WOMAN IN ME	Shania Twain (Mercury)
12	FRIDAY (OST)	Various (Priority)
13	ASTRO CREEP: 2000 SONGS OF . . .	White Zombie (Geffen)
14	HELL FREEZES OVER	The Eagles (Geffen)
15	POVERTY'S PARADISE	Naughty By Nature (Tommy Boy)

Billboard

5 YEARS AGO

1	SACRIFICE/HEALING HANDS	Elton John (Rocket)
2	NESSUN DORMA	Luciano Pavarotti (Decca)
3	IT MUST HAVE BEEN LOVE	Roxette (EMI USA)
4	IMONA	Craig McLachlan & Check 1–2 (Epic)
5	OOPS UP	Snap! (Arista)
6	WORLD IN MOTION	England/New Order (Factory)
7	CLOSE TO YOU	Maxi Priest (10)
8	U CAN'T TOUCH THIS	MC Hammer (Capitol)
9	HOLD ON	Wilson Phillips (SBK)
10	THE ONLY RHYME THAT BITES	MC Tunes vs 808 State (ZTT)

10 YEARS AGO

1	FRANKIE	Sister Sledge (Atlantic)
2	CRAZY FOR YOU	Madonna (Geffen)
3	AXEL F	Harold Faltermeyer (MCA)
4	CHERISH	Kool And The Gang (De-Lite)
5	YOU'LL NEVER WALK ALONE	The Crowd (Spartan)
6	KAYLEIGH	Marillion (EMI)
7	I'M ON FIRE	Bruce Springsteen (CBS)
8	SUDDENLY	Billy Ocean (Jive)
9	HISTORY	Mai Tai (Hot Melt)
10	JOHNNY COME HOME	Fine Young Cannibals (London)

15 YEARS AGO

1	CRYING	Don McLean (EMI)
2	FUNKY TOWN	Lipps Inc (Casablanca)
3	BACK TOGETHER AGAIN	Roberta Flack/Donny Hathaway (Atlantic)
4	EVERYBODY'S GOT TO LEARN SOMETIME	The Korgis (Rialto)
5	SIMON TEMPLAR	Splodgenessabounds (Deram)
6	JUMP TO THE BEAT	Stacy Lattisaw (Atlantic)
7	BEHIND THE GROOVE	Teena Marie (Motown)
8	XANADU	Olivia Newton-John & ELO (Jet)
9	WATERFALLS	Paul McCartney (Parlophone)
10	THEME FROM MASH	The Mash (CBS)

20 YEARS AGO

1	TEARS ON MY PILLOW	Johnny Nash (CBS)
2	I'M NOT IN LOVE	10CC (Mercury)
3	MISTY	Ray Stevens (Janus)
4	THE HUSTLE	Van McCoy (AVCO)
5	HAVE YOU SEEN HER	The Chi-Lites (Brunswick)
6	DISCO STOMP	Hamilton Bohannon (Brunswick)
7	DOING ALL RIGHT WITH THE BOYS	Gary Glitter (Bell)
8	MOONSHINE SALLY	Mud (Rak)
9	EIGHTEEN WITH A BULLET	Pete Wingfield (Island)
10	WHISPERING GRASS	Windsor Davies/Don Estelle (EMI)

25 YEARS AGO

1	ALRIGHT NOW	Free (Island)
2	IN THE SUMMERTIME	Mungo Jerry (Dawn)
3	GROOVIN' WITH MR BLOE	Mr Bloe (DJM)
4	SALLY	Gerry Monroe (Chapter One)
5	GOODBYE SAM HELLO SAMANTHA	Cliff Richard (Columbia)
6	COTTONFIELD	The Beach Boys (Capitol)
7	UP AROUND THE BEND	Creedence Clearwater Revival (Liberty)
8	IT'S ALL IN THE GAME	The Four Tops (Tamla Motown)
9	DOWN THE DUSTPIPE	Status Quo (Pye)
10	SOMETHING	Shirley Bassey (United Artists)

8 July 1995 New Musical Express—Page 9

Fig. 14.1

versions of certain singles made available. This is done by varying the formats used and, in some cases, releasing two different versions on one format with different tracks.

Some record companies supply shops with free copies of certain singles. These are then sold at a discount price. The lower price makes the singles more likely to sell and the sales of these records can help them to get a chart place, a 'Top of the Pops' appearance, etc.

These offers are made to audiences because the record company's need audience support to ensure success. If audiences reject the offers, it can have a long-term effect on the careers of the acts involved.

Other aspects of audience behaviour

Some other aspects of audience behaviour we need to consider are:

- loyalty

- the changing nature of an audience.

One example from the charts shown here allows us to consider both points.

Neil Young is the man pictured making a V sign at the bottom of the page. His 1995 album entered the UK charts at No. 4 in the week this chart was published. The album also made the top end of the US charts.

Neil Young's professional musical career goes back over 30 years and in that time he has gained the reputation as a musician who plays his own music and refuses to compromise. He is unique in pop music history for being sued by a record company on the grounds of making 'unrepresentative' music – his record company sued him for making records that were different to what they had expected when they signed him. Neil Young won the case and this victory earned him extra respect in the music industry.

Audience loyalty

At the time this chart was published, Neil Young was enjoying a high level of popularity because many fans of grunge music and similar styles were buying his records along with older fans, many of whom had been loyal to him for decades. Most of these fans value the fact that Neil Young tends not to change to please the demands of fashion but sticks to his own ideas of what is right.

Neil Young has had a longer and more successful musical career than most performers of his age but this has not always been easy. The role of his audience in this has been crucial. The fact that there are people prepared to support a peformer like Neil Young shows that loyalty among audiences does affect the behaviour of the industry.

If a record company were faced with a choice between signing Neil Young and signing a new pop band who had managed a couple of hits, the sensible decision would be to sign Neil Young because the loyalty of his fans suggests he will still be selling records in 10 years' time. The pop band *might* be selling records in 10 years' time.

Changing nature of an audience

The career of Neil Young also shows us something about how audiences can change. His audience in 1995 was quite different from the one which bought his records in 1975. Fans of bands like Nirvana discovered Neil Young when they realised that he had influenced the band's music. Many people bought the 'Mirror Ball' album listed in these charts because the backing band on the record is Pearl Jam, which has its own, much younger, audience. Most of Pearl Jam's fans had not been born when Neil Young started his musical career.

Other people discovered Neil Young as a result of coverage in the music press, which tends to value Neil Young because of his policy of not always doing what record companies want.

Conclusion

This example has shown us that audiences affect the way that the media work. They affect the products that are sold and the meaning that people find in these products. Most important of all, audiences affect the amount of money that is made.

The media make definite efforts to find and keep audiences. When audiences remain loyal, the chances are that the media can continue to make money for years from an initial investment. However, audience behaviour is not always easy to predict.

EXAMPLE # Categories of audience

We saw in the previous example that audiences were difficult to predict. Even so, there is a great deal to be gained from accurate predictions of audience behaviour. The more that is known about audiences, the more likely the media are to succeed in making profits.

For this reason, vast sums of money are poured into audience research. The aim is to build up a picture of the needs of a particular audience to enable media producers to target the right kind of products at the right people.

Tracking audience behaviour

Changes in technology in recent years have enabled an accurate picture of audience behaviour to be compiled. As people increasingly use credit and debit cards to pay for goods, it has become possible to monitor by computer the things that they buy. This means of **tracking audience behaviour** is still developing, although it is already used by supermarket chains to build up a fairly accurate picture of people's lifestyles from the household and food products that they buy.

Using social categories to identify audiences

As the monitoring of audience behaviour becomes increasingly sophisticated, the media will be able with more accuracy to aim the right products at the right audiences. Until now, much of this targeting has involved the use of some officially recognised general categories identified by social class or grade. These categories are based on the occupation of the head of household. A simple outline of these social categories and what they mean appears in Fig. 14.2.

The idea behind these categories is that people who fit the different groups will hold certain views, behave in a certain way and have a certain level of income. For example, it would be hard to get into the 'A' category without dedicating yourself to your profession and working hard to succeed. People who were not prepared to put in such effort but simply wanted a job in the 'A' category would be unlikely to get one.

This means, in effect, that it is possible to predict behaviour, which enables media producers and advertisers to target their audience.

One thing you will probably have noticed is that these categories do not fit everyone. For example, professional footballers at the top end of the game will have incomes that put them into the 'A' category, but they may not share many views on life with people in higher managerial jobs. They will have had to put in the same effort as many 'A' people to achieve their level of success but there are some things about their

Category	A	B	C1	C2	D	E
Description of category	Higher managerial, higher professional or very high level administrative	Intermediate managerial professional, or administrative	Supervisory, clerical with some responsibility, junior managers or professionals	Skilled manual	Semi-skilled or unskilled manual	Casual or seasonal, pensioners, any other description, unemployed
Example of job in category	MP, hospital consultant	Bank manager, commanding ranks in the armed forces	Shop manager, personal assistant	Plumber, machine operator	General labourer, cleaner	Persons on disability allowance
Population within category	Less than 3%	Less than 15%	About 25%	About 25%	Less than 20%	Less than 13%

Fig. 14.2 The social categories

employment which are different such as the lack of any real need for qualifications and the fact that many sports careers only involve a few years at the highest level.

A more usual example of people who are difficult to place is students. Many students have attitudes that would compare with people in the professional groups but incomes that fit the 'E' group.

While the media industry is using new technology to gain much more detailed feedback on the audiences for its products, advertisers and marketing departments still talk in terms of the groups outlined above. For example, The Family Channel mentioned in chapter 12 points out in its marketing material that most of the channel's viewers are in the top three categories on the list. This seems likely since it is the households in this bracket which can best afford the whole range of targeted cable and satellite channels.

Some people criticise the idea of putting everyone into categories. However, the existence of these has helped media producers to sell their work to the right market. This kind of targeting is effective since people's lives tend to follow certain patterns.

The scale of investment and the effort involved in making this forecasting more and more accurate shows how important it is to the media.

EXAMPLE

You as a media consumer

As we saw at the beginning of this chapter it will help you to make sense of audiences if you first see yourself as a media audience and then work outwards from this.

The previous two examples showed that the media take particular notice of sales of products and rate the success of products in sales terms, and that a great deal of time and effort is put into understanding audience behaviour.

You should now start to think about yourself as a media consumer. Answer the questions in this example.

Your expenditure on the media

❶ List the main media products you buy with your own money. Put these into categories of type of products – video tapes, magazines, etc.

❷ List any other expenditure of yours which may contribute to the profits of the media, for example, going to clubs which play records. You should think about this carefully because the background use of media, especially music, is a big industry in its own right and a lot of it is aimed at certain markets. For example, if you shop in particular clothes stores, you may find that they have their own radio stations which play the right kind of music for the customers of the shop.

Your own lifestyle

Compile a diary of your media use in an average week. Concentrate on the things that you do and try to categorise them in the following way:

● *Primary media use* – things you definitely decided to do, for example a film you went to see at the cinema or a TV programme you actually planned to watch.

● *Secondary media use* – media you use when you are also doing other things, for example, a radio show on in the background when you are having breakfast.

Your lifestyle other than the media

This is something that will make more sense after you have been through all of the other chapters in this section. At this point you should:

● try to work out where you and your family fit in the chart of social categories in the second example.

● Fill in the questionnaire opposite. This should provide some basic information about your own lifestyle which can be used to compare with other examples in this section.

The questionnaire includes some basic categories but these are the kinds of subject areas in which products are deliberately targeted at GCSE students. There are many other areas in which products, schemes, ideas, etc are aimed at young people. For example, the Duke of Edinburgh's Award Scheme is a programme aimed at developing initiative and leadership skills among the young. Churches often aim some schemes at the young

---

QUESTIONNAIRE

Rate your level of interest in the following. Circle the numbers as appropriate — ranging from 1 for not interested at all to 10 for extremely interested.

	Not interested						*Very interested*			
Politics	1	2	3	4	5	6	7	8	9	10
Going out with friends	1	2	3	4	5	6	7	8	9	10
Being successful	1	2	3	4	5	6	7	8	9	10
Art	1	2	3	4	5	6	7	8	9	10
Computers	1	2	3	4	5	6	7	8	9	10
Sports (watching)	1	2	3	4	5	6	7	8	9	10
Sports (taking part)	1	2	3	4	5	6	7	8	9	10
Music	1	2	3	4	5	6	7	8	9	10
Clothes	1	2	3	4	5	6	7	8	9	10
Television	1	2	3	4	5	6	7	8	9	10
Films	1	2	3	4	5	6	7	8	9	10
Travelling	1	2	3	4	5	6	7	8	9	10
Meeting people	1	2	3	4	5	6	7	8	9	10
Reading	1	2	3	4	5	6	7	8	9	10

and, statistically speaking, people of GCSE age and slightly above have a higher than normal level of interest in the paranormal. The kinds of interest just listed will attract some people from an age group, but not all.

Consider anything else that you would rate as an interest and add it to the questionnaire. You should now have a basic profile of your own interests. Compare your responses with those of your classmates. You may find that even close friends have different scores in some areas.

This is a basic exercise and it will only give an insight into your profile as a person. Even so, it should show that you are unique and important to the media. If the media can present products that meet your needs and reflect your levels of interest, they can make money from you. As we have seen already in this chapter there are people employed to do this, and this book is one example. It has been designed to meet the specific needs of GCSE students and the examples and chapter structures have been selected to meet the needs of as many students as possible. From the publisher's point of view, it is expected to generate a profit.

14.3 How these examples can help in your assignments

This chapter is unusual among the subject chapters of this book because it sets out to explain a concept. The information it gives will not fit neatly into a set area of an assignment. It is much too general for that. There are two main ways in which this chapter can help in your assignments:

- The basic ideas outlined here should be understood and noted. They are extremely important in media studies. Use the self-test questions to get this important information clear in your own mind.

- You can use the information you noted down about yourself to compare your own media use with other examples.

There are some possibilities of using the general ideas in this chapter in practical assignments. As has already been explained, successful people in the media often have the ability to use their enjoyment of media products as the start of a career making successful products of their own. You can use the same process in discussing your own practical work.

Practical assignments tend to have sections on evaluation in which students should consider how successful their work has been. If you can be clear about your work, the kind of audience it would reach and the value of your work to this audience, there are some marks to be gained.

Summary

1   'Audiences' are the people to whom media products are directed.

2   Their use of media products is called 'consumption'.

3   The media business is an industry – it could not survive without an audience and the money supplied by this audience.

4   The importance of the audience for media products is shown by the fact that the media spend huge sums of money trying to understand their audiences and obtain more information about them.

5   The developing technology of computers is allowing more detailed information than before to be gathered by the media.

6   The media use categories based on the occupation of the head of household to understand people, their interests and how they behave.

7   A number of different research organisations collect information on the sales of media products. Some of these are listed in the first example.

Self-test questions

1   In four or five sentences explain the meaning of the word 'audience' with regard to media studies.
2   In four or five sentences explain the basic reasons for the importance of an audience to the media.
3   BARB, ABC, RAJAR, MRIB are all organisations that research into the success of media products. What do the initials stand for and what does each organisation research?
4   In four or five sentences explain why the media are interested in 'targeting' an audience.

Chapter 15
Audience profiles

15.1 What you need to know

We saw in the previous chapter that people in the media rank audiences in terms of their behaviour, income, views on life, etc. The collective term for all of these things when applied to the way an audience behaves is **profiles**.

An audience profile means all the important information about a particular audience. The 'important' information includes anything that the makers of the media product, the advertisers and any other company – such as a parent company of a magazine – might want to know.

The importance of this information is that it can help everyone involved in the creation of a media product to be more effective in targeting their work. Put very simply, the understanding of an audience profile matters because it means a media producer can give people what they want.

The issue of audience profiles is not as simple as this short introduction makes it sound. However, you are not expected to become an expert on the subject. The second example in this chapter shows some of the limits of audience profiling.

15.2 Three examples of audience profiles

EXAMPLE   *She* **magazine**

This example shows the typical use of an understanding of audience profiles.

She is a long-established magazine for women. It might be termed a 'lifestyle' magazine. This means that the collected contents are built around the lifestyles of the readers. There are other types of magazines, such as special interest magazines – these focus on one subject.

The lifestyle aspect of the magazine reflects the audience profile because it includes the things that are of importance to the women who read *She*. The cover line on the issue shown here (Fig. 15.1) says 'For women who juggle their lives'. This is a good reflection of the way that readers of *She* see themselves. It suggests that *She* readers are women who want a lot from life and have to work hard to get it. The things that are being 'juggled' in this sense are children, jobs, relationships and the daily domestic routine.

The cover lines describing the features inside also help to establish the profile of the audience. Fig. 15.2 gives some idea of how the *She* readership can be broken down based on the cover headlines.

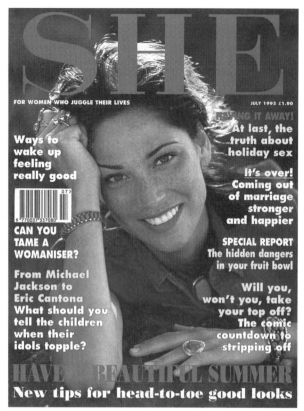

Fig. 15.1

When all of this information about *She* readers is added together, we begin to build up a picture of mature women who care about issues such as health, their families and the way they live their lives. These readers are not easy going, are probably better educated than the readers of many other women's magazines and are people who take control of their own lives. They often have their own ideas about what they want from life and are prepared to work to get this. At the same time, they want some fun and enjoyment.

Because there is a definite profile to these readers, the magazine can target them. It can also allow advertisers to target them.

The profile of advertisers gives a good insight into the kind of people reading *She*. Inside this issue, some of the adverts might be described as 'typical' of any women's magazine. They include adverts for female hygiene products and make-up. Some other adverts do not fall into this category. They include adverts for mortgages and new cars. *She* readers are the type of women who take out their own mortgages and buy their own cars. The readers of some other women's magazines are less likely to do this.

When we consider this example, we can see that the profile of the audience has allowed *She* to develop a clear identity for itself. It has also allowed the magazine to target a particular audience – 'Women who juggle their lives'. The advantage of this from the point of view of the magazine and the readers is that both feel a sense of loyalty to each other. The magazine can appear as an understanding friend to the readers and the readers will reward the magazine with regular sales. The magazine also benefits because advertisers are prepared to pay good rates to 'target' the audience that they want to reach.

The type of women targeted by this magazine have disposable income and their own thoughts on how to spend it. They are an attractive audience to a number of advertisers. Because the women who read *She* will have made different decisions on many issues – for example, they will vote differently in elections – it might be impossible to reach them with one advert in any other magazine.

Headline	*She* audience information
Ways to wake up feeling really good	Readers expect to be able to feel good when they wake up. They take their health, diet and fitness seriously.
Can you tame a womaniser?	Relationships matter to readers. They often take some initiative themselves and are prepared to work at relationships.
What should you tell the children when their idols topple?	Many readers are mothers who care about bringing up their children as well as possible.
New tips for head-to-toe good looks	Many readers want to make the most of their appearance.
At last, the truth about holiday sex	Many readers have active sex lives. Their interest in the subject includes considering the behaviour of others.
Coming out of marriage stronger and happier	Some readers are going through relationship breakups. Most readers want to feel they can cope on their own.
The hidden dangers in your fruit bowl	Many readers are health conscious and take notice of advice on foods and similar topics.
Will you, won't you, take your top off?	Issues of how to live life are important to readers and most of them think carefully about their decisions.

Fig. 15.2 Profile of *She's* audience

We can see from this example that the profile of the audience is at the heart of the success of this publication. Understanding the audience and knowing its profile makes this success possible.

EXAMPLE   *Viz comic*

This example shows some of the limits of understanding that exist in audience profiles.

The issue of audience profiles is not as simple as the opening section might suggest. One major complication is that profiling can only be done with any accuracy for media products that already exist. There are a number of limits you should note:

a   It is possible to investigate people's interests and get some idea of how these could be put into a media product. But, until the product is produced there is no guarantee it will be successful.

b   It is also possible to look closely at the audience profile for an existing media product and then try to produce an imitation, but this imitation may be rejected because it is not as good as the real thing.

c   There have been cases in which media products that were new or unusual suddenly became popular and produced new types of audience profile. Predicting this success would have been difficult.

A good example to show these points in action is *Viz* comic. The first *Viz* comic was produced in 1979 and sold 150 copies. At its height of circulation in the late 1980s, the comic was approaching 1 million sales per issue. Today the sales figure is not far below this and *Viz* has a long history of appearing in the top ten of the magazine sales chart.

Viz started life as a joke publication produced in the editor's home. For several years no major publisher would take it seriously and the comic survived on government enterprise money in its early days. Despite some publicity and slowly growing sales it took a long time for major publishers, distributors and shops to see the potential for success in *Viz*.

The important point to consider in terms of profile is that a publication with the huge sales of *Viz* must be appealing to a range of people. High street banks, major drinks companies and specialist companies such as those selling herbal smoking mixtures all advertise in *Viz*. A few readers will be interested in all three of these, some readers will not be interested in any.

The one thing that we can say for certain about the readership is that it shares a similar sense of humour which involves vicious jokes and 'toilet' humour. The adverts would suggest that this enjoyment is shared by people on high incomes as well as those with very little money such as students.

If a major publisher had seen the potential for a comic like *Viz* sooner, then the editor who started the project in his bedroom might never have become so successful. It is possible to start new products and profile audiences that have never been served by a product before, but this is difficult. Many people did not know that they wanted to read *Viz* until they actually saw a copy.

This example also shows some other problems in profiling an audience. Some audiences, particularly those of 1 million or above, are so big that it makes no sense to see them as people with identical interests. People who aim products at such huge audiences often accept that they must vary the appeal of what they are doing.

In the case of *Viz* comic, this is done by having a range of characters and subjects for humour. Television soap operas which, in the UK, can have audiences close to 20 million generally do the same thing by including a variety of characters and story-lines in each episode.

If you regularly read *Viz* or watch a soap, it is likely that you have favourite characters and remember some events within stories as being particularly good. Your interest in these products will add to the profile of the audience but you may find that there are others with an interest in the same products who are very different to you.

EXAMPLE   ## A profile of yourself

Use the self-profile sheet overleaf to draw up a profile of yourself that would be useful to the editors of a magazine. This should concentrate on your interests and does not

INTEREST 01:	Health and diet
INFORMATION 01	I am interested in eating the right foods to ensure that I lead a healthy life. I want to know more about diet to allow myself to stay as healthy and fit as possible.

SELF-PROFILE SHEET

Name: _____ **Age:** _____

Area in which you live: _____

INTEREST 01:	
INFORMATION 01	
INTEREST 02:	
INFORMATION 02	
INTEREST 03:	
INFORMATION 03	
INTEREST 04:	
INFORMATION 04	
INTEREST 05:	
INFORMATION 05	
INTEREST 06:	
INFORMATION 06	
INTEREST 07:	
INFORMATION 07	
INTEREST 08:	
INFORMATION 08	
INTEREST 09:	
INFORMATION 09	
INTEREST 10:	
INFORMATION 10	

have to pay much attention to your use of the media. You may find the questionnaire in the final example in chapter 14 provides you with some headings for your interest categories.

Consider your major areas of interest and list ten of these in the boxes provided. Fill in the information boxes to give a few more details of each. There is an example completed for you which is based on the kind of interests discussed for the readers of *She* magazine which featured in the first example.

You could expand this exercise to provide a useful class project. For example, you could photocopy the form and use it for a survey to help you to devise a media product to meet the needs of different groups of people that you identified from the answers.

Example

The information you have gathered should allow you to see yourself in profile terms. This is the kind of information needed by the makers of media products. You could do a number of useful things with this information. All of these activities would give you some insight into the way that the media work to an audience:

1. Compare your information with the diary of media use that you compiled in chapter 14. Select one media product from the diary and try to break this down. Do this in the way that *She* magazine was discussed in the first example. Consider the way that this product might be designed to fit the lifestyle of someone like yourself. This exercise is known as a **deconstruction**.

2. Take your profile and try to design an ideal media product for yourself. This could be in any media form, for example a magazine or radio programme. Include the kind of material that you would really enjoy.

3. Follow up your work by writing some advertising material. This should be aimed at people like yourself and it should try to sell *either* the real product from **1** *or* the product you developed in **2**. You can write an advert for any media – for example, television or a magazine – but you must make a real effort to state why this is the right product for a person with an audience profile like yourself.

15.3 How these examples can help in your assignments

Understanding audience profiles is central to understanding the way that the media work. You need to be certain in your own mind about the following:

- defining audience profiles – see unit 15.1.

- understanding how these profiles work – see the first example.

- understanding the limits of audience profiles – see the second example which shows these limits.

In terms of your coursework assignments, this understanding should provide you with a solid basis for arguments when you are discussing audiences and their media use. If you use the term 'profile', explain it and then discuss the way that audience profiles work. You should, of course, read all essay titles carefully and discuss any plans with your teacher to make sure that you are using this information in the best way to get marks.

Your own practical work will be aimed at some kind of audience. You may do some audience research of your own. Once again, you could gain marks by discussing your audience and the profile of this audience. If you target a product at an audience that has similar views and interests to yourself, you could bring in material from the surveys included in this chapter and other chapters in this section. You must discuss this with your teacher before attempting the assignment to double-check that this information will get you marks.

Summary

Advantages of profiling

1   An audience profile is an overall picture of the make-up of an audience for a particular media product.

2   The information included in an audience profile includes details of people's income, views on life, age, gender, hobbies, interests, etc.

3   Profiling audiences in this way is important to people in the media because it allows them to understand their market.

4   This understanding allows media products to reach the needs of their audiences.

5   A media product developed to reach such audience needs is said to be 'targeted' at this audience.

6   Targeting appeals to media producers because it allows them to build up loyalty to their products.

7   Targeting also makes it possible to get regular advertising because advertisers who wish to target a particular audience are likely to get a good response.

Disadvantages of profiling

8   There are some limits to the use of profiling.

9   A major weakness of profiling is that it is often hard to profile an audience that does not already exist. The example of *Viz* comic explains this point.

Self-test questions

1   In three or four sentences explain 'profiling' of a media audience.
2   In three or four sentences state why a media producer might benefit from profiling an audience.
3   Why are advertisers interested in profiling?
4   In three or four sentences explain the major weakness of audience profiling.

Chapter 16
The place of the audience

16.1 What you need to know

We have already examined the way that the nature of an audience makes a difference to the work produced by the media and the research that is done into audiences.

It is important you realise that the relationship between the different media and their audiences is two-way — the media have an effect on audiences and audiences, in turn, have an effect on the media. This effect on audiences can take a number of different forms, for example, changing people's behaviour, attitudes or the way that they shop.

If we consider the size of the media industry and the total size of media audiences, it is obvious that this subject is so huge that it could never be covered in one chapter. It is also impossible to cover this subject completely as part of a GCSE course. The examining boards recognise this and both simply want you to have an awareness of the relationship process and the way that it works.

We need to explore the place of the audience in its relationship with the media and get some idea of the way that this is seen by media studies experts. This will be done through the use of a number of terms. Sometimes these will appear as a short phrase such as 'engagement with the media'. This is because it is important to link the important word 'engagement' with the subject we are studying. The main words in this chapter are:

- interpretation

- expectation

- placement

- positioning

- identification

- engagement

- mode of address

- influence.

One point you should remember is that this issue is complicated. There are two main reasons for this:

❶ The size of the media industry and the number of people involved in audiences means that it is very hard to fit all of them neatly into a few categories.

❷ It is impossible to study the media on their own. The media are part of society. They cannot be studied in a laboratory like a chemical. This means that there are times when it is impossible to be certain about the links between the media and the audience.

This chapter explains the terms outlined by the examining boards and will help you to understand them.

> **TERMS**
>
> - **Exploring audience interpretation** – understanding what a media text means to an audience and how it comes to have this meaning
>
> - **Audience expectation** – understanding what the audience expects from particular products in the media
>
> - **The place of the audience in relation to the production process** – how the audience makes a difference to the business of producing media products. This can cover the way that audience needs and profiles (as seen in the previous chapter) are taken into account by media producers
>
> - **Audience positioning in relation to text** – the way that media texts offer different positions to an audience, for example, a camera in a horror film acting as the eyes of the viewer and taking him or her into dangerous situations
>
> - **Identification** – the way that audiences feel an attachment to things or characters within a media text
>
> - **Engagement** – the way that an audience reacts to a media text; the things it does in response to a media text
>
> - **Mode of address** – the way the media deal with us as individuals and groups. Modes of address build up relationships between audience and media
>
> - **Influence** – the way the media may influence us to make some change

16.2 Three examples of the place of the audience

EXAMPLE **Labi Siffre: *Nigger* – collection of poems**

This example shows how the different terms outlined in unit 16.1 can help us to understand the way an audience is placed within a text. It has been chosen because the text deals with issues relating to minority groups.

Labi Siffre is a songwriter, singer and poet who is probably best known for the song 'Something Inside So Strong'. Siffre's work explores a number of themes and in the book *Nigger,* many of the poems deal with issues related to being black and being gay.

The first verse of the poem 'Niggers' is reproduced below to allow a brief discussion of some of the issues of audience placement. Study the opening words of 'Niggers'.

We don't need Niggers
any more
We got something even better
Every colour
can abhor;
Most abuse is in the family
(convenient)
to ignore);
Thank God for Gays
We don't need Niggers
anymore

The idea behind the poem is that prejudice against gay people is so strong that it has replaced prejudice against blacks. The poem is very direct. It can make a reader feel uncomfortable.

Labi Siffre tends to 'spit out' the words when he performs this poem on stage – he sounds angry. By using a word like 'niggers', which has often been used as an insult, the poem deals with the subject of prejudice against black people.

The title of the anthology is taken from this poem and Labi Siffre's portrait appears on the front cover. This draws attention to his colour and suggests that the contents of the book will tell us something about his experiences.

The book and the verse of the poem reproduced here raise a number of points. If we look at the items listed in the GCSE syllabuses – see unit 16.1 – we can begin to understand the way an audience might make sense of this work.

Audience interpretation

This is very personal poetry. By comparing one prejudice to another, Labi Siffre points out that prejudice is simply unfair. People tend to link the points in the poem to Labi Siffre himself. If the poem had been written by a white poet or sung by a crowd at a football match would an audience get a different message?

Expectation

The cover of the book has a portrait of the poet. Many media texts use portraits on their covers. When we look directly at another person we tend to feel some kind of relationship to them. Labi Siffre's facial expression suggests that this is a serious book. The title suggests racial prejudice. The expectation is that this book will tell us something about the writer's own experience of being black.

If you look around your home, you should easily find other examples of media texts that use portraits and a few words to suggest the kind of material that is inside. Copies of the *Radio Times* or *TV Times* usually feature pictures of TV stars on the cover along with a short caption suggesting that you will find more about them inside.

It is also worth comparing Labi Siffre's book with the pop star pictures of Boyzone and David Cassidy in chapter 10. You could ask yourself how the expectations raised by the pictures of Labi Siffre and Boyzone differ from each other.

Placement of the audience

Because this poetry is personal, it places an audience in a number of different positions. Anyone who has experienced prejudice as a result of being black, being gay, or both may well feel that the poem and the book are offering them some support. Other people who don't share the same experiences are allowed to share Labi Siffre's own feelings.

Audience positioning within the text

The book and poem treat the audience as intelligent. The cover presents us with a title and portrait. The poem presents us with a series of ideas. We have to work to understand these and make sense of the messages they are giving us. This is similar to the way that we deal with people in real life. We often think about the things that other people say and try to make judgements about these people. This is especially true when we don't know them very well.

Identification

The poem and the book both give people the chance to identify with some very personal feelings. Because the issue of Labi Siffre's colour and gayness are both clearly presented, people who have experienced racial or sexual prejudice can identify with the ideas in his work.

Engagement

The reaction to this work is likely to be strong from the minority groups already mentioned. They will recognise the message and the idea behind the work. Because the poem makes prejudice look unfair and unattractive, it can also make people who have held prejudiced views feel uncomfortable.

Mode of address

The poem because it talks directly to people is a little like a speech. It makes points so generally that it can easily be read out at one of Labi Siffre's performances. At the same time it confronts people with some uncomfortable facts.

You may have seen other **confrontational media texts**, for example, leaflets explaining the work of charities and asking for a donation.

Influence

The book and the poem are designed to make people aware of the experiences of a person who has suffered prejudice. Poems like 'Niggers' are often used in school English classes because they can help to change people's opinions and make them more sensitive to problems linked to prejudice.

Deconstruction

We have been introduced to the term **deconstruction** earlier in this book – see chapter 6. This term also appears in the Glossary.

The terms explaining the relationship of the media and audiences outlined in unit 16.1 have allowed us to deconstruct some elements of Labi Siffre's work.

While this anthology would not appeal to everyone, it would particularly attract people who shared the poet's viewpoint.

EXAMPLE *Quick's Guide* **self-help leaflets**

This example shows how the relationship between the audience and the media can be extremely interactive.

The word 'interactive' means two or more sides in a relationship acting together.

As computer technology improves, more media are taking an interactive form. In the future study guides such as this may well be available on CD-Rom and computer disks that will allow some interaction.

Another example of media that verges on being interactive is the 'self-help' leaflet. This is aimed directly at the needs of the audience and its job is to give the readers ideas about how to do particular things. Study the example of three self-help leaflets shown in Fig. 16.1.

Once again, we look below at the terms that the examining boards use to discuss the placement of the audience within the media and try to make sense of the way that a media product works.

Audience interpretation

For these leaflets to have an appeal, the audience has to believe that the things they claim are possible. The leaflets make this appear to be so.

No. 169	No. 171	No. 176
Instant Inspiration	**Super Achievement**	**Developing Super Self Confidence**
How to turn yourself into a highly productive ideas factory	*How To Make It Big In Life*	*How to be more confident and improve the quality of your life*
☐ Unlock Your Natural Genius ☐ Relax And Be Inspired ☐ Inspired Daydreaming ☐ How To Be Inspired By Others ☐ Learn To 'Brainstorm' ☐ Where To Go For Inspiration ☐ How To Copyright Your Winning Ideas	☐ The People Who Super Achieve ☐ Picking Your Field Of Excellence ☐ How To Close The Credibility Gap ☐ How To Get On The Road To Super Achievement ☐ How to Make Sure You Stay There ☐ How to Avoid The Pitfalls ☐ The Super Achiever Checklist	☐ Lose your fear of people in authority ☐ Stop worrying about tests or exams ☐ Make decisions more easily ☐ Increase your willpower ☐ Magnify your chances of success ☐ Improve your social life

Fig. 16.1

Expectation

The audience expects that the information inside will make a difference to individuals' lives. In fact, it is up to individuals to make the changes but this information may give them the push they need to do this.

Audience place in relation to the production process

These leaflets, like many similar publications, have been based on market research. People have put time into finding out what an audience wants. It is important for the sales of these leaflets that audiences understand this.

Audience positioning

The audience is put in the position of having access to information that can positively change individual lives.

Identification

The audience can identify strongly with the titles of the leaflets because they offer positive changes.

Engagement

In response to reading these leaflets, many people will probably follow the advice listed in the bullet points.

Mode of address

The leaflets speak directly to people, but they don't do this in a personal way. The tone is more general, rather like someone lecturing an audience.

Influence

The intention of the leaflets is to influence people to make some changes in their lives.

Conclusion

We can see from these leaflets that people feel a strong need to change things in their lives. This example shows that the relationship between the audience and the media can involve a good deal of action on both sides. Leaflets like these are written once market research has indicated an audience need. Once people have these leaflets, they see them as the start of making changes in their lives.

We can also see from this example that there are some overlaps between the first example, which is basically an entertainment product, and this example. In both cases, the products deal directly with things that people might think about but not discuss openly. There are also some differences. The book makes points in an open and confrontational way. The leaflets have a very general kind of tone, like someone delivering a talk or lecture.

Both of these examples have shown that it is possible to use all the terms mentioned by the examining boards to give us a good insight into the relationship between audiences and the media. If you are going to use this information and these ideas to help you get more marks in assignments and exams, it is important that you are familiar with these terms. You should also get some practice in using the ideas and writing arguments. The third example gives you the chance to start doing this.

EXAMPLE Yourself

This example gives you some practice at using the terms mentioned by the examining boards.

Use the chart overleaf to make some notes about your own use of media products. You could also use this chart as part of a survey in class if your teacher sets you work along these lines.

You should list a few media products that mean a lot to you and then make notes about these in the boxes provided in the chart. If you choose products like TV programmes, you should base your answers on one single episode or one single programme.

This exercise will get you used to using the terms discussed in this chapter. This exercise should also help you to understand how these words describe your own use of the media.

Type of media product: _____ **Name of media product:** _____
INTERPRETATION: What kind of meaning does this product have for you?
EXPECTATION: What did you expect from this product before you saw/heard/read it?
PLACE OF AUDIENCE IN THE PRODUCTION PROCESS: Note some ways in which this product appears to have been put together to appeal to you.
POSITIONING IN RELATION TO THE PRODUCT: What kind of viewpoint does the product offer you? For example, does it give you a look at people's lifestyles, does it treat you like a friend, etc?
IDENTIFICATION: Do you identify with a message, character, etc?
ENGAGEMENT: How did you react to this product?
MODE OF ADDRESS: How does the product address the audience? For example, does it talk to people as if they are individuals, does it expect people to understand a lot of things, does it seem to be aimed at a group of people?
INFLUENCE: Did the product make you do anything or think differently about any subject? Did it support any of your opinions?

16.3 How these examples can help in your assignments

Because the audience issues involved in this chapter are so complex, the examining boards will not expect you to do entire assignments on any one issue. However, you will be able to gain marks from a simple understanding of the terms used like 'engagement'. As long as you know the meaning of these terms and can describe them together with an example, you will be able to gain some marks.

In terms of coursework assignments, you can bring these ideas into any discussion that asks you to consider the audience for a media text. It is important that you discuss this with the teacher who has set the assignment. It is also important that you plan your essay before writing it.

Use the charts on pages 130 and 134 to remind you of the important terms and their meanings. They will help you to plan your essay and ensure that you mention the terms and discuss them.

Planning will enable you to include all the information in your assignment without taking up too much space. There is a danger in trying to write about these ideas without planning because it is easy to get bogged down in a long discussion – you do not get extra marks for being long-winded. Brief arguments that show an understanding and use a good example to prove a point tend to impress teachers and examiners.

If you have to write an assignment about your own media use, the third example in this chapter should help. You can discuss the way that you fit into the different terms used by the examining boards and you will already have the examples you need.

You will probably have to write an evaluation of your own practical work at some point in your course. Brief use of the words outlined in unit 16.1 and some consideration of how your own practical work would 'engage' an audience, how this audience would be 'placed', etc should gain you some marks.

You will probably get extra marks if when discussing your practical project you compare it to a real media product. For example, if your project is a video, you could compare the opening shots with a real TV programme. By discussing the way these two sets of shots deal with audience 'expectations' and the way that the audience is 'placed', you should gain more marks. Once again, you should talk to your teacher about this and plan your work before writing.

Summary

Look at the charts on pages 130 and 134 to remind you of the terms used by the examining boards. Some other general points are listed below:

1 The relationship between audience and the media is complicated and a number of terms are used to explain this meaning.

2 The important words are:
- interpretation
- expectation
- placement
- positioning
- identification
- engagement
- mode of address
- influence.

3 These words explain our relationship with the media.

4 These words also help us to understand what we are really saying when we talk about media products being 'good' or 'bad'.

Self-test questions

1   Briefly explain the meaning of audience 'interpretation' of a media product and use one example to support your answer.
2   Briefly explain the meaning of audience 'expectation' of a media product and use one example to support your answer.
3   Briefly explain the meaning of the 'placement' of an audience within the production process and use one example to support your answer.
4   Briefly explain the meaning of audience 'positioning' in relation to a media text and use one example to support your answer.
5   Briefly explain the meaning of 'identification' with a media text and use one example to support your answer.
6   Briefly explain the meaning of audience 'engagement' with a media text and use one example to support your answer.
7   Briefly explain the meaning of 'mode of address' and use two examples as comparisons in your answer.
8   Briefly explain the meaning of 'influence' on an audience and use one example to support your answer.

Chapter 17
Issues in audience study

17.1 What you need to know

Issues in audience study refers to the ideas that support much of the material included in chapters 14–16. These are **theoretical** ideas.

A theory in media studies terms is a belief about something supported by facts that helps us to predict and understand the workings of the media.

Both of the examining boards expect students to know a little about the theory and issues behind audience study. You are not expected to be an expert, simply to understand the main terms and to have an idea of how these apply to the media.

Passive versus active

The theoretical terms used refer to the way that audiences relate to the media and revolve around two different and conflicting ideas:

- Audiences are **passive** – they receive information (media products) but do nothing in response.

- Audiences are **active** – they do things in response to the media; they do not simply absorb information, but use it.

Since it is impossible to take the media away from society, we cannot absolutely prove which of the two ideas above is the truth. For this reason conflicting ideas in media studies tend to continue with each side gathering the best information it can to support its argument.

This chapter looks in particular at schedules, as part of the active audience theory.

Gathering information on audiences

There are some basic patterns of gathering information on audiences. This chapter considers the topic by looking at the way that asking different questions tends to produce different results.

An overview

When considering issues in audience study, we can see that there is a good deal of overlap between the supporters of passive and active ideas and the different ways in which information is gathered:

- Those who support the passive theory of audiences tend to use certain types of research involving the gathering of simple statistical information.

- Supporters of the active theory employ more active kinds of research like questionnaires and surveys that consider the ideas of audiences.

The examples in this chapter are varied and illustrate the way that media research has gathered information and drawn conclusions.

17.2 Three examples of issues in audience study

EXAMPLE | **'The War of the Worlds' radio broadcast, 1938**

This and other examples explain the ideas behind the 'passive' view of media audiences.

This radio play, broadcast in the USA on 30 October 1938, remains one of the most famous events in broadcasting history.

The play concerned the invasion of Earth by Martians, and it used such a realistic style of presentation that many listeners thought it was a real event. The play caused panic in some areas, with people trying to flee their homes and fearing that the end of the world had come. The panic was so great that a research project was set up to try to make sense of the whole event.

What the researchers found

Over a period of a few years the researchers managed to find a number of different causes for the panic:

- They discovered that people trusted the voices of radio announcers because the announcers had proven reliable in the past.

- They discovered that other things in people's backgrounds, like their religious views, had played a part in whether or not they panicked.

- The most important point in deciding whether or not people panicked had been the time at which they had tuned into the show. Many had joined it after the start and had missed an announcement stating that it was a play. By the time another announcement was made, many of these people had panicked.

The findings at the time suggested that the media had produced the panic. For many who had an interest in the media this suggested that the power of the communications industry could be turned on audiences to produce a number of effects. At the same time as this broadcast was being made in the United States, Hitler was rising to the height of his power in Germany and his propaganda machine was helping him.

Other examples of media influence

There have been many more examples since of cases in which the media have been blamed for all sorts of behaviour. For example, many people blame violent videos for violence in society.

One example that is often quoted when referring to media influence is the way that the popularity of certain sports leads to more people taking them up. For instance, tennis courts in Britain are more heavily booked than usual during Wimbledon fortnight.

The hypodermic idea

There is clear evidence to suggest that when people are subjected to pressure in some way from the media, they will react. The study of this phenomenon started seriously after 'The War of the Worlds' broadcast and there are now many studies and different ideas about how it works.

The term **hypodermic model** has been used to describe this process. The suggestion is that the media work very much like a hypodermic needle – the information they pump into the audience goes one way and has an effect.

Most researchers think that the hypodermic idea is too simple to explain the way that the media work but there is still a lot of opinion and research to suggest that information from the media has an effect on audiences which simply soak this up. The view of an audience being affected in this way is an example of **passive** audience behaviour.

EXAMPLE ## TV schedules

The TV schedules and other material mentioned in this example illustrate the 'active' view of media audiences.

Look at the two sets of TV schedules for 28 August 1995 – Fig. 17.1 is from the *Guardian* and Fig. 17.2 is from the *Radio Times*. Both suggest choices for the day's viewing, but these vary. The choices also tend to ignore some of the programmes that will actually get the highest viewing figures. Even on a Bank Holiday Monday, as this day was, the popular soaps like 'Eastenders' and 'Coronation Street' tend to get some of the highest viewing figures.

The *Guardian* guide in particular picks programmes that will be of interest to its readers. The paper sells around 360,000 copies a day, less than a tenth of *Radio Times's* sales. These choices show us that a lot of thought is put into viewing decisions.

Different people decide what they are going to watch on television in different ways. The *Guardian* guide is designed for people who want to expand their knowledge and awareness of things. Programmes like 'Secret History' which it recommends tend to attract very small audiences when compared to popular drama like 'Runway One' or 'Prime Suspect 2'.

We should also look at the way that both guides describe the same programmes. The *Radio Times* tends to be positive about the footage of the alleged alien 'autopsy' in 'Secret History', while the *Guardian* is less enthusiastic – in its preview of 'The X Files' it refers to the film and 'grainy rubber-slicing', making it clear that it thinks the 'alien' is made of rubber and therefore a hoax.

Both guides give 'The X Files' a high profile. The *Guardian* concentrates on its production values and the quality of the programme, while the *Radio Times* tends to concentrate on the story. This suggests that *Guardian* readers are more concerned about the meaning of the whole programme, while readers of the *Radio Times* are more concerned with the basic story.

TV & Radio Monday

Preview

The X Files
9pm, BBC2

The BBC's "coincidental" scheduling of the reopening of The X Files against C4's Roswell footage (actually the only interesting part of the channel's absolutely tragic Sci-Fi Weekend) presents fans of the freaky with a difficult choice; which to tape? But really, how can 20 minutes of grainy rubber-slicing compare to this, possibly the most atmospheric piece of television you'll ever see? Having grown tired of Mulder and Scully's supernatural snooping, the FBI has separated them. Mulder is worrying himself scruffy with his search for evidence of alien contact (we actually get to see the abduction of his sister, a defining moment if ever there was one), and receives word from a senator friend that he may find it at a disused radio telescope in Puerto Rico. From then on it's an intricately plotted white-knuckle race with the military, accompanied by the ongoing promise of … contact. (RJ)

Fig. 17.1

Secret History: The Roswell Incident
9pm, C4

The case for the defence in this all-time video dilemma: can The X Files's Little Green Men truly compare to the real thing? The Roswell Incident is hot news – a 1947 crash-landing near a nuclear-strike airbase, which supposedly produced footage of an alien being's autopsy and subsequent Federal cover-up. What difference if it's true? With an ever-increasing flood of visitation-themed TV, only the live-on-news state visit of the Galactic Emperor could provoke the hysterical apprehension of the Cold War decades. (AP)

Film **Legend**
(Ridley Scott, 1985)
6.30pm, BBC2

The story's hardly original, but what legend is? And Scott is a master at creating fantastical, violent worlds (Alien, Black Rain, Blade Runner). So a lord of darkness (Tim Curry) aims to savage a sylvan earth by ensnaring the last unicorns, and only a toothy young Tom Cruise stands in his way.

Film **Soylent Green**
(Richard Fleischer, 1973)
10pm, C4

Adapted from Harry Harrison's novel, Make Room! Make Room! An ecovicious New York 2002 is packed with 40 million souls, existing on the Soylent Corporation's synthetic foods. Detective Charlton Heston, investigating the death of wealthy Joseph Cotten, stumbles on the secret ingredient of Soylent Green: people. Memorable mainly for Edward G Robinson's touching final screen appearance.

Film **Taxi Driver**
(Martin Scorsese, 1976)
10.30pm, BBC2

Potent drama that charts a descent into the abyss of a squalid New York. Robert De Niro's Travis Bickle is his finest incarnation, a taxi driver who seems inured to the seamy underworld until involvement with a teenie hooker, stunningly played by Jodie Foster, sparks extreme violence. From the fun of "You talkin' to me?" in the mirror to Mohican-haired menace, De Niro exudes a demonic force. (PH)

Uses and gratifications model
The fact that we each select our media for different reasons has led to research that tries to understand this. Researchers often use the **uses and gratifications model** to describe it. The model is based on the idea that we use the media to meet our own personal needs and when we make decisions about media use.

This idea sees audiences as **active** because it suggests that they can decide things for themselves and they are able to resist the ideas contained in media products. This view disagrees with the passive view in the previous example.

Active audiences
Another example to illustrate the point that audiences are 'active' is Andrew Ridgeley's solo album. Andrew Ridgeley was half of Wham!, the most successful British

MONDAY 28 AUGUST BANK HOLIDAY
TODAY'S CHOICES

NATURE

Zoo Watch Live

From 1.35pm BBC1

The great zoo debate gets a good airing this week. Last night and tonight, *State of the Ark* revisits some terrible zoos and reviews a year of international lobbying to improve conditions. Tonight and throughout the week Rolf Harris, Emma Forbes and Steve Knight offer the other side of the story as they report from two exemplary zoos, London and Whipsnade.

Many new characters are introduced over the next five days including Tiny the too-tall giraffe, and Spiny Norman the sleepy echidna. "It's a great privilege to be so close to these animals," says Rolf Harris, "but I am conscious all the time that they are wild, and shouldn't be bonded with and turned into household pets."

FACTUAL

Victoria Wood's Dirty Weekend

7.30pm BBC1

In February, Victoria Wood went to Zimbabwe to make a short film for Comic Relief. Tonight there's a chance to see the full story of her visit with "dry land" farmers in one of the dustiest places in the world.

The climate in Zimbabwe just keeps getting hotter and drier. Living with the Masara family during a drought, Wood discovered how people are adapting to a life where every drop of water counts.

See page 7 for news on how *Radio Times* readers helped raise money for Comic Relief.

DRAMA

The X Files

9.00pm BBC2

More spooky shenanigans are afoot as the massively popular sci-fi series returns. The last X file may have had "closed" stamped on it, but Agents Mulder (David Duchovny) and Scully (Gillian Anderson) refuse to let official disbandment halt their alien-hunting quests.

Having been relegated to the FBI equivalent of traffic duty, Mulder is suffering from depression and self-doubt. Only when he is tipped off by a sympathetic senator about possible evidence of alien contact does his old spirit flame.

Running through the episode is a clever motif about electronic listening: while Mulder is assigned to a routine wire-tap, the aliens are picking up and sending back signals via the *Voyager* probe. And watch out for the Watergate allusion. It ends in spectacular fashion but as Mulder ruefully remarks: "Once again, nothing but evidence and again, no evidence at all."

FACTUAL

Secret History

9.00pm C4

By an unfortunate scheduling clash, the new series of *The X Files* launches against a documentary offering convincing and controversial evidence of alien contact with Earth. The Roswell incident took place in July 1947, when something crashed in the New Mexico desert. A press release from the nearby military base said that a "flying disk" had been found; this was retracted in a second statement that identified the wreckage as a weather balloon.

In 1978, a retired intelligence officer claimed this was a cover-up, and in 1993, film was unearthed of what some believe to be an alien undergoing an autopsy. It seems that the truth has not yet emerged.

PLUS

Prime Suspect concludes (9pm ITV)

TODAY'S FILM CHOICES
Random Harvest (8am BBC2) ★★★★
Around the World in 80 Days (10.50am BBC2) ★★★★★
An American Tail (3.35pm BBC1) RT Choice
Soylent Green (10pm C4) Barry Norman's Choice
Taxi Driver (10.30pm BBC2) Barry Norman's Choice
The Brother from Another Planet (12.25am C4) ★★★★

Fig. 17.2

pop act of the mid-1980s. George Michael, the other half of the band, went on to become a highly successful solo artiste, but Andrew Ridgeley's album flopped.

Despite press releases stating that the album was good and George Michael's appearance as a singer on the record, the album sold very badly and ended up in bargain bins. One shop even refused to put a price on it in a sale and simply used a sticker that said 'Make us an offer'.

This example shows that audiences do decide on the value of media products. Andrew Ridgeley's previous success and his publicity failed to convince people that they wanted to buy his solo record. This shows an audience making an active choice.

Needs of an audience

When researchers study the way we use the media, they tend to list four main types of need in audiences:

❶ **Escape or diversion**. To get away from everyday worries. Good examples of such media use are fantasy adventure films like 'Batman' or 'Jurassic Park'.

❷ **Companionship**. The media is seen as a friend and people tend to talk about what they find in the media, for example, a group of football fans watching a match on TV and arguing about the refereeing decisions.

❸ **Personal identity**. People compare their own experiences with those they see in the media like the girls who read articles like 'My guilty secret' featured in chapter 7. Problem pages in general tend to appeal to both sexes for this reason.

❹ **Seeking information**. To keep in touch with all kinds of event, for example, through TV and newspaper news.

Active or passive?

We can see from both these theories about audiences that there are disagreements. These disagreements are hard to resolve because both sides of the debate have good points.

Those who claim audiences are passive are right when they say that the media bombard us with messages and we tend to do things as a result of taking in these messages. They are also right when they point out that in a few cases – like 'The War of the Worlds' – media messages have produced extreme reactions in people.

On the other side of the debate, people who claim that audiences are active also have a point. They are right when they say that audiences make choices and reject messages. They are also right when they point out that there is evidence that audiences can decide the meaning of a media product for themselves.

The debate continues and the examining boards will not expect you to be able to solve it. They will expect you to be aware of the meaning of 'passive' and 'active' and to be able to explain these in some detail.

EXAMPLE **Yourself**

This example is designed to give you some insight into the arguments put forward in the first two examples. It may also give you some material that could be included in assignments.

Complete the questions below. By thinking about the answers as you give them, you should begin to decide for yourself where you fit into the debate about passive and active media use.

QUESTIONS

Passive

1 Can you think of any important decision in your life that has been influenced by information that you receive from the media?

2 Has a media message ever prompted you to buy things, go somewhere, etc? If so, how often?

3 Do you have heroes in the media? If so, how much do you want to be like them?

4 What do you think about the following subjects? Try to write two or three sentences that sum up your opinions.

   a   Politics
   b   Equality of the sexes
   c   The country you live in
   d   Law and order

5 When you think about the above subjects how much is your opinion linked to pictures or programmes that you have heard or seen in the media?

Active

6 Name some media products that have been aimed at you but which you found uninteresting. Say, very briefly, why you didn't like them.

---

7   Have you ever used a media product in a way that was not intended by the makers? For example, have you ever laughed at a serious story on the news or made fun of a programme like a quiz show that was intended as entertainment?

---

8   List some adverts you think are uninteresting. Why don't they appeal to you?

---

9   Choose a favourite media product such as a record, video or book. Does this have any personal meaning to you? If so, try to sum this up in two or three sentences.

---

10 Keep notes on your use of the media on one evening. Write down the times at which you used any media product and when you stopped or changed this use. Consider whether this was done in the way the makers of the products intended – did you switch off a radio or TV programme only at the very end, for example?

All of the information gathered in this survey on yourself should help you to make more sense of the ideas in the first two examples.

The answers you gave will, of course, be different to those of your classmates since each of you has your own tastes in the media. There isn't any one piece of advice this book can give that will mean the same to every reader at this point.

Some points about the survey

The first five questions should give you some insight into the passive side of your use of the media. To make sense of these, you need to think a little about the answers you have given. For example, the questions about media heroes and individuals' views on various subjects usually show that people's opinions are influenced by the media. If a pop star is a role model to you, then it is likely that the images that he or she has chosen to put across in the media have impressed you.

This is connected to passive views of the media because pop stars tend to present complete images that are linked to people's ideas about things that are important. For example, Boyzone in chapter 10 showed us a band that was presented as the perfect boys. When people accept images like this, it can be said that they are making decisions passively. If your views on a subject such as politics came from one media source, like one programme, once again this is an example of a passive response.

In terms of active media use, it is important that you are clear in your own mind about how you make decisions. The questions here should help you to focus on this. The key to getting some understanding of active media use is considering whether you simply use media products in the way the makers intend or whether you make your own meanings out of them. If, for example, you watched a popular quiz show with friends and made jokes about the contestants and the presenter you would be using the programme in an active way. The purpose of doing this might be to enjoy yourself and to share your view of life with your friends.

Consider how you start and stop your media use. If you listen right through a radio programme because an interesting item is coming at the end, then you are probably doing what the station intended when it put in a trailer for the item. If, on the other hand, you stop reading a newspaper story half-way through because you are bored, you have made your own active decision.

Conclusion

This chapter cannot conclude the debate on active and passive media use – media experts are still researching this issue. There is truth in both views and your own work on the third example in this chapter should give you some insight into how you see the debate.

17.3 How these examples can help in your assignments

Although it isn't possible to end the active/passive debate, this needn't be a problem when it comes to getting marks. What really matters is making sure you understand the terms and what they mean. It is also important that you can discuss them and use some examples from your own experience or study to explain your understanding.

It is very unlikely that you would be set an entire assignment on issues in audience study. You will, however, certainly get an assignment on audiences. You should be able to discuss the points in this chapter within your audiences assignment.

Whether you fully cover these points will depend on planning your answer well and making sure that you have consulted your teacher about what you intend to say before completing your work. The marks you get in discussing something like passive versus active views of audiences will depend on how clearly you explain these points and how well you choose your examples.

It is possible that your audiences assignment will be linked to your practical work. If it is not, there will certainly be some part to your practical work that will ask you to evaluate your efforts. Whatever happens, you should be able to discuss the way that an audience would use your media product and consider whether you would expect their use to be passive, active or a bit of both.

You should be able to make the most of your use of these arguments by mentioning both passive and active ideas and discussing how they are both understood before making your own conclusion. As with all such points making the most of the arguments also involves good planning for an essay and discussing your ideas with your teacher if you are unsure.

Summary

1 Passive views of audience use suggest that audiences are fed media material and they are then influenced by this.

2 Passive views see audiences as having little power in this relationship.

3 There is some evidence to support the passive view of audience use.

4 Active views see audiences as making their own meanings and decisions about media products.

5 Active views suggest that audiences have a lot of power to make decisions and make sense of the media for themselves.

6 One idea of active media use is based on the **uses and gratifications** model which suggests that people use media products to meet personal needs.

7 There is some evidence to support the arguments about active media use.

8 The two arguments are opposites and both sides of the debate have supporters among media researchers.

Self-test questions

1   In five or six sentences explain the idea of 'passive' use of the media, and include one example.
2   In five or six sentences explain the idea of 'active' use of the media, and include one example.

SEG controlled test

What you need to know

The SEG **controlled test** does the job of an exam and can be thought of as an exam. From 1997 50 per cent of the marks of the syllabus will be awarded for your work in this controlled test. However, there are some important differences between this test and a more traditional exam:

❶ Flexible date and time – your school or college will organise the date and time of the test and other schools/colleges will be doing the same work at slightly different times.

❷ Flexible sessions – the length of each test session and the number of sessions needed to complete the whole paper can also be decided by your school or college.

❸ Emphasis on your own ideas – there are certainly right answers to test questions, but a large part of the controlled test depends on you developing and explaining your own ideas. As long as you develop reasonable ideas and good arguments as to why they should work, you stand to gain marks.

Format of the test

The test takes four hours and includes four questions. It starts with a **scenario** – this gives you some background information about your situation and explains what you are expected to achieve. The questions test your understanding of different aspects of this situation and ask you to produce some of your own original work.

The questions and marks are divided as follows:

❶ Knowledge-based question (40 marks). This will ask you to explain something about an area of the media. It is looking for knowledge with good arguments and examples about why things happen in a certain way.

❷ Idea-based question (15 marks). This will ask you to suggest an idea for a media product and plan it out. It is likely that the question paper will tell you which audience you should be considering.

❸ Practically based question (30 marks). This asks you to do something practical to develop your idea. You will be told clearly what you are expected to do and what you are supposed to achieve.

❹ Evaluation question (15 marks). You will be asked to weigh up the good and bad points of your own work. You will gain some extra marks by using the right media studies terms.

Sample controlled tests

This chapter includes six sample controlled tests based on different media. Each should take four hours of student time.

Sample controlled test 1: Video

Background

You work for Down Home Video. Your company is a small provider of specialist titles and in the last year you have managed to earn substantial profits from cheaply produced videos for small markets. Your range of titles now covers subjects as far apart as gardening and choosing the right GCSE courses. Your tapes sell in bigger video stores and gain extra income from major rental outlets. You want to develop an idea for a new title.

Task 1

Define the area in which this company operates. Make clear distinctions between specialist video and the strengths of television and publications. Conclude by outlining the appeal of your kind of product to an audience. (40 marks)

Task 2

Write a proposal (or brief summary) of your ideas for a successful new title for your company. This should include ideas about audience, likely cost, existing competition and running time. (15 marks)

Task 3

Storyboard a sequence from the video that would give a likely investor a clear idea about the style, angle, content and appeal of the video. Include details of where this sequence would appear in the tape and how it would fit with other contents. (30 marks)

Task 4

Write a summary of the unique selling points of your tape and consider the way that these will work to give it a strong appeal to the target audience. (15 marks)

Sample controlled test 2: The press

Background

You work for International News, a worldwide news organisation. Your company has interests in newspapers, television, films, news programmes and magazines. The company wants to make more money from its news gathering and has decided to produce weekly newspapers covering world events to be sold in selected countries. You are in charge of developing a UK edition.

Task 1

Outline the features of a major newspaper. Pay particular attention to all of the elements that may be linked to other activities of a company like International News and explain why companies involved in newspapers may also have interests in other media.
(40 marks)

Task 2

Select between 6 and 10 items for inclusion in your new paper. Briefly explain why each would be included and what kind of audience it would attract. Give your paper a name.
(15 marks)

Task 3

Produce material for an advertising campaign for the new title. Choose between a poster campaign or television commercials. Outline when and where this campaign would appear. You should design and include a logo and develop some clear 'angle' for your paper. (30 marks)

Task 4

Compare your product to existing newspapers. Identify the strengths and weaknesses of the competition and weigh up the likely chances of success for your new title.

(15 marks)

Sample controlled test 3: The film industry

Background

You are the managing director of BRIT Films Ltd (BFL). BFL has been established to make films about British subjects that will appeal to audiences around the world. You have already had two major successes with a romantic comedy – *Four Weddings and a Funeral* – and a historical drama – *Remains of the Day*. You are now looking for a third success.

Task 1

Summarise the points that make a successful film. Draw on examples of film success. Consider what audiences want and pay particular attention to the variety of successful films on the market and the different audiences that exist for films.   (40 marks)

Task 2

Write a treatment (or summary description) for your planned film. This must include details of likely budget, location, plot and some idea of the star(s) you want.   (15 marks)

Task 3

Storyboard the opening sequence of the film which will establish the story and at least one main character. This sequence should be clearly angled to meet the needs of the likely audience.   (30 marks)

Task 4

Account for the decisions taken in the first three tasks. Consider the options rejected and explain why the decisions you made will help your film to succeed.   (15 marks)

Sample controlled test 4: Television

Background

You work for OFF THE WALL productions. This is an independent company that manages several well-known comedians. The success of your acts on the stand-up circuit has given the company the money to develop new television ideas to promote the acts to new audiences. You want to develop a new sit-com aimed at an audience under 40 and suitable for a major channel (BBC1 or ITV). You have meetings scheduled with programme buyers from both companies.

Task 1

Write an account of the main elements that make a successful television situation comedy. You should pay particular attention to the way these programmes appeal to their audiences. Use as many examples as you wish and compare some comedies on smaller channels (Channel 4, BBC 2, satellite and cable) with the comedies on major channels.

(40 marks)

Task 2

Write a proposal (or brief summary) of your ideas. This should include ideas about set design, characters, likely audience and placement within a television schedule. (15 marks)

Task 3

Storyboard a trailer for the first episode of your show. This should clearly establish the characters and the plot for the first episode.   (30 marks)

Task 4

Consider the strengths and weaknesses of your proposal and outline your own expectations about the channel most likely to buy the show and its chances of success once bought.   (15 marks)

Sample controlled test 5: The music industry

Background

You work for BIG records. BIG is a major label covering most areas of pop and rock music. BIG has decided to launch a major new act into the mainstream pop market. The act should aim for hit singles, sell-out concerts and maximum television coverage. BIG will recruit the people it needs once it has established the image and ideas for the act.

Task 1

Summarise the main elements you would expect to find in a successful pop act, using examples to illustrate your answer. Discuss the way that these pop acts meet the needs of their audiences. (40 marks)

Task 2

Write a plan for the first year of your new act including realistic achievement targets. Add simple profiles of two people you would want to recruit to ensure success.

(15 marks)

Task 3

Produce publicity material for the act that will attract the right target audience and give the act a clear image. Produce this material for a poster campaign to launch the act and magazine adverts promoting the first single. (30 marks)

Task 4

Analyse the chances of success of your act. Consider the problems of competition, audience and finance. Give the strongest arguments you can to show how your act will succeed. (15 marks)

Sample controlled test 6: Magazines/comics

Background

You work for Little Wonder Magazines. This company has only been trading for two years and in that time it has taken advantage of the falling cost of magazine production to launch new titles with a very small circulation. By attracting some advertising and obtaining distribution deals with the larger branches of W. H. Smith and John Menzies, the company has made impressive profits. Now you are looking for a new title aimed at a very selective market to add to the profits.

Task 1

Write an outline of the things that make a successful magazine. Consider the way that changing costs in production have had an influence on the industry and use examples to illustrate your points. (40 marks)

Task 2

Write a proposal for a new title. Invent a title, consider likely sources of advertising and identify the target audience. (15 marks)

Task 3

Produce a mock-up of a front cover and one feature from inside the magazine. This should clearly show angle and visual style. The cover should aim to provide a strong attraction for your target audience. (30 marks)

Task 4

Write an evaluation of your idea outlining the reasons why the company should expect it to make a profit, the likely competition and briefly considering the reasons for launching the publication this year. (15 marks)

Controlled test – sample answers

This section aims to give you some idea of the way that high-quality answers would appear in a SEG test. The six tests above have been organised to give you some idea of the way that SEG would approach six different media. To answer all six tests in detail would make this chapter needlessly long. To give you an insight into the way that students should plan answers to SEG controlled tests we have selected two tests – number 1 on video and number 2 on the press. This will show you the kind of thinking that goes into media products and the kind of thinking that SEG wants to see in the answers to its tests.

Sample controlled test 1

Background to the sample test answer

This test asks students to produce products for a small and selective market. In other words, the video idea will have to find an audience who all share a similar interest. This interest will have to be the kind of subject that attracts people from around the UK but doesn't have a massive following. There are many such subjects and one useful exercise for you might involve trying to list 10 from your own imagination. We have listed 10 below:

- rock climbing
- horse riding
- collecting model cars
- belonging to a film club
- making your own clothes
- writing poetry
- aerobics
- joining a political party
- having foreign pen-friends
- train spotting.

All of the interests above have organised groups and there are media products that exist for people involved in all of these activities. There are also adverts for many of these activities in general magazines, radio, etc.

There are other types of interests that may be called major interests. These are activities that most people know and understand, even if they don't take part. Activities like going to football matches fall into this category.

The controlled test answered in this chapter has been developed on the minority interest of UFOs (unidentified flying objects). It has also been developed by using a real media product that deals with this subject. This is to allow you to see how the real media deal with a minority interest subject.

Before we look at the controlled test we will briefly outline the way that the subject of UFOs presents a good example of a minority interest subject.

Most people may have seen brief bits of media coverage on UFOs. This could be factual like a newspaper report or fictitious like the film *ET*. Like the subjects listed above, UFOs are generally understood but not really a major part of people's lives. The number of people involved in investigating them or even reading books on the subject is small compared to the interest in subjects like football, fishing or fashionable clothes.

The interest in UFOs tends to come from a small group of people and these people are scattered all over the country. They are very unlikely to meet and this means that media products that are put together properly will be useful to these people because they will give them new information and keep their interest alive.

One important thing about media products that have a small audience like this is that they often make a good substitute for talking about an interest. People who wanted to talk about football or pop music in your school or college wouldn't find it hard to get a conversation. How easy would it be to find somebody with opinions and knowledge about UFOs?

When media producers consider subjects for their material, they think about the level of interest and consider the way that this will affect their product. You will see this in the way that the points outlined above are used in the answers to the controlled test.

About the controlled test answers

These answers have been based on a real media product. This does not mean that you will be expected to come up with answers that would certainly work in the real world. You will be graded on your understanding and the arguments you develop. The answers here are simply examples of how you should go about this work. The wording of the answers is based on the demands of SEG and not the demands of the real media industry.

Answers

Task 1

Down Home Video operates in the area of video. Companies in this area make money from selling their tapes. Some of these tapes are sold to video shops and libraries where they can be rented. This usually leads to profits for the shops and the libraries but it can bring in some more money for the video company. Down Home Video is a maker of 'specialist' titles. This means that it makes titles for audiences with small numbers. Titles from a company like Down Home Video might sell a few thousand at the most. In the past companies like this couldn't survive very easily because making videos was very expensive and the only way to get the money back was by selling lots of copies of the video once it was made. These days making videos is a lot cheaper than it used to be and this means that small companies can find their own type of market and put out a few videos to reach this market.

There are a few things that make small companies like this one different from other, bigger companies. One of these is the way that their videos are sold. They can only get into bigger shops that sell lots of titles because small shops without much stock tend to stick to the best-selling titles. This means that companies like Disney which make really popular films can get their videos everywhere while companies like Down Home who are putting out videos on subjects like fishing will probably see their tapes in the very back of a shop like Blockbuster. On the other hand, if tapes deal with a special subject like fishing or passing exams they could be sold in places that don't usually stock videos, like fishing tackle shops.

The area of videos on special subjects is changing for a number of reasons. First, it is a lot cheaper now than it used to be to make tapes. This means that a company can make a profit from selling a fairly small number of tapes. In the past it made sense for big companies to release videos because they could make tens of thousands of them and get them into big shops like Woolworths and W. H. Smith. These days lots of places sell tapes and there are places everywhere that will copy them and make them. Most towns have their own videos and even schools and colleges have their own promotion videos. Another reason for the area of tapes to be changing in the media is that the type of competition is changing. Because video tapes can be bought on all kinds of specialist subjects the real competition to them is books or specialist magazines. Things are different with videos of big films where the real competition is television and the cinema.

New competition is also coming into the market. CD-Roms and other ways of storing information in computers have now really good graphics and this means that they can offer the same things as videos. At the moment a company like Down Home Video can make some money by offering videos on a specialist subject such as passing exams. These videos appeal to people and they have some advantages over other types of media. But the area in which this company is working is being expanded all the time by new companies trying to make money and by new types of media that are trying to do the same things that are done by video.

People buy and rent videos for lots of reasons. Some of the time people simply want to be entertained. They also want education from videos or they simply want to collect them and watch them over and over again because the videos deal with subjects that they like. There are some advantages to videos in comparison to television. One of the main advantages is that videos can allow you to watch exactly what you want when you want. You can also do this by taping programmes from the television to play back at another time, but a company like Down Home Video won't suffer from people taping television programmes because there are not that many dealing with the kind of specialist things that are covered in their videos.

This leads us to another good point about videos. Many of the videos about special subjects appeal to people with a really strong interest. This means that these people will want to own lots of videos, books, etc on their favourite subject. Groups of people interested in particular sports or certain subjects might be big in numbers but if they are really keen to buy videos, books and magazines they can make a loyal audience. This means that people making things like video tapes can expect some profits from their work and can probably predict fairly well how many copies they will sell.

Videos have some advantages and disadvantages over other products in terms of the way that people use them. One advantage is that videos offer the chance to see moving pictures. This means that they can illustrate things and show them in real detail. People often find this easier to understand than a lot of written words and a few pictures. Videos are not so demanding, you don't need to concentrate as hard on a video as you do on a book. This point is a real advantage when the video deals with a subject where actually seeing something is a lot better than simply reading about it. For example, if you get a video about a racing driver's career and you can see crashes and bits of races, it makes things clearer than simply trying to imagine them. You can watch a video with friends and if you have an opinion about it, you can talk about this as the video is going on. If you really want to concentrate on something, you can stop the video and go back to see the thing again.

There are some disadvantages to videos. You often have to give them all your attention. If you have a radio programme or a tape this isn't true. Because videos need to be played back you can't very easily take them many places. You can read papers or books on a train or a bus or even in a tea break. You have to plan at least a little bit to watch a video.

Despite the disadvantages videos are popular, easy to use and fairly cheap to buy. Easily cheaper than a lot of books and computer products, this means that at the moment they have a large and steady market.

Task 2

My proposal is for a video on the subject of UFOs. This subject gets a lot of interest and almost everyone has an opinion about whether UFOs exist and what they are if they do exist. I think this video would appeal to a slightly varied audience. First, there are people who are really interested in this subject and want every piece of information they can get about it. These people buy books and magazines and would read anything in a paper or watch anything on television about UFOs.

There are also a lot of people with a general interest. Many of these people watch programmes on television – like 'The X Files' – that have some material about UFOs in them. These people might not want to read a really detailed book but if they could see people being interviewed about their own UFO experiences and get a quick update from a few experts on UFO information, they would be interested. The video would give them an easy way to find out more about the subject.

People like 'The X Files' because the programme collects lots of information on strange phenomena and puts it across in a popular way. I would do the same with a UFO video and I think that calling a video 'The UFO Files' would suggest it was like 'The X Files'. It would make people think about the fact that there are a lot of different things to know about UFOs.

It might be possible to take serious UFO people for granted because there will be some who would buy anything with a UFO idea behind it. To make this video successful it would be important to keep the price fairly low and offer reasonable value for money. There are lots of videos that sell for around £10 and run for around one hour. I would want 'The UFO Files' video to be around both of these figures because the evidence suggests this price and running time appeal to audiences.

I'm not a complete expert on this subject but I think that this specialist area would be likely to have the kind of competition you see for videos of some sports and other interests. This means that 'The UFO Files' could expect to compete with a few other tapes on the same subject as well as books, a few magazines and maybe some software for computers. I think that my title would help because of its 'X Files' link. I also think that the title promises real cases and information. If the first one was numbered '1', suggesting that there were more to come this would add to the appeal because it would promise anyone with a real interest the chance to build up a collection.

There would be no 'typical' member of the audience. I would think they would be young – 16–25. This age group has more time to watch videos and tends to buy more than others. Older people tend to rent a lot more than they buy. Because these subjects appeal more to boys I think there would be more males than females in the audience but this needn't be too many more. I think you might find that the audience for this tape would be better educated than most people. You do need some imagination and knowledge to understand arguments about strange and weird things. The audience might also be slightly better off than average because it is only people with a bit of extra money to spend that can afford to think about building up a collection of videos and the idea of my tape is, partly, to encourage people to start collecting a series.

Task 3

The sequence I have storyboarded is from the opening of the tape. This shows a number of the key shots from the first few minutes and I will briefly explain how they fit in.

1 The title 'UFOs and Paranormal Phenomena': This says something about the content of the tape. The title is clear and I have used very plain letters to suggest straightforward information. The idea of making the title different to the title on the cover of the video is to suggest that this is just one part of 'The UFO Files'. If the series continued, other tapes could have different titles and serious UFO persons would want them all.

2 Expert talking to camera: It is important to suggest right from the start there are knowledgeable people who can tell the viewer something about UFOs. An expert simply talking like this might be cheap to use but he or she can suggest things that are coming up later on that viewers will want to see.

3 Drawings by witnesses: These show some of the things that people investigated by the expert have drawn. These back up his claims about what is happening to people and keep viewers interested without using up all the best film of UFOs at the start.

4 Shot of radar station: This suggests people on Earth looking for UFOs and tracking them. The commentary could talk about this. The idea here is to suggest that military people are always hunting UFOs. This creates some tension for the viewers.

5 Shot of Earth: After talking about military people looking for UFOs I think that this shot will show that we are out in space on our own and might suggest the way that the Earth looks to other life. This gives another viewpoint and helps build up the idea of UFOs and the Earth or 'us and them'.

6 Plane circling with light in the sky: After introducing all the UFO ideas in the previous shots this shot would show a UFO-type light. This is still at the stage when the tape is introducing the whole idea and I would have a voice-over talking about the kind of things that people see. This shot would probably be a special effect at this stage because I would want to keep any real UFO pictures for later in the tape. I think that this shot would be useful because it would start showing UFO pictures and this would show the viewers that they were going to get more than people simply talking about UFOs. I would use a normal plane and a bright light to make this shot short and simple.

7 Drawings of UFOs: This would be a good follow-on from the previous shot. I could use a lot or drawings of different UFOs because in this introduction it would be important that people got an idea of the whole range of UFOs. Because I had the shot before generated by computer I think I would use a number of drawings after that to keep costs down.

The video would follow up this general introduction by doing investigations of real cases, talking to witnesses, talking to experts and using any real pictures and film that we could afford. After this introduction each case investigation would be a few minutes long, a bit like a small 'X File'. Using all of these cases would fit in with the 'files' part of the title, and the 'paranormal' part in the title of this tape would be covered by having cases where lots of odd things happened. This would mean that other tapes would have a different theme, like UFOs in history. I could save costs a bit more by using some of the same shots in all of the tapes. Many documentary tapes in a series do this. I think that the shot of Earth and the radar would have the same use in all my tapes.

These opening shots would provide a start for the other things in the tape. They would set the scene and by the end of this opening people would know that they should expect good information from experts, a number of different cases, and witnesses talking about their experiences. The different cases are probably the most important thing to keep people interested and I think the real strength of using a lot of different UFO pictures near the start is that viewers will know that one case won't tell them everything. This is true in a programme like 'The X Files' because some of their stories are similar but each case has its own different features.

Task 4

There are a number of good selling points of this tape. First, the subject itself. If people are really interested in strange phenomena, then they will feel better buying one tape full of information on this than they will buying up a load of newspapers and magazines that might have just a little bit of information. The attraction here is that this tape will concentrate a lot of what they want to know into one hour of their time.

This tape also combines lots of things. The expert opinions mean that the audience can use arguments from experts to help them build their own ideas. The witnesses in the tape will also help with this and the viewers will be interested to see real people talking about things that happened to them. The viewers can probably identify with witnesses, especially if they are varied for age and gender, etc, and this will help them to feel involved. Using witnesses can be cheap and it could be a regular feature of these tapes if they ran for a long time as a series.

Finally, an audience that is interested in strange things wants some evidence. It would be great to collect every film and picture on this subject and put them into the one tape but this would cost a lot and I've already decided to keep this tape at around £10. I think that using some real film, some drawings and a few special effects should provide enough evidence for the viewers and keep the costs down.

I think that the target audience I discussed earlier will value this mix of evidence and price because they will want the tape to be affordable. If it is reasonably priced, it is possible that libraries and other places might buy up copies that can be borrowed. This would increase sales. If Down Home Video lost a few sales of the first tape because people borrowed it from a library instead of buying it, this would not be too serious. I think the company could do well out of this in the end because if the tape was part of a series, people who had borrowed one tape in the series might decide to buy others.

I think that there is a real advantage in trying to make a series of these tapes. Really keen people with an interest in UFOs will want the lot and that means that there will be some sales guaranteed for as long as the series keeps going. The tapes are going to go out to a small market and so the longer the series keeps going the more likely we are to get good sales. Down Home won't be able to afford proper advertising on such small sales but, if their tapes are out for a long time, they will be able to build up an image for themselves. This last point is not guaranteed because there is another problem with special interests like UFOs and that is that the market for the tapes can be filled if too many tapes are released in too short a time.

Sample controlled test 2

This test follows the development of a newspaper. In this case, the answers are not based on any real publication. This test asks you to think about the connections between gathering news information and making a product. A good mark in this test would depend on your ability to see the connections between products, audiences and the way that a major media company is organised. One central theme of this test is linking the gathering of information with the development of one product.

A useful exercise you could complete to get yourself thinking along these lines involves trying to link a number of products produced by one industry. Start with some popular item you know well like one record, one TV show, etc. and then think of the ways it has been developed or could be developed. This may sound confusing but there is an example below to help you.

Example

Basic product: Hit single

Other items using this: pop video, film (as part of soundtrack), pop magazine (could print lyrics or feature pop act talking about their single), television show (may feature act performing single), radio show, television advert etc.

Companies exploit a basic product in this way because they are always trying to make the maximum amount of money out of an investment. This second controlled test is based on this idea and all of the tasks revolve around developing an idea for a newspaper. Marks could be gained in this test from understanding that a big news organisation would want to develop ways to make extra money from its world-wide news gathering. Further marks could be gained from understanding that the right type of newspaper, aimed at a particular audience, could make this extra money.

Task 1

Newspapers cover news events. They tell readers about things that are happening and also include some comments on the news. The kind of news covered depends on the readership of the paper. For example, 'Motor Cycle News' covers developments in motor bikes and motor bike racing whilst daily papers like 'The Sun' cover national news events like disasters, events in the royal family, etc.

There are many standard features within a newspaper. One such feature is the name of the paper presented in some recognised way, this is called the masthead. Most papers have a well-known look which is based on using a particular kind of typeface, sometimes with some graphics around it. Other features include the use of big headlines to get the attention of readers and eye-catching pictures. It is quite common for many of these pictures to appear in colour, however, the amount of colour depends on the amount of money that the publication can make.

Photographs and headlines are used to attract readers, by grabbing their attention and encouraging them to read further. One good example of this tactic occurred in 'The Sun' when the headline read 'Freddie Starr Ate My Hamster'. This was at the top of an article that told an unusual story about a television personality. It created a stir and many people bought the paper that day just to read about this story.

This example also demonstrates another typical feature of a major paper. That is the way it can scoop big stories that are sure to generate lots of interest from the public. Major papers are in a position to pay well for stories, which they use to get their money back by attracting a big readership.

Another feature of newspapers is the dividing up of the paper into different sections. This happens because a paper must have a range of readers before it is going to be really successful. For example 'The Sun's' Monday edition has a special section called 'Goals', which is about football. On Mondays it also publishes the top 30 or 40 singles. On Wednesday it has a women's section and on a Saturday it lists all the forthcoming television for the next week. All of these sections are designed to appeal to certain people. There are men who read the paper regularly but probably never read the women's section on a Wednesday.

Another common feature of large-circulation newspapers are listings of general information such as TV schedules or weather reports. Such general information shows that these papers are catering for a large market, this contrasts with specialist publications that often limit their television coverage to particular programmes. For example, sports magazines that only mention what is on a sports channel.

Mass circulation newspapers have an 'Editorial' section in which they express their own opinion. Usually this is on the inside of the paper and is tucked well away, to avoid putting off readers who do not share the same opinion. Occasionally, papers put their opinion on the front page. For example, when a terrorist bomb has gone off in this country some of the popular tabloids have said on the front page that we shouldn't give in to violence like this. Papers only push their opinions in this way when they are sure that most of their readers will strongly agree with them.

Many daily newspapers have weekly editions or links with weekly papers which means that the same news can be used more than once. Some papers also have links with television and radio which allows them to use the news that they gather in a number of different kinds of media. Huge companies like News International and The Mirror Group have links with areas like book publishing, which means that they can use the information that they gather to make books.

One other important point about the links with different media is that most of the work of gathering information is now done using computers. Information held on a computer is easy to access and to edit. In the past newspapers were made by people working on typewriters and printers moving metal blocks around to print the paper. Now that computers do much of the work, the same information can be called up by different people. One story can easily be used as part of a newspaper, book, radio programme or some other kind of product like a leaflet.

Newspapers also list lots of information which can easily be loaded into things like teletext and computer files. Computer-based publications are now known as examples of 'Electronic publishing'. Big newspapers have lots of chances to use their computers to gather and send out information and this is becoming a bigger and bigger part of what they do.

Task 2

My paper will be called 'Eastern Voice'. It will sell to people in the UK who belong to the Asian community. It will cover a range of material that people in this community would not find in the other UK papers. Much of the material will be news but there will also be other things that appeal to people with an Asian background.

My newspaper will offer different things to other papers aimed at this community. One of these will be the fact that it will focus on a lot of things that are happening in other Asian communities around the world. This means that it will not just focus on the UK and Asia.

I have outlined six items that will be part of this paper.

1 – Voice of the People: this is a column in which people who understand Asian affairs will be able to pass some comments. It will use experts but there will be a range of these. This is because many experts on Asian affairs take one type of view, for example, supporting a certain religion like Hinduism. If there was just one person who supported one religion making comments, this would leave out a lot of potential readers. There are strong divisions between the different Asian groups and for this reason I will let a number of different people be the 'Voice of the People'. I will also stick this feature on an inside page to avoid offending those people who do not agree with the various experts.

I think that this item will appeal to readers because they are unlikely to find too many other papers pushing personal opinions about Asia. They will also see that this is balanced by taking lots of different opinions. This means that even if they don't agree with some of the things they read, they will still see that the paper is trying to provide a balanced view.

2 – Listings: the Indian film industry makes more films that any other. There is a real demand amongst some of the Asian community for these films in cinemas and on video. Most of the time the other papers don't cover these.

There are other products aimed at the Asian community including music, television, theatre, etc. This listings section will be different to other listings in a number of ways.

i) It will cover all the UK television aimed at the UK market and will feature short snippets and interviews with people involved.

ii) It will make a point of listing other products, like TV documentaries, theatre, etc. that is not just aimed at the Asian community but does include Asian themes or things that would interest this audience. For example, a documentary that looks at laws on immigration.

iii) It will feature items on people that are not well-known, like new musicians, etc. This will try to expand their audience so they can appear in the listings later on.

3 – Past to Present: this will be a regular feature looking back at some important news item on an anniversary and comparing the way it was seen at the time and the way it is seen now. This would appeal to older people who remember the old news and also younger readers who could find out about some part of history that affected them. This feature could include things like Indian independence but also might look at a case of racial harassment that came to court in the seventies. One useful spin-off from this is that over a period of years the paper could collect lots of information that would be useful for other projects, like books. Various audiences could be catered for by focusing on different countries and religions.

4 – Sports: this will cover some of the same sports as other daily papers because there is a following in the UK Asian community for sports like football. However, the appeal of this item will be that it mixes these sports with others, like Kabaddi, which have a following in the Asian community. This kind of coverage would appeal to a range of people in the community because it would offer them enough general sports coverage to stop them buying other papers and enough specific sports coverage on Asian-based sports to make them want to buy 'Eastern Voice'.

This sounds complicated but in practice it would be easy because most of the major coverage on sports like football could be fed to 'Eastern Voice' from the news operation run by the parent company.

5 – Focus: this will take an important person every day and profile them (a feature which appears in the so-called 'quality' papers). This will be done in a fast and effective way. I've seen a thing called 'Pass Notes' from 'The Guardian' that does this. 'Focus' will be like that but a bit less jokey. This presentation of leading figures will appeal to the readers because many people in the UK are aware of Asian issues but lack all of the background knowledge to keep right in touch. Younger readers without any experience of living in Asia could use this item as a way of building up knowledge about things they have heard discussed by older people in their community.

6 – WWW – The Web: 'Eastern Voice' would have its own web site. This would feed letters and views to the paper. Furthermore, many views and opinions in the Asian community disagree with others making it impossible for some opinions to appear in the paper. The web site would provide people with the chance to talk about their experiences to a wider audience without upsetting the readership of the paper. The paper could publish a selection of opinions and advise readers that there was a web site that can discuss these issues further. This would allow the paper to keep the printed material tame enough to avoid turning off readers and at the same time allow a chance for all opinions to be covered in a different media. This would be a hard balance to keep but it would pay off by leaving a lot of people feeling a link with the paper.

Task 3

I have decided to produce a television advert for 'Eastern Voice'. This will aim to show people in the Asian community that this is their paper. It will also demonstrate that this paper is different to the other national papers on the market. I would expect this commercial to run on TV in breaks in programmes aimed at the Asian community. I would also run it on cable and satellite news channels and programmes. The advantage of running it on a news channel is that it would reach people who are really interested in knowing a lot about news and this might lead to some people outside the Asian community buying the paper. It would also reach some more people in the Asian community because many Asian people subscribe to 24-hour news channels because these channels provide the most news coverage on Asian issues.

The angle that I have developed in this commercial suggests that many people in the UK see themselves as Asian and see some of the things that they get from the media today as unimportant. This isn't presented as a criticism of other ideas but it does suggest that there are people who have something missing from their lives. 'Eastern Voice' will fill this gap.

Storyboard for commercial

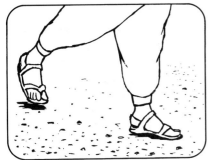

"Sometimes the world seems familiar…

… sometimes the world seems strange.

However the world seems we all need a little help to make sense of things.

If some of the messages don't matter to you…

… Here's one that will."

Task 4

There are two areas of obvious competition to 'Eastern Voice'. One of these is the existing popular daily papers. These tabloids, like 'The Sun' and 'Daily Mirror', appeal to many people, regardless of their racial background. These papers cover popular news and deal with famous people. They have lots of competitive advantages, for example, they can make huge payments for exclusive stories. They could outbid 'Eastern Voice' for the best stories coming from the Asian community if these stories were of interest to the whole country. For example, if a story involved a huge lottery win it is likely that 'The Sun' would pay the most to get an exclusive.

However, 'Eastern Voice' will be a paper in a big news organisation, so it will share some of these advantages. If another paper in the organisation got an exclusive on an event like a coach crash that involved a group of people from an Asian community, it is likely that 'Eastern Voice' could also use that information and might run a different kind of story, maybe one that dealt more with the community and less with the disaster.

The tabloid papers will certainly be more entertaining and appealing and probably less serious than 'Eastern Voice'. This means that this new paper will not be able to compete for popularity. However, the appeal of 'Eastern Voice' is that it offers an alternative to the popular press in the UK. It is feasible that it will sell to some people who also buy another more entertaining paper.

The main competition will come from the serious papers like 'The Independent', which provide lots of news coverage about major world events. 'Eastern Voice' will win readers from these papers if it can give the readers more of the coverage they want. The one big advantage for 'Eastern Voice' is that it will be taking angles that the Asian community recognise. On the other hand, the paper will have to ensure that it contains enough information about day-to-day events in Britain to appeal to a lot of readers. Many people in the Asian community follow things in the UK as much as anyone else: items such as football coverage will have to be good for these reasons. There will be lots of good news information available from the parent company but the hard thing for 'Eastern Voice' will be to make sure that this is presented with the right balance to keep everyone interested.

There are already papers aimed at the Asian community in the UK. 'Asian Times' and 'India Times' are British and they cover the kind of news that 'Eastern Voice' will include. These papers are trusted and have steady sales. They are independent and so trusted by the Asian community. If 'Eastern Voice' was too closely linked to a big news operation some people might not trust it because they would see it as just another part of a huge business empire trying to make money. They might link it in their minds with other papers and other things that came from that business empire.

On the other hand, the link with a big company would ensure good distribution, good advertising and money to run things like competitions. This would boost sales and take readers away from the existing publications for Asians in this country. The paper could afford to run at a loss for a while until some of its poorer rivals had gone out of business. It could also afford good quality production and use its news contacts to get exclusive stories from Asia ahead of the other papers. It could also be advertised by the parent company in a way that kept its profile high. The parent company could advertise 'Eastern Voice' on its own cable or satellite channels or in its other papers.

I think there are some problems for 'Eastern Voice'. These are to do with striking the right balance and not offending any one minority. The paper would also have to get some definite ideas about exactly where it would draw the line on coverage. Should the paper focus on people with roots in India, Bangladesh and Pakistan? Or should it cast the net wider to places like Vietnam?

I think that Eastern Voice could be a success, it would get support from a big company and find readers that were not buying anything else made by that company. It could use a lot of information gathered within the one company and run on a small staff as part of a much bigger organisation, thereby keeping costs down. This paper could take on the rival publications and probably beat them in their own market.

WJEC written paper

Tackling the written paper

From 1997 onwards the written paper will count for 50 per cent of your final assessment and is the last element in the assessment process. It will seek, in timed conditions, to draw on the knowledge, concepts and skills which have been developed by the coursework element of the syllabus.

The best preparation is working hard on all the elements of the course. There is little advantage for you in last-minute swotting. The teaching approaches developed for the coursework element of the assessment are also appropriate for preparation for the written paper. Experience also suggests that if you know how the written paper works and have experienced working under time pressures, you can improve your performance.

The intention of the written paper is to allow you to show your media knowledge, understandings and skills on unseen segments of media texts drawn from the areas of study specified in the syllabus. In addition two questions (5b and 10b) on the paper are set which allow you, if you wish, to respond to more general issues and concepts which are specified in the syllabus and the Notes for Guidance.

Format of the paper

The written paper lasts for two and a half hours in total; half an hour of this time is given over to reading the questions and scanning the resource material for Section B: 5 minutes for the print-based material and then 25 minutes which is given over to the viewing/listening to of audio/visual material.

The written paper seeks to test all three groups of the assessment objectives:

❶ knowledge and understanding

❷ description and analysis

❸ production and evaluation – questions 4 and 9 are designed as practical activities which encourage evaluative commentary.

The paper has two equally weighted sections.

Section A will consist of questions which focus on either film or television or radio or video.

In each year of the examination specified areas are offered. Only one of these is chosen. The intention is to allow you to put into context the area of study so that you will be prepared to deal with an unseen segment(s) of media text(s). It is not intended that you should be prepared for the written paper in a way that anticipates what these segments will be. You will be prepared best for this section by regularly working with media texts within the specified area of study.

All the material presented in this section will have been broadcast during the period of the examination (i.e. for 1997 from 1995 to 1996, for 1998 from 1996 to 1997). So it is a good idea to check the listings on a regular basis to see what material is being broadcast or shown in the cinema during your course. This will provide you with lots of material to use in the examination room.

In 1997 three areas are specified:

- police/detective series (television)
- documentary (radio, television, film)
- the science fiction film.

In 1998, after one of these has been used in 1997, it will be replaced by popular music programmes on television and radio.

Section B will consist of a similarly structured set of questions which will focus on still images or print drawn from newspapers, magazines, comics or advertisements. Material will again be chosen which seeks to reflect current media practice and issues. More than one text may be chosen. The best preparation for this section is again a regular reading of a range of appropriate materials.

In both sections then more than one text or segment of text may be used. However, you will not always be expected to deal with all the material presented. The questions will be determined finally by the nature of the stimulus material.

In general terms the questions will get more demanding and this is indicated by the marks allocated to each question. Experience suggests that you must take notice of the marks allocated to each question in writing your responses to questions. Usually, the lower the mark allocated to a question the shorter the answer.

Specific prompts within questions also guide you in terms of the length of an answer. 'Briefly' really does mean briefly. 'Identify' or 'list' often means a single word answer. Note form is appropriate, especially on questions 4 and 9.

How does the paper work?

Section A – audio-visual stimulus material

Qu. 1   You are often asked to describe the material/part of the material. You will be rewarded for demonstrating awareness of forms and conventions in that description. It is very important to keep answers brief. It is a very common mistake to write too much on this question.

Qu. 2   This often requires you to 'read' the material/part of the material in some way. Reading means considering how the chosen media text works. Again your answer needs to be brief.

Qu. 3   This often raises knowledge and understanding of concepts and/or technical issues raised by the material. It is often a slightly more difficult question. In recent years this has developed into a question which allows you to refer to material you may have knowledge of from other contexts than the stimulus material itself.

Qu. 4   This is a practically based question (practical as defined by the syllabus) which allows you to develop some of the ideas/concepts/conventions raised by the first three questions in a practical way. In recent years stronger prompts are being given to you to encourage you to annotate your suggestions. You can do this as a section in the answer book or by text-marking your work on the resource sheet.

Qu. 5(a)   This is an essay-based question which is clearly linked to the specified area for study for Section A. It is intended as an 'open' question which encourages lots of different answers depending on which programmes and films you know or have studied. So you may use the information built up over the first four questions and extend it. Or you may use different material entirely. You should try to show the examiner what you know. In recent years it has developed a three-part form: definition, description, comment to help you to shape your responses.

Section B

This section is organised in a similar way to Section A. It is particularly important to know about the ways words and images interrelate in print-based material.

Questions 5b in Section A and 10b in Section B will either be based on a key term (for example, schedules, ratings, censorship, advertising campaign in past papers) in the syllabus or will encourage you to show your knowledge and understanding of a media concept (stereotype, target audience), issue (violence, effects, media presentation of the royal family) which has been current in the period of study for the examination. These will always be 'open' questions which encourage lots of different responses by allowing you to use examples which you know about. These may be drawn from a range of media forms and genres not simply those specified for study in the section.

Worked examples from past papers

One of the best ways of improving your performance on the written paper is to study answers to previous papers to see what the examiners are looking to reward in the answers to questions. This section looks at a range of answers to the kinds of questions that occur in the written paper.

A Questions which ask you 'to describe briefly': questions 1 and 6

Activity 1

In 1994 one of the specified areas for study was situation comedy on television.

The examiner chose four trailers for various programmes which had been broadcast in 1993. Of these the overwhelming favourite was 'One Foot in the Grave'.

Look at the following answers to the question 'Describe briefly one of the trailers'. Which, in your opinion, gained full marks? Why?

a In 'One Foot in the Grave' there is a man with short brown hair. He's about 30. He dresses quite old. He is taking a picture of two women in the same dress and an old bloke. He tells the old bloke 'If you step to your left, you will step in dog muck' but before he finished the sentence the old bloke stepped to his left. Then the bloke taking the picture said smile and took the photo. Then it goes on to where they are all stuck in a boat on a lake. The old bloke says 'Let's go for a nice day out in the country and we end up on the set of "Apocalypse Now"'. Then it goes on and the old bloke is going up from a field to an old spooky looking house.

b The trailer begins with a close-up of the photographer, who tells Mr Meldrew that if he steps to the side he will be standing in a large pile of dog mess... There is a shot of some swans and a voice-over says 'What could be nicer than a summer's day in the open air'. You then see a long shot of Victor, his wife and her friend stuck in a pond. Next there is a low angled shot of Victor walking up to a dark, mansion-like house, followed by a close-up shot of Victor's hand pulling the door bell. Throughout this the voice-over says 'But it's only just begun. Will Victor have more than one foot in the grave?' You see a freeze frame telling you the show is in half an hour. Screen fades to black.

The answer is obviously **b**. The reason is that the candidate uses appropriate media language accurately to describe the trailer. To gain high marks you need to know the appropriate media language for the areas specified for study on the written paper. You can practise your description skills by choosing short extracts (two to three minutes only) of the types of programme which are specified in the area for study.

Activity 2

Look now at these two answers to a print-based question which was question 6 in the 1994 paper.

Candidates were asked to describe the front cover of a computer magazine.

a The front cover is very colourful. It has pictures of a computer, the Supernes and Gameboy. It has got a new game on which is a picture of a cat smiling and winking.

The words to go with this new game are 'Exclusive BUBSY the BOBCAT. Faster than a speeding hedgehog'.

b The front of the magazine is made up of three main parts. The first part is the name of the magazine. Also grouped with this are the price, the date of issue and the fact that it is the biggest console magazine. The main part of the cover is a picture of Bubsy the Bobcat, an exciting cartoon-like piece of artwork. Also in this section is a mention of a game included in the magazine. There is also more information about a free offer. The barcode is situated in the bottom right-hand corner. The third section is on the left-hand side of the cover showing three systems made by Nintendo and the games that can be played on them.

Again **b** was awarded full marks. The reason for this is that the candidate is clearly aware that front covers are constructed and organised, while **a** is only able to identify some of the elements of the front cover.

You need to study the front covers/front pages of newspapers a lot for Section B of the written paper. You need to know how they are constructed and organised. You will need to think about layout and design.

B Questions 2, 3, 7 and 8

These questions test your ability to identify and comment on specific elements in the material. Obviously, they are determined by the material itself.

a In 1995 an extract from a 'Flintstones' cartoon was used. One of the most important things about cartoons is humour, so a question was set which asked candidates to say what two aspects of the extract audiences might find funny. Obviously, there are several potential reasons: the jokes, the situations, the animation, the setting, the characters. More marks were gained by those candidates who went on to explain how an audience might find them funny.

b In 1992 the extract consisted of the title sequences of five regionally based soap operas. One of the most important points about the organisations that produce soap operas is that in the UK they use region as a selling point to attract audiences. This is particularly true of the ITV companies – 'Coronation Street' is a flagship programme for Granada which is an organisation based in Manchester. So one of the questions asked candidates to use the information in the title sequences to show how they represented the region in which the soap opera was set.

c In 1993 in Section B a story from *The Beano* and one from *Mandy and Judy* were used. One of the most important things about the representation of characters in comics for young people is stereotyping. So a question was set about Dennis the Menace which encouraged candidates to explore how his behaviour was stereotypical in the story. The best candidates could show how his character was an exaggeration, how he was simplified into a series of typical behaviours and how these identified him as a typical character who had an audience appeal to young boys especially.

d In 1995 two display advertisements from newspapers were used in Section B – one for Tesco and one for Kwik Save. One of the most important things about advertisements of all kinds is the target audience. So the question asked candidates to identify the target audience. The best candidates were able to use elements of the advertisements to support this identification.

To prepare for these questions you will need, with your teacher's help, to identify the most important aspects of the chosen areas for study.

Here, for example, are key areas in the study of situation comedies (set in 1994):

● character (well-known star/personality/stereotype)

● setting (region/class/race/gender)

● situation (often workplace/family/home)

● circular structure of narrative

● audience expectation/humour/comedy.

You cannot study situation comedy without looking at these key elements. What should be clear from this is that to deal with these questions, the study of almost any situation comedy will be useful. Even alternative situation comedies such as 'Red Dwarf' draw attention to these.

So make sure you know the specified areas of study for the year you sit the written paper and the most important aspects of them.

It is essential that you deal with the first three questions in each section quickly and efficiently so that you can deal with the questions that carry the bulk of the marks.

C Questions 4 and 9

These are practically based questions which ask you to use the issues raised in your mind by the earlier questions in a practical way. The most common tasks often involve storyboarding, design, layout as these are important media skills as well as story-lines, scripts, ideas, suggestions. It is always best to support your visual ideas with brief notes to explain them. You are provided with resource sheets to carry out these tasks. The examiner is interested in your ideas not your drawing skills!

Your coursework should have developed these skills. Here are some typical questions:

a Make suggestions for a trailer for a new series of your favourite situation comedy. You may use the storyboard provided to help you. (1994)

Fig. 19.1 shows one answer to this which gained a good mark.

  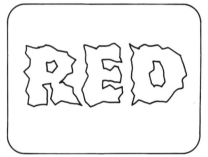

Establishing shot. A picture of space. Writing scrolls into the distance. Fade to black.

Close up of one of main character's face (Lister) looking puzzled.

Fig. 19.1

If the candidate had made more notes on the storyboard, the examiner could probably have awarded more marks. It is very brief but very clever. The examiner, for instance, might be impressed with the use of the scroll in the first establishing shot because it uses a convention drawn from the film *Star Wars*. However, the candidate has not noted this on the storyboard as part of the evaluation and commentary on the ideas. Nor has the candidate explained the use of RED in the final shot. So examiners need you to explain your ideas, though you do not need to write an essay! Brief text markings are enough.

b Make suggestions for a title sequence for a new soap opera to be based in your region. You may use the storyboard to help you. (1992)

c Design a contents page for a special interest or hobby magazine. Explain the reasons for your design. You may use the blank page in the Resource Material to help you. (1994)

d Make suggestions for a new cartoon character who works for the environment. Suggest a possible story-line that might be used in the cartoon series. (1995)

The more practice you have had in shaping, discussing, explaining and justifying your ideas, the better prepared you will be for these kinds of questions.

D Questions 5 and 10

These questions are the ones which carry the most marks and so you must make sure that you make a good effort with these questions. They are usually broken down into parts to help you to organise your answers effectively.

Questions 5(a) and 10(a) always link back to the stimulus material; so if you are really stuck you can use the stimulus material to help you with the answer. However, to get better marks you should use these questions to show what you know about the area specified for study.

Here, for instance, is a question set in 1994 on situation comedy:

Describe a situation comedy which you know. In what ways is it typical of the genre?

Study the following answer which gained a high mark. You will see how the candidate uses knowledge of the media language appropriate to situation comedy to describe 'Keeping Up Appearances' and in doing so clearly identifies the elements which are typical of the genre. The candidate also begins to explore the relationship of the programme to the viewing audience.

In 'Keeping Up Appearances' the three basic guidelines of a sitcom are easily found. Firstly, the location must always stay the same. This is true enough as the main set is Hyacinth's lounge and kitchen area yet the action does take place nearby. The social conflict is most definitely there. The embarrassment to Hyacinth of her lower class relations and really the abandonment of her 'Daddy' now it seems he is not the respectable man he used to be. She always has to be better than any of her friends and with her rich sister owning a large house with a swimming pool and a pony, she never misses an opportunity to make sure that everyone knows this. Her son attended a boarding school which is another typical stereotype of an upper class child and Hyacinth being the ultimate snob manages to forget or hide anything that might bring her name down, or lower the standards of her reputation about town.

The character relations also remain the same. Hyacinth being married to the much quieter, patient husband, who however much he disagrees with her will always stand by her and eventually give in to her. The neighbours and most of the town are 'scared' of Hyacinth <u>because</u> she is so dominating and do their best to avoid her because they know that once they are faced with Hyacinth they will be unable to refuse whatever she asks of them.

'Keeping Up Appearances' like other sitcoms contains many stereotypes: Hyacinth the snob and her working class brother-in-law to name just a couple. We know what to expect of each character after regular viewing and by using stereotypes thoughts and jokes written by the creator can much more easily be expressed to the viewer so that the preferred meaning is received.

Repetition is important for continuous laughs. For example we know that in each episode someone will call Mrs 'Bouquet' Mrs Bucket and that when Hyacinth walks past her relations' dog she will fall in the bush. We therefore can anticipate what is going to happen raising a chuckle and then a laugh when it finally does happen.

All of these 'roles' for a sitcom including when everything seems terrible in the first five minutes and the rest of the programme is how to resolve the situation and by the end of the episode everything is back to normal are conventions for all situation comedies and when this formula is followed quality programmes usually appear.

Questions 5(b) and 10(b) are more difficult to prepare for in that they deal with central concepts and issues defined by the syllabus rather than being on specified areas of study. You should make sure that in your course you have a good working knowledge of the main mass media. The amount you need to know about each of the main media is described in the Notes for Guidance which your teacher will have.

GLOSSARY

A

Access   The opportunity to make media products. Access to the media puts people in a position of influence. There are a number of forms of access including:
- ownership of the means to make media texts
- involvement in some area that makes a person attractive to the media and leads to regular appearances
- well-organised pressure groups working to get their own messages and views noticed by people within the media.

Alternative media texts   Opposite to 'mainstream' media texts. Alternative products tend to be developed as items that are deliberately different to popular or 'mainstream' items. Some other common features also unite most – but not all – alternative products:
- Centred on views of audience.
- Take similar form to popular texts but use this to make fun of popular texts in some way.
- Aimed deliberately at a small selective audience.
- Often want to stay small scale rather than find large audience.
- Often take extreme or unusual views.

Alternative working practices   New patterns of working. With the growth of technology allowing people to make their own media texts, ways of making and distributing alternative media products have seen different working practices develop. The following points are often – but not always – true of alternative working practices:
- Concerned more with enjoyment than profit.
- People often treat their media work as a hobby and want operations to stay small scale.
- People undertake a range of jobs themselves rather than pay professionals.
- Systems of distribution are kept small and targeted, often avoiding traditional routes like shops.

Audience   People who actually use a media text. The idea of the audience is central to media studies because it is audiences that decide on the success or failure of texts. Audiences also make decisions about how good or bad texts are and what they mean.

Audience engagement   The way that an audience relates to a media text and makes changes as a result of being exposed to the text.

Audience expectations   The things that audiences expect from the media. The existence of genres, narratives and other forms of regulation in the media mean that a great deal of the content of media texts is predictable.

Audience identification with the media   The ways in which members of the audience relate to the media. The attachments that they feel to characters and things within these texts.

Audience placement within the production process   The way that the media take account of audiences to the point of involving them in the process of making media texts.

This ranges from people in the media just being aware of what audiences want and trying to make the right texts to actually involving members of the audience in the making of texts, for example, by giving them opportunities to make their own TV programmes.

Audience placement within a text   The idea that the media address their audiences in a number of different ways. Examples include: telethons that expect audiences to do something active like make phone calls; TV programmes that expect audiences to do nothing other than watch; and records that are designed to get people dancing.

B

Bias   Distortion or changing of a message in the media. If a media text is biased, it supports one message, one side of a debate, one view of life, etc. Bias can occur in two main ways:
- Media texts are put together with biased material which has deliberately been prepared to be included.
- Media texts are edited to omit a particular message and leave another untouched.

Broadsheet   Newspaper of a certain size, shape and content such as the *Guardian* and *The Times*. *See also* tabloid.

C

Case study   A way of investigating the media. This means studying one particular example as a way of gaining a greater understanding of a particular area. For example, chapter 9 on working practices includes three case studies, each of which provides some understanding of an area of working practice within the media.

Codes   Systems into which media representations are organised. By following the same pattern of presenting images, sounds, etc, a media product can give a particular message to an audience. For example, fast cutting from shot to shot in an action sequence during a movie presents a code that is understood to mean excitement and danger. This leads to another point about some codes, that is, some codes are based on things we might recognise from real life. In real life dangerous and exciting situations often present us with quick images and little time to react. This quality can also be seen in the example of a media code described above.

Construction   The way that media texts are made up of a number of elements. For example, the title sequence for a TV show usually features music, written titles and some shots that tell you about the contents of the programme. There may also be a logo featuring the title of the programme. Each item listed here is part of the overall construction of the title sequence. *See also* deconstruction.

Control   Anything that controls the media. Some controls are obvious such as the age limit on who can rent or buy certain video tapes. Other controls are less clear, for example, controls from the market on what people will and will not buy. Areas of control include:
- **formal controls** such as the law
- **informal controls** such as the attitude of a potential audience
- **market controls** such as the competition for a product
- **technical controls** such as what can/cannot be created within a certain area of the media.

Convention   The usual way to present something. For example, the title sequences of films usually display the name of the star in huge lettering while the names of other people involved, such as those who do minor technical jobs, are shown in smaller letters.

Cult   A type of audience group, usually small and linked by a common interest in a particular media text. Members of cult audiences often share similar views on life, styles of dress, etc. Different to other kinds of audiences, like mass audiences or family audiences, because their interests in their chosen media tend to be strong and very important to their lives. Cult audiences are often attracted to extreme types of media texts such as thrash and death metal music, unusual horror films or TV programmes that make no attempt to appeal to huge audiences.

D

Decoding   The study of media texts for the purpose of finding codes within them. The process of study that breaks down a media text and isolates the pieces of the text that allow it to do its intended job. Decoding is possible because media texts use the same codes for the same reasons and we can find these codes in a range of texts, such as action shots of sportsmen/women.

Deconstruction   The study of individual parts of a media product to discover meanings within these parts that will help in the understanding of the whole product. For example, if you consider the opening titles of 'News at Ten' you can easily begin to understand both construction and deconstruction. The classical music gives a strong feel to the opening, the sounds repeat and create a tension, the shots of the news building with people working suggests a lot of information being gathered and the word 'News' in the title sequence tells you that the programme will deliver information on the important events of the day. Added together these elements create a meaning for the opening of the programme. If we take any one of these, such as the music, we can see how this meaning is created. *See also* construction.

E

Editing   The process of selecting some information and rejecting other material. Most people are familiar with the word 'Editor' when it is applied to the person selecting material for a magazine or newspaper, but it is important to realise that editors are employed throughout the media and any decision that involves selecting information to go into a media text is an editorial decision.

Explicit message   One that is contained in a media text and is clearly stated. For example, the opening line in the late evening news on BBC 1 states: 'This is the Nine O'Clock News from the BBC'. This statement identifies the programme and cannot easily be given any other meaning. Explicit messages are often compared with **implicit messages**.

F

Fanzine   A small circulation publication usually produced and sold independently. The word 'fanzine' comes from the fact that these publications started with groups of fans producing their own magazines about football teams, pop groups, etc that did not get much coverage in the media. As the technology to produce such magazines has become cheaper, there are now fanzines on so many subjects that they have become impossible to count. Anyone with something to say and the time to devote to putting a magazine together can now produce their own fanzine.

G

Genre   A group of media texts that show a similarity of style and content. Genres develop for economic reasons. This means in practice that once a type of text has become a proven success, it is imitated. Genres will continue for as long as the demand for a particular kind of product continues. Genres suit audiences because they help them identify their favourite kind of products. They also suit producers because placing products in a particular genre increases the chance of success. Most genres are identified within one media but some commentators believe genres cut across different media, for example, 'horror' which exists in films, comics, etc. *See also* sub-genres.

I

Impartiality   The practice of not taking sides in an argument or any other area that involves conflicting opinions. Impartiality is the opposite of bias. There are some areas, such as political coverage on television, where the law states that media producers have to be impartial.

Implicit message   One that is contained in a media text but not openly stated. Examples occur in advertising – people shown using advertised products, like beers, are often successful in whatever they are doing in the adverts. The implicit message is that drinking a particular beer might make you more likely to be successful. However, the slogan will not say this. Implicit messages are often compared with **explicit messages.**

Inferential reading   A detailed type of study of media texts. Different to reading of media texts, which simply identifies the different parts of texts and the jobs that they do, because inferential reading infers or draws conclusions from looking at a media text. These conclusions usually involve finding material that would help in an understanding of the meaning of the text. *See also* reading.

Influence   The ways in which media texts change audiences. These changes can be very small, for example, gradually changing an individual's opinion. They can also be massive like a telethon prompting its audience to donate millions of pounds to a particular charity.

M

Mainstream   Opposite to alternative. Describes media texts that are aimed at large audiences and include views shared by a great many people.

Market   The entire potential audience for a text – everyone likely to buy it, watch it, hear it, etc. The understanding behind the existence of markets is that there are groups of people in the world with similar interests who would all be likely to buy a particular product. With this in mind, most media products are promoted and marketed to the kind of people that are thought to be the most likely to take an interest.

Media form   The form taken by a media text or a part of a media text. For example, a single record comes in several forms including CDs, tapes and vinyl.

Mediation   The act of channelling a message through the media. The word 'media' actually comes from 'mediation', and people involved in media studies see the job of the media as being to put messages into different forms and present them to an audience. The act of putting a message such as a news report into different forms like television or radio is an act of 'mediation'.

Mode of address   The way that media texts speak to audiences and make a difference in the relationship between the audience and the media. There are a number of ways in which this can be done. For example, a newspaper editorial addresses readers directly and seems to suggest that we share views. By contrast, a study of television schedules for one evening shows that companies treat audiences in a 'domestic' way – they provide different programmes for different people at different times. It is possible for modes of address to be aimed at any size of audience from an individual to an international audience.

N

Narrative   The way that a story is told. Can be broken down into two parts:
- plot – a simple outline of the story
- narration – the point of view from which the story is told.

Narrative can be found throughout the media but different media use it in their own ways. For example, pop song writers tend to give brief details of stories and leave out details like the age and background of people involved in the stories. Audiences are used to filling in this information for themselves.

Narrative code   The usual pattern for the media to develop a narrative. The media tend to use the same ways of developing narratives time and time again. Different media have their own particular ways. This allows us to spot codes in which certain elements have their own meaning. For example, in a sitcom we expect that the main character walking into a scene will move the story forward in some way.

O

Ownership   The individual or company owning a media product or having the means to produce media products. There are obvious ways in which ownership can make a difference within the media, for example, an individual buying a newspaper to allow that paper to print the person's opinions. Media ownership may have an influence in other ways. For example, one television company may take over another to get ownership of all the programmes made by that company. The company taking over would then be able to fill its schedules with newly acquired programmes and so save money on making new programmes.

P

Products   The things actually made or produced by the media. The term is usually used to describe complete pieces of work such as a video tape or comic.

R

Reading   The study of media texts to make sense of them. All of the examples in the chapters involve reading a media text in some way. *See also* inferential reading.

Role model   A figure from the media who presents behaviour, advice, values, etc which influence other people. In some cases role models may be created such as crime-fighting super heroes like Batman. In other cases the media may present ordinary or real-life figures as role models. This is not exclusively a media phenomenon. People who study behaviour of individuals accept that we all have role models and in some cases these are people we simply know at work, school or college, etc.

S

Sub-genre   Small groups of products within genres that have their own particular peculiarities of style and content. They tend to have a lot in common with the other items in the main genre but also some clear differences. *See also* genres.

Symbol   A sign, object or action, etc that represents something other than itself. Audiences recognise the meaning of symbols and tend to use them in a particular way, for example, the red rose used as a symbol on advertising and other literature by the Labour Party. When the party uses the emblem of the rose, it doesn't carry the meaning of being a flower. It is understood as a symbol of the political values of Labour.

Syllabus(es)   Used in this book when discussing the intentions of the two examining boards.

T

Tabloid   Newspaper of a particular size, shape and content such as *The Sun* and *Daily Mirror*. *See also* broadsheet.

Technology   Equipment of any sort used in the making or production of media texts. Much attention in media studies is paid to studying the effects of new technologies, such as satellite broadcasting systems, on the whole media industry. 'Technology' in media studies ranges from the equipment used to manufacture CDs to the computer packages used to produce a leaflet.

V

Viewpoint   The point of view taken by a media text. Some media texts make explicit statements – others make implicit statements and some combine both types. *See also* explicit messages and implicit messages. As media texts are put together or 'constructed' with audiences and profit in mind, it is usual for media producers to think about the point of view the texts will take. They usually contain similar views to those held by the audience.

W

Working practices   The ways in which people work within the media. Major areas of working practice studies include:
- the ways in which people work together to make decisions – does one person decide or a whole group, for example?
- the way that changes, such as changes in technology within the media, have had an impact on working practices in certain industries.

INDEX